CATHOLICS, PEASANTS, AND CHEWA RESISTANCE
IN NYASALAND 1889-1939

Catholics, Peasants, and Chewa Resistance in Nyasaland 1889–1939

IAN LINDEN

with Jane Linden

HEINEMANN

LONDON · NAIROBI · IBADAN

Heinemann Educational Books Ltd
48 Charles Street, London WiX 8AH
P.M.B. 5205, Ibadan · P.O. Box 45314, Nairobi
P.O. Box 3966, Lusaka
EDINBURGH MELBOURNE TORONTO AUCKLAND
HONG KONG SINGAPORE KUALA LUMPUR NEW DELHI

ISBN 0 435 32530 2

Printed in Great Britain
by Richard Clay (The Chaucer Press), Ltd,
Bungay, Suffolk

Contents

List of Illustrations, Maps, and Tables

N.B. 'Mlanje' as spelt on the maps is the modern spelling of 'Mulanje'.

Acknowledgements

We acknowledge with gratitude the contribution to this book made by Malawian Catholics, Bishops, Priests, Sisters, Brothers, and laymen. We are equally grateful for the help and hospitality afforded us by the White Fathers and Montfort Fathers in both Italy and Malawi. Since none of the many informants cited in this book, and the many who helped us, may concur fully with its conclusions, and indeed may deplore them, our debt to them cannot be exaggerated.

The archival research was greatly facilitated by the kindness and co-operation of Gordon Hazeldine of the University of Malawi Library; Father Réné Lamey of the White Fathers' Archives, Rome; and Mr. Drew of the National Archives of Malawi. We would like to thank them all along with Father Van Asdonk of the Montfort Fathers whose *bons offices* proved invaluable.

We thank the University of Malawi for a research grant which partly covered the expense of the project, and those of its members, like Rev. Dr. J. M. Schoffeleers, Dr. Martin Chanock, Dr. Leroy Vail, Lois Chanock, and Prof. Margaret Kalk, whose encouragement, company, and intellectual stimulation, partly covered its emotional and intellectual costs.

Earlier drafts of this book were read by Prof. George Shepperson of Edinburgh University, Prof. Terence Ranger of the University of California at Los Angeles, and Prof. Richard Gray of the School of Oriental and African Studies, and we are indebted to them for scholarly criticisms and suggestions.

Finally we have two outstanding debts. One is to the painstaking anthropological research of Dr. Matthew Schoffeleers which provided us with the social framework for this book. The other is to Dr. Martin Chanock whose political and economic insights into Malawi's colonial history informed and reinforced our interest in the Chewa peasantry. Responsibility for our conclusion is, of course, entirely our own.

Author's Preface

The old-style mission histories, an expansion of the nineteenth-century mission magazine article, were intended to reinforce the commitment of European Christians to bring the 'Gospel to the Dark Continent'. They were aimed at the heart and purse-strings of the pious reader. Today they provide invaluable insights into the society and values of Victorian Christians and, after careful sieving, useful ethnographic data about Africa. With their explanations of missionary success and failure in terms of Divine Grace, superstition, or wickedness, they do not give African Church History a respectable ancestry.

The publication twenty years ago of W. H. C. Frend's *The Donatist Church*[1] and Roland Oliver's *The Missionary Factor in East Africa*[2] finally rescued African Church History from being a quaint literary genre. A long tradition of scholarly analysis of the Early Church culminated in Frend's monograph about the first Independent African Church, while Oliver applied the normal techniques of a colonial historian to nineteenth-century missions in East Africa.

The treatment of Christianity as an aspect of colonialism could not survive the ideological restraints of African nationalism and the growth of indigenous Churches in independent African countries. In Shepperson and Price's *Independent African*,[3] published in 1958 at the height of the nationalist movement in Malawi, a history of the Providence Industrial Mission and radical Protestantism in colonial Nyasaland is transformed into the biography of a nationalist martyr and the Christian élite around him. Similarly Ajayi in his study of nineteenth-century missions in Nigeria focuses on the figure of the Black Anglican bishop, Samuel Crowther, and the Creole élite in the Niger Mission.[4] The theme in both books is the same, the growth of political and religious independence as a result of the clash between Black élites and Europeans.

The importance of the political dimension of African Christianity is taken up in McCracken's thesis on the Livingstonia mission[5] in which African innovation and initiative is stressed. It discusses the mission as a transforming agency and investigates how, and if, it instigated social change. In Ross' study of the Blantyre mission[6] the same themes are present but the case is presented with less sophistication. The history of Malawi is the story of the generation of African leaders, fostered in the Scots missions where they received their education, who finally swept the country into the era of mass nationalism. Behind every pew there seems to lurk a proto-nationalist.

Roman Catholic missions in Nyasaland did not produce leaders of modernizing movements and suffered from a dearth of creative writers like Laws,[7]

Scott,[8] and Hetherwick.[9] Not surprisingly they have been ignored. Yet there are over three-quarters of a million Catholics amongst Malawi's four million people, mainly peasant subsistence farmers. A historian studying the Catholic missions is obliged to concentrate on a peasant Church whose essential conservatism calls in question, or at least balances, the élitist slant of the Protestant mission histories. There is something more, then, to the historians' indifference to the role of Catholic missions in Malawi than a legacy of Protestant mistrust for 'heathenism and the Pope'. Catholic missions do not fit tidily into the box marked Christianity and Progress.

This is not to say that Catholic missions have not produced, and undergone themselves, meaningful and progressive changes during the colonial period, only in the world of several hundred thousand illiterate peasants, and over a period of only two generations, the magnitude of this transformation is seen to be small indeed. Similarly, there were erudite priests whose knowledge of village life was second to none, but individualism was not encouraged and their reflections and observations ended up as jumbled notes in the mission cupboard rather than in English bookshops.

The missionaries were neither drab nor stupid but, unlike their Jesuit and Dominican predecessors on the Zambesi, they had left Europe at the low-water mark of Post-Tridentine Catholicism. With their French Catholic values of loyalty and obedience the priests brought to the African societies of Nyasaland a Christianity filtered through centuries of European peasant culture. It is this juxtaposition of conservative Catholicism and Malawian peasant culture that provides the setting for this monograph. But the wider framework is the interaction between the diverse interest groups that made up Nyasaland between 1889 and 1939, the different aims of missionary, peasant, planter, and administrator, in the colonial period. As Engels says, it is this interaction that makes history.

> Men make their own history, whatever its outcome may be, in that each person follows his own consciously desired end, and it is precisely the resultant of these many wills operating in different directions and of their manifold effects upon the outer world that constitutes history.[10]

The focus of this book is, then, the micro-events around Catholic mission stations, the interaction of European Catholic and African peasant conservatism, each with its conscious aims and goals and view of society.

The change of perspective is not an artificial historiographical device employed to bring African mission history into harmony with the main emphases of social historians in Europe. It is dictated by the available material. It is also surely desirable. To move from élites to peasants, and from Native Associations to Nyau Societies, is to explore the experience, not of a handful of men, but of the vast majority of Chewa-speaking Africans in the colonial period. Once mission history is investigated at the fine-grain level of village society many features appear important and prominent that would otherwise form a hazy anthropological background. Christianity begins to appear in the context of

African religious systems rather than national politics and therefore as part of the historical study of African religion.

But if the Africanist moves into the field of Church History, does this make it any the less an arcane discipline? Is it important what went on between Catholic missionaries and African peasants? Most people thinking in terms of Modern Europe would be inclined to say no. But in Africa the Catholic Church has emerged in many independent nations as one of the largest unified hierarchical institutions. Whenever the Church finds itself in such a position, as in the Middle Ages, Church History has serious political overtones.

It is easy to see that in reaction there can be *raisons d'état* for falsifying Church History. In Africa the psychological satisfaction of making the missionary a scapegoat may coincide with political expediency. In countries such as Zaïre, Uganda, and Guinea, conflicts can arise and have already arisen. The history of Catholicism in Africa is not the study of some minor and unimportant religious aberration but the story of the growth of what is today a powerful and central African institution.

It is my sincere hope that this book will not be grist to the mill of anyone wishing to denigrate the Catholic Church in Malawi. But neither can it be Catholic apologetics. For the Church in Malawi needs an objective historical consciousness. Without this, the real needs of peasants and subsistence farmers cannot be served, nor will the local leadership be forthcoming that will enable them to 'make their own history'.[11] This was the task the missionaries set themselves and one for which they surely need not apologize.

REFERENCES TO PREFACE

[1] Frend W. H. C. *The Donatist Church* Oxford 1952
[2] Oliver R. *The Missionary Factor in East Africa* Longmans 1952
[3] Shepperson G. and Price T. *Independent African* Edinburgh 1958
[4] Ajayi A. J. F. *Christian Missions in Nigeria: 1841–1891* Longmans 1965
[5] McCracken K. J. *Livingstonia Mission and the Evolution of Malawi: 1873–1939* Doctoral Dissertation, University of Cambridge 1967
[6] Ross A. *Origins and Development of the Church of Scotland Mission, Blantyre, Nyasaland: 1875–1926*. Doctoral Dissertation, University of Edinburgh 1968
[7] Robert Laws, born 1851, went to the University of Aberdeen in 1868. After qualifying medically he was ordained a minister of the Free Church of Scotland and went on the pioneer expedition of 1875 that founded the first Livingstonia station at Cape Maclear. Laws remained active in Protectorate affairs until the 1920s, see Livingstone W. P. *Laws of Livingstonia*. London, undated (c. 1930).
[8] David Clement Scott worked at the Blantyre Mission from 1881 to 1898. Although he shared Laws' views on the development of industrial enterprise, he was more ecclesial in his thinking and favoured ecumenism. His magazine *Life and Work* served as a channel for his thinking and Blantyre Cathedral provides a permanent memorial to his vision. He died in 1907, in Kenya.
[9] Alexander Hetherwick retained much of the roughness of his Aberdeenshire farming background. He spent from 1883 to 1928 as a missionary, mostly at the Blantyre Mission. Respected by colonial officials and planters, he was able to attack colonial policy. His book *The Gospel and the African* is helpful in understanding the attitudes of the Blantyre mission-

aries in the early twentieth century: see Livingstone W. P. *A Prince of Missionaries* London 1932.

[10] 'Ludwig Feuerbach and the End of Classical German Philosophy' in *Karl Marx and Frederick Engels Selected Works* London 1968, 623

[11] Chanock M. L. 'Development and change in the history of Malawi' in *The Early History of Malawi* ed. Pachai B. Longmans 1972, 445

Introduction

I do not mean that I am against the Roman Catholic Religion. They are very kind people than any other Missionaries in the country. They show real love towards everyone. They can eat and chat together with anybody without respect of colour. I will (be) very sorry if some of my remarks will cause other people feel [*sic*] when reading them (that I was against the Roman Catholic Religion), surely I did not mean it, if I meant it 'Ruat Coelum' on me.

George Simeon Mwase[1]

Before briefly discussing the Portuguese antecedents to nineteenth-century mission activity in Malawi, it will be helpful to provide some introduction to the country's major ethnic groups. The Chewa-speaking peoples of Malawi trace their origin to a dispersal point in the Eastern Congo. At the end of the first millennium A.D. groups of iron-age Bantu migrants moved south and east to displace or assimilate an earlier Bushman culture. A major group of invaders sharing a baboon totem, the Phiri clan, came from the region around Lake Tanganyika in the fourteenth century and seem to have been the first to produce a political organization above the level of lineage and village cluster. The Banda clans whom they found appear to have had only religious and ritual leaders who were believed to control rainfall and ensure the fertility of the land and its people.

By the sixteenth century one Phiri chieftancy, the Karongaship, had achieved pre-eminence. Situated in a fertile plain to the south-west of Lake Malawi the kingdom had a dense population and an army to control the ivory trade with coastal Arabs. The Karonga's position was contested by other Phiri chiefs like Lundu, whose capital on the Lower Shire allowed him privileged access to trade routes along the Zambesi. The Portuguese knew the people of these chieftancies as the 'Maravi', though the name originally referred only to the Phiri invaders.[2]

Although the Portuguese called the people to the north-east of Tete 'Cheva', the idea of the Chewa as a 'tribe' only grew up in the colonial period as the clans of Central Malawi needed to establish an ethnic identity in distinction to the culturally different nineteenth-century invaders, the Ngoni from South Africa and the Yao from Mozambique. The idea was reinforced by colonial administrators who needed convenient labels and large units. Lundu's kingdom was sufficiently isolated from Central Malawi by the Blantyre escarpment for linguistic and cultural differences to develop and the clans in the Lower Shire Valley to be called Mang'anja rather than Chewa. Their identity was reinforced by the arrival of the Lomwe and Sena from Mozambique in the twentieth century. Similarly the lakeshore Chewa were called Nyanja and those around Lilongwe, Chipeta, but I will try to avoid these distinctions, as they have less justification.

The Ngoni, who were few in number, soon lost their language, and Chewa is *lingua franca* from Kasungu to the Mozambique border in the south. To the north-east of the Shire Highlands in the Yao heartland ChiYao is spoken while many people around Mulanje only speak ChiLomwe. The missionaries were therefore in the fortunate position of being able to make do with a single language and transfer without difficulty from station to station. Climate was tolerable, if not extremely agreeable, in all but the Lower Shire stations. A wide range of crops and fruit trees thrived. Rainfall was uncertain and famines did occur, but rarely with the severity of those in countries like Rwanda which had a similarly dense population. The Ngoni kept cattle, the Chewa goats. Villages could always produce a few chickens and Lake Malawi provided a plentiful supply of fish. The staple was and is *nsima*, boiled maize flour, usually supplemented with a relish, *ndiwo*, of pumpkin leaves, beans, fish, or game. The major Chewa industry of iron-smelting did not survive the introduction on a large scale of European-made hoes, knives, and utensils. For mission sites the priests could choose between the Kirk Range which divided off a long lakeshore plain and was called Central Angoniland, the Shire Highlands, and the extensive plain around Lilongwe stretching to the Dzalanyama range in the west along the Mozambique border.

The Catholic missionaries who arrived in Nyasaland in 1889 and returned again in 1901 were latecomers to the country. For the different Protestant missionary bodies which had evangelized the area since 1875 they were interlopers. But in their own eyes the priests and Brothers were continuing an almost unbroken tradition of Catholic mission activity on the Zambesi that had begun in the sixteenth century. They evoked the glorious days of St. Francis Xavier and of Jesuit and Dominican penetration of the interior. The more faded and tarnished the glories of Rome, the more they were passionately recalled. They were, after all, the representatives of a Church that had sent missionaries around the globe from South America to Tibet and that had dominated the intellectual life of Europe for centuries. More nostalgic than real, their claims to Central Africa offered protection against Protestant hostility and a pervasive sense of inferiority inherited from nineteenth-century Europe.

The first Catholic missionaries to arrive in East-Central Africa were a by-product of the Portuguese colonization of Goa. Mozambique Island, that had begun as 'a kind of hostelry for the refreshing of the Portuguese, worn out with a long, toilsome voyage',[3] became a staging post for travellers into the interior. Further inland along the Zambesi was the town of Sena where in October and November 1560 the Portuguese Jesuit, Gonçalo da Silveira,[4] is reputed to have performed over five hundred baptisms. A year later he was murdered in the MweneMutapa's capital on the instigation of Arabs at court.[5] The Mwene-Mutapa had agreed to accept baptism and the Arabs rightly feared Portuguese encroachment on their trading interests.

The prize luring the Portuguese into the interior and along the Zambesi was gold. The rich ivory supplies of Malawi did not promise such immediate profits and involved the problems of porterage to the coast; [6] no valuable minerals had been discovered north of the Zambesi, so Portuguese interest in Malawi was initially minimal. Missionaries who always moved with trading expeditions or as military chaplains only rarely contacted the Maravi. In 1570 two Jesuits, Francisco de Montclaro and Estevo Lopes, [7] accompanied a Portuguese expedition intended to take control of Zimbabwe, the MweneMutapa's capital.

The first fruits of the Counter-Reformation, drawn mainly from noble families in Europe, the Jesuits who came to the Zambesi were intellectually sophisticated and recorded ethnographic information with some objectivity. Occasionally they showed their training in the chivalrous codes of European courts; Father Andre Fernandes felt that African women were treated 'no higher than cows' [8] and all condemned the practice of polygamy. On the other hand, Father Gaspar Soares [9] in an annual report for 1611 dealt sympathetically with the problem of ancestor veneration. [10] Unlike the mission to China, few concessions were made to indigenous culture. Father Montclaro wrote of Chief Chombe who lived in Maravi territory:

> A Kaffir chief on the side of Bororo opposite the land of the Mongazes [11] . . . wished to become a Christian but because of his many wives and other customs which it would have been most difficult to turn him from . . . this wish was not attended to. [12]

By 1583, Dominicans had reinforced the Jesuits and occupied the three major Portuguese towns of Tete, Sena, and Sofala. [13] Communications between the garrison towns were tenuous and dangerous. The first contact with the Mang'anja in the form of Lundu's warriors, the Zimba, [14] gave Malawi its earliest 'martyr'. In 1592, a Portuguese Dominican, Nicolas do Rosario, who had been shipwrecked on the East African coast while on his way to Goa, offered his services as chaplain to Fernandes da Chaves, the captain of Tete. He accompanied a military expedition of 130 mercenary troops sent to relieve Sena, beleaguered by the Zimba. The column was ambushed in thick forest on the north bank of the Zambesi. The Dominican Superior in Mozambique, Dos Santos, gave this account of Rosario's death after making a number of visits to Sena and Tete in the 1590s.

> There they bound him hand and foot to a high tree-trunk and finished killing him with arrows, in hatred of our holy religion, saying that the Portuguese only made this war upon them by the advice of their (priests). . . . Thus ended his life and labours with this merit more, and another very considerable to follow, which was to become the food of these ferocious eaters of human flesh, roasted and boiled. [15]

Although the account is apocryphal and modelled on the martyrdom of St. Sebastian, the words Dos Santos puts in the mouth of the Zimba are telling. The Portuguese clergy were sometimes instrumental in encouraging punitive raids and saw the best hopes for Christianity in Portuguese conquests. [16] Montclaro considered the 1570 expedition against the MweneMutapa a 'just war', [17] and it

3

cannot be denied that missionary work outside the narrow confines of the garrison towns was hazardous without a measure of stability. By 1624, there were nine priests at Sena who might have exercised some influence over the Governor.[18]

The vision of contacting the Kingdom of Prester John to form a Christian front against North African Islam was still very much alive amongst priests at the beginning of the seventeenth century. Father Luiz Mariano, a Jesuit at Tete in 1624,[19] took an interest in the geography of Malawi in the belief that Prester John's kingdom began somewhere to the north-east of the lake. But the Karonga was most valuable to the Portuguese for the troops he was willing to supply as mercenaries against the MweneMutapa.[20] In exchange he asked for carpenters' tools to build boats for the lake, perhaps to open up alternative trade routes to the coast.[21] The Karonga was an unreliable ally and by the 1630s, after he had finally defeated his Phiri rival, Lundu, Maravi warriors marauded as far as the coast[22] and the Portuguese were no longer safe north of the Zambesi. This was the high point of Maravi power. The Karonga was described as an 'Emperor'[23] and according to Jesuit reports his burial was accompanied by the mass slaughter of his concubines, wives, relatives, soldiers, and friends.[24]

Even had Portuguese missionaries reached the Karonga's court it is unlikely they would have made many converts. The Phiri royal house controlled important rain-shrines where worship was directed to the High God, Mphambe, and to deceased Phiri chiefs, in order to obtain rain.[25] A Portuguese trader, Theodosios Garcia, who reached the Karonga's court in 1679 remarked on a sacrifice made 'on a high hill'.[26] The cult system, with its hierarchy of officials and annual sacrifices, was an important element in the authority of the Phiri ruler. An intrusive religious system would most likely have been seen as an attack on the chieftancy, or at least on the shrine priests.

Despite repeated reverses,[27] the Portuguese clung to their settlements along the Zambesi and colonizers arrived in small numbers. In 1667, there were sixteen churches standing along the Zambesi Valley, nine staffed by Dominicans, six by Jesuits, and one with a secular priest.[28] Preaching was in Portuguese and little evangelization was attempted. Although Portuguese records testify to 239 baptisms carried out in a period of nine months at Tete in 1699, the converts were all slaves of local Portuguese and baptized in batches of fourteen to twenty at a time.[29] In a brief period of reform the Jesuits began a seminary for Portuguese boys and the sons of local chiefs in Sena in 1697 while Father Francisco da Trinidade, a Dominican at Tete, produced two catechisms in local languages.[30] There was considerable contact with the Mang'anja who were interested in locally-made cloth and later traded slaves with Sena on a regular basis.[31]

Missionary activity remained at a low ebb in the eighteenth century. The development of an extensive *prazos* system of Crown estates along the Zambesi, with its particular form of slavery, provided the priests with a ready-made flock. Obliged for financial reasons to farm or trade, the priests were more a part of the mixed Portuguese/African *prazos* culture than active missionaries. Father Pedro da Trinidade, who increased his flock at Zumbo from 262 in 1734 to 478 in 1749, appears to have been a zealous priest. He was also the civil authority, mining boss, and, it is said, had 1,600 African clients.[32] It was not the modern conception of the missionary but one that was in some measure imposed on priests along the Zambesi.

With the opening of mines at Maano in the middle of the eighteenth century the Portuguese were brought directly into contact with the Chewa. Maano was at the heart of the kingdom of Undi, a Phiri chief who had displaced the Karonga as Maravi paramount. The returns of Father Caetano Alberto, the Dominican in charge of the local church, gave 199 baptized Christians in 1751.[33] It was rare for more than ten per cent of the population to be baptized even in the towns.[34]

Figures, of course, provide no indication of the degree of Christian influence. The baptized *prazeros* of mixed blood consulted diviners, believed in witchcraft, and knew no Christian doctrine. An edict had to be promulgated from Goa in 1771 forbidding ritual intercourse after Catholic funerals and it is apparent that all the Church rites had been invaded by elements of local culture.[35] This was not the result of conscious adaptation but a syncretism caused by inadequate supervision. A chain of command running from Goa to Mozambique and then along the Zambesi to the isolated *prazos*, visited most infrequently by undertrained clergy, meant that baptized Christians were effectively cut off from instruction and direction.

The weak dose of Christianity emanating from the Portuguese settlements along the Zambesi did make some impact on African societies in the neighbourhood over the centuries. The M'bona shrine in the Lower Shire Valley[36] controlled by the Phiri chief Lundu incorporated some Christian themes. M'bona, the guardian territorial spirit of the Mang'anja was given the titles 'Jesu wakuda' (the black Christ) and 'mwana wa mulungu' (the son of God) reputedly before the arrival of the South Africa General Mission at Chulwe in 1900.[37] Similarly the nyau societies amongst the Mang'anja[38] still have a figure strongly resembling a Portuguese cavalry horse. Generally, though, it was the person of Mary, the Virgin Mother of God, that survived the centuries and became incorporated in traditional religious thinking.

The Barwe to the south of Sena were reported by Von Sicard as naming their great ancestress in the first fruits ceremony as 'Maria',[39] and 'Maria' also occurs in witchfinding movements amongst the Mang'anja[40] and the Bemba.[41] Both Duff[42] and Hetherwick mention a Tonga rowing song that could be heard on the lake and in the Lower Shire at the beginning of the twentieth century 'I have no Mother. I have no Father. Who will take care of me but our Mother Maria' (Sina Mama, sina Baba. Wakelewa naye. Nusutanaye Mama ndi Maria). Duff reports that the Tonga said the song had been taught to them long ago by Jesuit Fathers.[43]

The retention of this Catholic symbol amongst the predominantly matrilineal peoples of Malawi was certainly more than a product of Marian devotion amongst the Portuguese. Women as mythical ancestors play an important role in Chewa oral traditions. Such figures as Nyangu,[44] Mangadzi,[45] and Makewana[46] shared features of the Catholic idea of Mary; they were either virgin

5

brides of the otiose High God or stood in the relationship of perpetual mother to Phiri semi-divine rulers such as Karonga and Undi. Even today reverence for motherhood is very high in Malawi. The expression 'Your mother is second only to God' (Mai wako ndi Mulungu wachiwiri) is a not uncommon way of according respect and 'Mothers' Day' is a feast in the national calendar. The Catholic symbol of the Virgin Mary fitted easily into Chewa patterns of thought and served to mark off the 'Aroma' from their Protestant rivals.[47]

The Catholic saints were also incorporated to some degree into local rain-making ceremonies. When the Montfort Fathers went down the Shire river to the region of Massingire *prazo*[48] in the 1920s they found that statues taken from a ruined church were being used for rain-calling.[49] Portuguese priests who ministered to congregations were scarcely less in need of a religion that could explain, predict, and control,[50] their precarious lives, than the Africans around them, and thought nothing of parading statues around the town to bring rain. Livingstone was interested to find such a procession in Sena in the mid-nineteenth century.[51] St. Antony was the most popular of the saints in the Portuguese settlements and the object of many superstitious devotions. But even in Europe statues of the Virgin Mary would be dipped in water to ensure good rains for the crops.[52]

The nineteenth century almost saw an end to Portuguese missions on the Zambesi. As a result of the development of Shaka Zulu's military state in Natal bands of armed refugees began moving north from South Africa in the 1820s. By the 1830s what had been small groups of Zulu and Swazi in flight were now powerful marauding bands settling for periods of years and then moving north. These waves, known as the 'Mfecane', swept through the Portuguese settlements on the Zambesi, razing Zumbo and seriously threatening Sena.[53] When Livingstone reached Tete in the 1850s he was greeted by the sight of decayed churches and priesthood, to confirm his Protestant Faith. With his exploration came the end of the Catholic monopoly of missionary activity along the Zambesi.

The first Protestant missionary body to reach Malawi under the influence of Livingstone's glowing accounts of the Lower Shire Valley was as catholic as the flexibility of the Anglican Church could allow. The Universities' Mission to Central Africa was led by men profoundly influenced by the Oxford Movement whose momentum had already taken John Henry Newman into the Roman Catholic Church. When the U.M.C.A. reached Cape Town in 1861, its leader, Mackenzie, a young Cambridge mathematics tutor, was ordained Bishop and began his episcopate with a forthright condemnation of race relations at the Cape. Once in Malawi the missionaries were soon involved in a skirmish with a Yao slaving party after they had freed some Nyanja slaves. The expedition was doomed. Even had the evangelistic naïveté of the Anglican priests not vitiated their efforts, the political condition of Malawi was totally unconducive to missionary penetration.

Since Livingstone's first visit the Yao traders who had their major villages to the east of Lake Malawi had moved round to occupy its south-western shores. The Mang'anja in the Shire Highlands had fallen prey to Yao slave-raiders from the north, and from the south came raids by half-caste *prazos* owners along the Shire river. In 1862 an unusually severe famine, the result of repeated poor rains, threatened to annihilate the population of the Lower Shire and left them open to domination by the handful of Kololo who had been Livingstone's porters.

Further north the Ngoni bands which had swept through Malawi had returned to settle permanently. The Maseko Ngoni were making their headquarters in the Kirk Hills and raiding for captives to increase the size of their regiments. When the Scots missionaries arrived in 1875 the Maravi were already a colonized people. The last of the Phiri Karongas, Sosola, had been killed by the Mangoche Yao, the Phiri shrines had been sacked by Chikunda slavers from the *prazos* and Ngoni regiments, and the last vestiges of Phiri territorial rule obliterated. The Chewa peoples had become vassals of the expanding Ngoni states led by Mpezeni at Chipata, Chikusi at Domwe and M'belwa in northern Malawi. Around the lake they either fell under Yao rule or were prey to slave-raids. In a few cases well-fortified Chewa villages on hilltops maintained a precarious autonomy. Yet despite these depredations the Chewa people maintained their language and village-level religious institutions. They expanded their food production to pay tribute to the Yao and Ngoni and accepted the protection this temporarily afforded.

The Scots missionaries both at Blantyre and at Cape Maclear had to come to terms with the African colonial rulers of Malawi. The Ngoni states, with their huge numbers of assimilated captives and penumbra of vassal villages ruled by an appointed *nduna*, were significantly less stable than the fortified and tightly-knit Yao towns. Whereas the Ngoni paramounts were willing to countenance the presence of missionaries, provided they stayed at the capital, the more powerful Yao were either uninterested or positively hostile. Both Ngoni and Yao were united in opposing too great a missionary influence on tribes considered to be their vassals.[54]

The European invasion of planters, colonial officials, and missionaries after the declaration of a Protectorate in 1889 halted the growth of the Ngoni kingdoms and brought the Yao slave trade to an end in the 1890s. Johnston[55] with his Sikh, Tonga, and Makua mercenaries controlled most of south and central Malawi before the end of the century. For the first few decades of the colonial era the Ngoni retained their assimilated captives and maintained their aristocracy in a weakened form. But for the Yao who had relied on the slave trade, and whose Islamic religion had equipped them for the role of traders within the dominions of the Sultan of Zanzibar, the advent of the *Pax Britannica* was an unmitigated disaster. They alone put up a sustained resistance to Johnston's punitive raids and their defeat left them isolated within a Protestant Nyasaland.

Missionary activity in colonial Malawi went on in a very complex social environment. The small European population was by no means homogeneous and could be divided into planters, administrators, and missionaries, with some overlap between each of the groups. Among Africans twenty years of Protestant missionary effort had produced a small mission élite whose political consciousness was permeated by biblical imagery. In contrast many of the traditional Ngoni chiefs and Chewa headmen had grown up in an environment of intertribal and inter-village politics and showed a more pragmatic grasp of political realities within the Protectorate. The different groups within colonial Malawi held widely disparate views as to the future of the Protectorate and its African population, and asked widely different things of the religious systems to which they belonged.

Each one of these groups saw the Catholic missions in the light of its own needs and aims, whether immediate and financial, secular or religious, short term or strategic. On their side the missionaries saw in each group or individual a potential ally, or opponent, for the achievement of what they saw to be their principal goal, the building up of the *corpus christianum* they hoped would one day encompass all Nyasaland.

As latecomers the Catholic missionaries found themselves on the edge of colonial society. It was a position they were used to in increasingly secular Europe. And on the whole their converts came from the edges of African society, the marginal men and latecomers to Nyasaland like the immigrant Alomwe and Sena.[56] They looked after lepers and coloured orphans and visited condemned men in Zomba gaol. Nuns championed the rights of women and priests protested against abuse of women in the village. The most profound difference from their Portuguese predecessors was that they represented an intellectually discredited Church in a foreign, Protestant, colony. The most profound similarity, they understood themselves to be the emissaries of the One, and only Holy, Catholic and Apostolic Church outside of which there was no Salvation. The result was a missionary body at once both aggressive and seeking acceptance, otherworldly yet fighting for every inch of territory and penny of Government aid, triumphalist yet amongst the poorest members of society.

REFERENCES TO INTRODUCTION

[1] Rotberg R. (ed.) *Strike a Blow and Die* Harvard 1967, 65

[2] Schoffeleers J. M. 'The Meaning and Use of the name *Malawi* in oral traditions and pre-colonial documents' in *The Early History of Malawi* ed. Pachai B. Longmans 1972, 91–104

[3] Hakluyt Society *The Voyages of François Pyrard de Laval Vol. II* London 1887, 224, quoted in Brodrick J. *Saint Francis-Xavier 1506–1552* London 1952

[4] Gonçalo da Silveira was born into Portuguese nobility in 1526 and joined the Jesuits at Coimbra in 1543. After becoming Superior of the Jesuit House in Lisbon, he was Provincial-Superior of Goa from 1556–9. He left Goa for Africa on 6 January 1560 and died in March a year later.

[5] Theal G. M. *Records of South-Eastern Africa Vol. II* Cape Town 1898, 118–28 and Schebesta P. *Portugals Konquistamission in Südost-Afrika* Steyler-Verlag 1966, 66–76

[6] da Silva A. *Mentalidade Missiologica dos Jesuitas em Mocambique antes de 1759 Vol. I* Lisbon 1960, 164–5

[7] Courtois R. P. *Notes chronologiques sur les anciennes missions au Zambèse* Lisbon 1889, 9

[8] A letter from Goa to his superiors in Rome, 1562, Archivum Romanum Societas Iesu, Goa 39 1 fl. 146 quoted in *Mentalidade* 214. The ideal of womanhood can be glimpsed in Peter Canisius' *De Maria Virgine Incomparabili* published c. 1577 see Graef H. *Mary: A History of Doctrine and Devotion Vol. II* London 1965, 18.

[9] Soares was a Portuguese Jesuit born at Ponto do Lima in 1562. He began his missionary career in Goa and only came to Africa in 1610. He died at Sena on 9 February 1612.

[10] A.R.S.I. Goa 33 1 fl. 351–2 quoted in *Mentalidade* 43

[11] The 'Mongazes' lived on the south bank of the Zambesi west of the Shire confluence. They may have been part of the Mang'anja under the jurisdiction of the MweneMutapa.

[12] Theal *Records Vol. III* 239. The ban on polygamy was ratified in a Papal ruling of 1631.

[13] Schebesta *Portugals* 90–4. Their first foundation was on Mozambique in 1577.

[14] The Zimba were first suggested to be Lundu's forces by E. A. Alpers 'The Mutapa and Malawi political systems' in *Aspects of Central African History* ed. T. O. Ranger London 1968, 21. Fieldwork undertaken by J. M. Schoffeleers has fully supported this hypothesis; see 'The History and Political Role of the M'Bona cult among the Mang'anja' *The Historical Study of African Religion* ed. Ranger T. O. and Kimambo Isaria, Heinemann 1972, 73–94.

[15] Theal *Records Vol. I*, 384–7. The suggestion of cannibalism may have been due to the Zimba's eating of a part of their victim's body, for example the heart or brains, to gain their power. In the 1920s rumours were rife in Nsanje near Lundu's capital that Europeans were planning to eat Africans' heart and brains, see *Nsanje District Book* 2 November 1928, District Council Meeting Vol. IV 129, National Archives of Malawi, Zomba. The Yao used to eat the heart of captured Ngoni, see *Mponda Mission Diary* 1 March 1891, White Fathers Archives, Rome.

[16] *Mentalidade Vol. I* 96, *Vol. II* 60–8

[17] *Guerra justificada* was an important theological principle at the time. There were legitimate wars in which slaves could be taken, and illegitimate raids whose only purpose was the capture of slaves. Wars that resulted in the conversion of the Heathen were considered justified, and slavery beneficial inasmuch as it brought Africans into the orbit of missionaries and helped their conversion.

[18] Courtois *Notes* 12

[19] Luiz Mariano was born c. 1580 and came from Brescia in Italy. He joined the Jesuits in 1600 and spent a period in Madagascar as a missionary before dying in 1634.

[20] Langworthy H. *A History of Undi's Kingdom to 1890 : Aspects of Chewa History in East-Central Africa* Doctoral dissertation at Boston University, 1969, 167–8.

[21] Alpers op. cit. 23

[22] Alpers E. A. *The Role of the Yao in the development of trade in East-Central Africa : 1698–c. 1850* Doctoral dissertation at University of London 1966, 24–60. This has the fullest coverage of Maravi/Portuguese relations in this period.

[23] *Mentalidade Vol. I* 271. A letter written by Father Manuel Barreto s.j. describing the extent of the Karonga's kingdom in the 1660s.

[24] A letter written by Father Michael Boym s.j. from Mozambique on 11 November 1644 A.R.S.I. Goa 34 1 fl. 150

[25] Linden I. 'The Karongas' shrine at Mankhamba: some problems in the religious history of Central Malawi'—a paper presented at the Lusaka Conference on African Religion. September 1972.

[26] Axelson E. A. *Portuguese in South-East Africa : 1600–1700* Johannesburg 1964, 153–4

[27] The most serious attack came from the Changamire dynasty led by Dombo from 1692–4. The Portuguese were driven from south of the Zambesi into their fortified towns.

[28] Theal *Records Vol. III* 488

[29] Courtois *Notes* 14

[30] Schebesta *Portugals* 180–200. These reforms were the product of Father Antonio da Conceicao's leadership as Augustinian Administrator of the Zambesi Mission. Courtois *Notes* 15.

[31] Isaacman A. F. *Mozambique. The Africanization of a European institution: The Zambesi Prazos, 1750–1902* University of Wisconsin Press 1972, 48

[32] Mudenge S. I. *The Rozvi Empire and the Feira of Zumbo* Doctoral dissertation at the University of London 1972, 181–8

[33] Theal *Records Vol. V* 215

[34] Schapera I. (ed.) *Livingstone's African Journal: 1853–1856 Vol. II* 439 gives Livingstone's entry for 28 March 1856 that only seven per cent of the population at Tete were baptized.

[35] Isaacman *Mozambique* 62

[36] Schoffeleers J. M. *M'bona the Guardian Spirit of the Mang'anja* M.A. dissertation at University of Oxford 1966

[37] Schoffeleers *M'bona* 367–9

[38] Schoffeleers J. M. *Symbolic and Social Aspects of Spirit Worship among the Mang'anja* D.Phil. dissertation at University of Oxford 1968, 320–421. Secret dance societies for men who perform at female initiation rites and mortuary rites.

[39] von Sicard H. 'Eine Afrikanische Bundeslade' *Studia ethnographica Uppsala* No. 5, 56 quoted in Schoffeleers *M'bona* 370

[40] Marwick M. G. 'Another modern anti-witchcraft movement in East-Central Africa. *Africa* XX 1950, 100–12

[41] Richards A. I. 'A modern movement of witchfinders' *Africa* VIII 1935, 448–61

[42] H. L. Duff arrived in Nyasaland in 1898 and rose to be Acting-Deputy Governor during the First World War. His undisguised racism in *Nyasaland under the Foreign Office* London 1903, provides a useful standard for comparison in judging the attitudes of European missionaries towards Africans

[43] Duff *Nyasaland* 246, and Hetherwick A. *A Romance of Blantyre* London c. 1930 103' The tune became the melody of Hymn No. 211 in the *Native Hymn Book* used at Blantyre Cathedral.

[44] The perpetual mother of the Phiri chiefs e.g. Karonga, Undi, Kaphwiti, and Lundu

[45] The Banda wife of the High God, Chiuta. The sense of the word in Mang'anja is a betrothed woman who is not yet cohabiting with a husband.

[46] The great Chewa prophetess at Msinja see Rangeley W. H. J. 'Two Nyasaland Rain-Shrines: Makewana the mother of all people'. *Nyasaland Journal* Vol. V July 1952, 31–50.

[47] The White Fathers were, of course, 'La Societé des missionaires de *Notre Dame* d'Afrique.' and the spirituality of the Montfort Fathers was strongly Marian in tenor. The Montforts' real title was 'The Company of Mary' but the abbreviated form of Montfortian, 'Montfort' will be used here as it is the commonest usage in Malawi.

[48] The *prazos* were originally Portuguese Crown estates. They later became hereditary principalities under the rule of powerful half-caste families independent of Portuguese jurisdiction. The *prazos* owners were a serious threat to Portuguese authorities and the church was probably destroyed during the Massingire rising of 1884—see Newitt M. D. D. 'The Massingire Rising of 1884' *J. African History* Vol. XI. No. 1 1970, 87–105.

[49] *Nsanje Mission Diary* December 1926. Nsanje is the name for the old 'Port-Herald'. Names now change rapidly and some of the nomenclature used here may be out of date.

[50] Terms used by Horton R. 'African Conversion' *Africa* Vol. XLI. No. 1 April 1971, 85–108

[51] Wallis J. P. R. (ed.) *The Zambesi Expedition of David Livingstone 1858–1863, Vol. I* London 1956. Entry for Sena 20 March 1859, 87.

[52] Eliade M. *Patterns in Comparative Religion* London 1958, 196

[53] Omer-Cooper J. *The Zulu Aftermath* Longmans 1966

[54] The initial fear amongst the northern Ngoni was that conversion to Christianity would weaken the martial personality of the Ngoni. On the other hand the paramount, M'belwa opposed the activity of the Livingstonia missionaries amongst the Tonga as did Matapwiri and Mponda amongst the Chewa vassals of the Machinga Yao.

[55] Harry Johnston was born in London on 5 May 1858. His career as a colonial officer began in the Oil Rivers in 1887 after a previous exploration of the Niger Coast in 1882. It was Johnston more than any other man who shaped the future Nyasaland Protectorate between 1889 and 1896. His desire for a 'Crown Colony' and his policy of 'divide and rule'

resulted in the forcible subjugation of independent indigenous authorities and left an indelible mark on colonial Malawi. See Johnston H. H. *The Story of My Life* London 1923, and Stokes E. 'Malawi Political Systems and the Introduction of Colonial Rule: 1891–1896' in *The Zambesian Past* ed. Stokes E. and Brown R. Manchester 1966, 352–75.

[56] The Alomwe were migrants from Portuguese East Africa who began coming into Malawi at the beginning of the twentieth century. The major influx was c. 1920–30, providing the bulk of the labour force in the Shire Highlands. The Sena began moving into the Lower Shire Valley after the Makombe rising of 1918 until today they form the dominant group south of Chikwawa. The Sena, like the Alomwe, represented a number of different peoples and clans and are only treated as a unified tribe for convenience to distinguish them from the Chewa-speaking peoples of Malawi.

CHAPTER I

The White Fathers in Yaoland

Finally a small detail, which might if the occasion arises be of some use to
Your Eminence; the advances made us by Major Serpa Pinto, and the over-
tures from the Portuguese Government have, I believe, as their main aim, to
make use of your influence on their behalf to offset English designs around
Lake Nyasa.

Father Deguerry to Cardinal Lavigerie [1]

By the middle of 1888 possession of the triangle of territory from the southern
tip of Lake Nyasa to the Zambesi, and from Tete to the Indian Ocean at
Quelimane, had taken on inordinate importance for the British and Portuguese
governments. It lay at the intersection of grandiose imperial dreams, on a line
from the Cape to Cairo, and from Angola in the west to Mozambique in the
east. Through it ran the Shire river, marshy and mosquito-ridden, with
awkward cataracts and sandbanks, but consecrated by Livingstone as the principal route to Nyasa and the great lakes of Tanganyika and Uganda.

Behind the British claim to the heart of this territory, the Shire Highlands,
were the commercial interests of the African Lakes Company, and a decade of
missionary settlement. Although the Portuguese had never permanently occupied the area, their interest in the region of the lake dated from the sixteenth
century. They had assumed that their jurisdiction extended from the coast and
the Zambesi into the interior. No foreign power had seen fit seriously to challenge it before.

From the arrival of the Scots missionaries in 1875, the Portuguese authorities
at Quelimane and Mozambique began to have misgivings. After the explorer,
Chirnside's, publication of 'Discreditable Disclosures' [2] about the Blantyre missionaries, within five years of their settlement in the Shire Highlands, it became
apparent that the Portuguese fears had not been misplaced. Some of the Europeans at the Blantyre mission had assumed powers reminiscent of Calvin's
Geneva.

There was little the Portuguese could do to bring the Protestant missionaries
to order. At the disposal of the Governor-General of Mozambique were less
than 1,500 troops, mostly *degredados* [3] or virtually untrained Africans, to
garrison 2,300 miles of coastline and the Zambesi valley as far as Zumbo. [4] Even
if Portuguese jurisdiction had been more than nominal, the main water route
from Sena and Quelimane, up the Shire, passed through territory controlled by

the half-caste *prazo* owners, and by the Kololo. Neither could be guaranteed to allow unimpeded passage of Portuguese military expeditions into the area of the lake.

An outbreak of hostilities between the agents of the African Lakes Company [5] and the Arab slavers at Karonga, the Mlozi war, accentuated the predicament of both the imperial powers. While the Portuguese were continually irritated by the large-scale shipments of arms into the interior in 1887 to 1889, the British began to chafe at customs and import restrictions that slowed down what they felt to be a legitimate campaign against slavery. A boat of the African Lakes Company, *James Stevenson*, was impounded by the Portuguese and a long drawn-out diplomatic war between the two countries began.

It was forcibly impressed on the Portuguese that the vanguard of British occupation of the Shire Highlands was the highly articulate Scots and Universities' Mission to Central Africa missionaries, who followed Livingstone. In July 1888, secret instructions were sent to Antonio Maria Cardoso,[6] an explorer with fifteen years experience on the Zambesi, to establish contact with chiefs in the region of the lake with a view to establishing a rival Catholic mission, which would counteract the influence of the British Protestants.[7] The site chosen for the mission was the village of the Yao chief, Cuirassia, who had accepted vassalage to the King of Portugal during the expedition of Cardoso's namesake, Augusto, in 1886. Cardoso reached his destination on 12 December 1888 to find the Portuguese protegé in hiding in the hills, and eager to gain protection from the powerful Masininga Yao chief, Makanjila, whose town was by the lakeshore to the north.[8]

Rather than found a mission near such an obviously weak chief, Cardoso set about fulfilling the second part of his mandate, to extend Portuguese influence in the lake region. In a remarkably successful treaty-making expedition he persuaded a number of chiefs to accept the Portuguese flag. The most important of these were Mponda, who controlled the Mpinganjila crossing of the Shire, and Matapwiri, strategically placed on the western slopes of Mount Mulanje. The assessment of the treaties by Ross, the Vice-Consul at Quelimane, as, 'just the sort of thing anyone in authority could get an ignorant Native to do for a few pieces of cotton and a gaudy flag',[9] showed more pique than insight. Both Mponda and Matapwiri were well aware that the treaties were a form of alliance. While they did not foresee the long-term implications,[10] it was no coincidence that these two chiefs, controlling important trade routes, had accepted Portuguese vassalage at a time when the Scottish African Lakes Company was making its presence felt on the lake.

As Cardoso was setting off to obtain the goodwill of the lakeshore Yao, two prominent Portuguese with strong interest in the colonies were on their way to Paris to negotiate the foundation of a mission with Cardinal Lavigerie, the head of the White Fathers. Serpa Pinto,[11] surrounded by all the glamour of explorers in the Victorian era, and Henrique de Macedo, were both keenly aware of the value of missionaries. Macedo felt that

There is simply no excuse for a country abandoning territory it has already conquered to the enemy because no importance is ascribed to the political and other advantages which missionaries can offer.[12]

The only problem was that the Portuguese Church, happily embedded in a compliant peasantry, had produced no Religious Orders dedicated to mission work such as the French had in the nineteenth century. The Bishop of Mozambique, Jose Antonio Barroso, felt the same way.

The English know that a missionary is worth more than thirty bales of cotton-wool. Our practice however is to consider them less than a trainee-sergeant.[13]

The Portuguese did need what the French Ambassador to the Vatican called a 'milice ecclésiastique'[14] to consolidate their position on the Zambesi but they were obliged to turn to foreign missionaries to recruit one.

The policy pursued in the Shire Highlands was a continuation of a diplomatic offensive that had been waged largely at the Vatican between 1881 and 1886. The Portuguese incumbents on the coast at Loanda and in Angola had attempted to secure ecclesiastical jurisdiction over territory in the hands of French and Belgian explorers.[15] Their claims were justified by the *padroado* agreements made between the Pope and Portuguese King, before the formation of the Propaganda Fidei in 1622, which gave the Portuguese ecclesiastical control of large and ill-defined areas of Africa. Cardinal Lavigerie had remarked ruefully of these tactics that 'if you have to go back to the sixteenth century to justify the grants made by these Bulls, you might as well go back to the Flood'.[16] But in a Church dominated by precedent and Papal Infallibility, sixteenth-century Bulls could not easily be forgotten, and the Vatican was obliged to struggle to regain control of mission fields once handed over to the Portuguese Crown.

Cardinal Lavigerie's prestige was high in Europe. His anti-slavery crusade had taken him to a number of countries and his reception had been invariably warm. In case a recent visit to England had clouded his judgement, the Portuguese envoys were charged to dispel from the Cardinal's mind 'any prejudices stemming, to some degree, from an unfavourable view of Portuguese Dominion, produced by the tenacious and persistent efforts of adversaries of that Dominion'.[17] Serpa Pinto's and Macedo's efforts in the realm of public relations were no less successful than Cardoso's. Two weeks later Lavigerie was in Rome for consultations.

The White Fathers were enthusiastic about establishing a mission in the Nyasa region. The fortunes of their missions in Equatorial Africa had declined seriously during the year. As a result of the 'Muslim Wars' in Uganda, all European missionaries had been forced to flee the Ganda capital.[18] The Abushiri rising against the German colonization of Tanganyika had temporarily closed routes to the interior through Bagamoyo.[19] Captain Joubert and his *zouaves*, who were to protect the missionaries, were cut off from supplies. Within a few months the White Fathers were forced out of Kipalapala by the Nyamwezi chief, Isike.[20] A water route up the Shire and through the Great Lakes seemed the best hope of resupplying the White Fathers in East-Central Africa. A station at the south end of Lake Nyasa linked to a supply centre in Quelimane would be a stepping stone to Lake Tanganyika. Lavigerie was sufficiently concerned at the plight of his men not to feign indifference.

The gravity of the White Fathers' situation in 1889 can be gauged from their losses after twenty years in Africa. Between 1868 and 1878 there were 175 priests ordained in the Society; 46 of them were dead before the end of 1889.[21] Unlike members of the Universities' Mission to Central Africa, who might perhaps be accused of courting martyrdom, the White Fathers looked after themselves. It would be no exaggeration to say that when Lavigerie went to Rome he was facing a possible collapse of his Central African missions.

However, the initial discussions between Martens, the Portuguese Ambassador to the Vatican, and Simeoni, the Cardinal Prefect of the Propaganda, revealed that Lisbon was in no hurry to dispatch missionaries to the Shire Highlands. The Vatican charitably put down the dilatory character of the talks to the Portuguese desire not to annoy the British with whom they had agreed to combat slavery on the coast. It was more likely that the Portuguese believed England to be uninterested in the region around Lake Nyasa and therefore gave action south of the Zambesi higher priority.[22] With the Pope and Propaganda fully aware of why the Portuguese wanted missionaries for the area,[23] it served Martens well to delay and hold out for the best possible terms.

The mission's mandate was to be 'the teaching of the Catholic Faith to the natives; agricultural development; the mission should bring to a halt the slave trade by all means at its disposal; it should build schools, churches, chapels and fulfil other obligations of its mandate'.[24] But the medium of instruction was to be Portuguese, and all establishments founded by the mission, while belonging to the White Fathers and for their use, would be considered Portuguese property. In exchange 50,000 francs were to be made available for the foundation and an annual subsidy of 20,000 francs paid until the station was self-supporting.[25] No *zouaves* would be permitted.

If Martens wanted the role of the mission in the secular city well defined, he was no less insistent about its status in the *civitas dei*. Lavigerie first held out for Vatican control:

> Missionaries would, in religious matters, be exclusively under the authority of their Religious Superiors in the Congregation, to whom they would owe their allegiance, and who would ask for and receive from the Holy See for their subordinates those spiritual powers necessary for the exercise of their apostolic ministry.[26]

Martens, an experienced Vatican diplomat, produced a Papal Bull of 21 January 1612, 'In Supereminenti', in which the region of the Zambesi valley, and an ill-defined territory around it, were conceded to the spiritual jurisdiction of the Portuguese.[27] Although, it was agreed, missionaries were to be directly answerable only to their Religious Superiors in the White Fathers, their spiritual powers, the right to hear confessions and say mass, were going to be under the control of the Portuguese Bishop of Mozambique.

The issue of spiritual jurisdiction, on which Lavigerie was defeated, was more than an impressive display of canonical legerdemain by Martens. The Portuguese wanted, and got, a national mission, both temporally and spiritually dependent on Portuguese goodwill. On Mozambique Island the Bishop was the right hand of the Governor-General, and acted in his absence. After their experience with the Scots, the Portuguese authorities were wary of giving any missionaries more freedom of action than was necessary. To have allowed the White Fathers, and the Vatican, spiritual jurisdiction would have opened the door to a degree of autonomy unacceptable to Lisbon.

Lavigerie gained a small concession; any Portuguese priests attached to the mission should undergo training as White Fathers. For his co-operation in Portuguese colonial expansion, he received the Grand Cordon of the Order of Christ from His Most Faithful Majesty, and the distant hope of getting supplies through to Tanganyika from the Zambesi. And it did, indeed, appear in the spring of 1889 that Portugal had the spiritual and temporal powers to dispense in the Shire Highlands. In April, Johnston in Lisbon brought Barros Gomes[28] to the point of shelving the age-old Portuguese dream of a swath across Africa, from Angola to Mozambique, in an extraordinary feat of diplomatic skill and cosmopolitan charm. The price was the Highlands, and with them, the Blantyre Mission. As the negotiations between Martens and Lavigerie drew to a close, the Cardinal had every reason to suppose that Blantyre was shortly to find itself in Portuguese territory.

In early February, the first practical steps towards founding a mission were taken. Father Deguerry was sent from Algiers to check that the route from Blantyre to Tanganyika was economically feasible.[29] He was impressed, both by the friendly attitude of the Portuguese towards the idea of a mission and by the convenience of the service offered by the steamers of the African Lakes Company. On the other hand, he complained that the prices of the Company were very high compared to the cost of overland porters, and estimated the travelling time between Quelimane and Karonga at six weeks. The negligible Portuguese control over the Upper Shire and lake region was duly reported to Lavigerie. In April 1889, Deguerry wrote back that the African Lakes Company had a monopoly of communications, but the Portuguese had put a ten per cent customs duty on goods passing through Quelimane.[30] It did not require great perspicacity to foresee an international conflict of interests in the area.

Deguerry returned to Maison-Carrée[31] in June, suffering from malaria, and personally confirmed his written reports. On 23 June 1889 the five missionaries chosen for Nyasa, after several weeks training in the Portuguese language with Messrs. Quefellec and Jeanselme from Marseilles, were given a formal farewell from Lavigerie in the Basilica of Our Lady of Africa.[32] Lavigerie had doubtless seen the ominous implications of Deguerry's reports, but was in no position to vacillate. His speech to the missionaries had all the marks of bravado used to disguise profound apprehension.

Abandon our missions, missions that have been growing for ten years in soil watered by our very blood. People who talk this way can have no idea what manner of men we are. It is because the danger for them is so pressing that we

17

cannot desert them. Desert our neophytes, our catechumens, our bought slaves, just to save our skins for a few more days on this earth. Never, my dear brothers in Christ. Never![33]

The religious glories and maritime history of Portugal were then extolled. The ceremony was closed by the Portuguese National Anthem introduced by the Cardinal: 'This was the tune St. Francis Xavier once listened to, and I wanted it to be ringing in your ears, my children, at the moment of your departure.'[34]

Not surprisingly, the Scots and Universities' Mission to Central Africa missionaries around the lake found the prospect of the Portuguese National Anthem ringing in their ears far less pleasurable. Angry rumbles went up from the Shire Highlands as the results of Johnston's diplomacy in Lisbon became public. In Scotland, ministers and church elders collected over 10,000 signatures to an anti-Portuguese petition to be sent to Westminster on behalf of the Presbyterian Church.[35] The combination of Anglican and Presbyterian churchmen, Glasgow businessmen, and loyal Scottish members of Parliament, formed a powerful lobby. Lord Salisbury,[36] preferring the 'wrath of Portugal' to that of Scotland, needed little coaxing to ignore Johnston's agreements in Lisbon.[37] By the end of July, Johnston, with £2,000 of Rhodes' money[38] in his pocket, had been dispatched to Quelimane to attempt a more muscular solution to the problem.

After forcing the Chinde mouth of the Zambesi in a British gunboat, H.M.S. *Stork*, Johnston continued up the Shire, making treaties with every willing chief. At the same time Serpa Pinto moved north overland with more than 700 armed men, ostensibly an escort for two engineers who were to survey the region of the Shire cataracts, with a view to extending a projected railway between Quelimane and the Zambesi, into the region of the lake. The Portuguese railway was the answer to the steamers of the African Lakes Company. Four days after Johnston had chatted amiably in Portuguese with Serpa Pinto, Buchanan, a Zomba planter and Acting British Consul, declared on 15 August 1889 that the territory of the Kololo and the Shire Highlands north of the Ruo junction with the Shire was under British protection. Johnston, frightened by the strength of Pinto's forces, had issued the order on arriving at Katunga, the last stop on the Shire below the Blantyre Escarpment.[39]

Serpa Pinto, who was then three days march from Mopeia, managed to telegraph the news back to Quelimane by 22 August.[40] His expedition had already come under sporadic fire from the Kololo who were being encouraged by the British to start a major incident. Agents of the African Lakes Company were reported to be smuggling gunpowder to the Kololo and, on one occasion, were themselves seen firing on the Portuguese forces.[41] One of the Portuguese engineers, Ferraz, retaliated by sacking a Kololo village, and the main body of Pinto's troops moved north to Mpassa. A colonial war seemed likely. Serpa Pinto managed to get back to Quelimane for consultations in a fourteen-day marathon using forced marches, *machila*, boat, and steamship.[42]

It was into this microcosm of the scramble for Africa that the Catholic missionaries on board the Castle-Mail *Dunkeld* steamed from Mozambique to

Quelimane on 19 August 1889. The caravan had already lost a Brother from Metz, Chrétien Hermann, who, barely three weeks after leaving Marseilles, died off Zanzibar from a fall down the steps into the hold of their ship, the *Mendoza*.[43] The group was led by Father Adolphe Lechaptois, 36 years old, ordained in 1878, but with barely three years experience of mission work, and that amongst Algerian Arabs; he had been for the other eight years a teacher at a minor seminary, and master of novices at Maison-Carrée. A man of almost pathological humility, he later became Vicar-Apostolic in Tanganyika. His greatest praise was for Father Joseph Mercui, his assistant, who Lechaptois felt should have been made Superior of the mission. Mercui too had pursued a fundamentally academic career in Algeria as head of the philosophy school at Maison-Carrée. A more driving personality than Lechaptois, he was more at home amongst archives than Machinga villagers, whom he seems to have seen less as persons than as interesting subjects for his prolific writing. A third priest, Heurtebise, whose immunity to Jesuit spirituality was endearing only to later generations, was 'inclined to be difficult to deal with when ill'.[44] That one, at least, of these priests was unable to accept endless bouts of haematuria and dysentery with angelic equanimity, is somehow reassuring. With them, as 'hewer of wood and drawer of water', was the remaining Brother, Antoine Verkuylen from Utrecht.

The missionaries were obliged to wait in Quelimane while Portugal reacted officially to Buchanan's declaration. It was an unpleasant surprise for them to find, despite much talk about the religious glories of Portugal, that the churches were almost empty. It was a first indication that the religious aspect of the Portuguese mission amongst the Yao was something of a charade. They had become, unwittingly, a pawn in a diplomatic game played between Lisbon and London. But at Quelimane they were on the wrong side of the board, and by August 1889 the Portuguese had fallen several moves behind Johnston. On 2 September Lisbon cabled the Governor-General to get the priests moving.

> It is absolutely indispensable to establish the Mission, accompanying the missionaries with all the forces necessary to ensure their complete safety, and making preparations for boats to navigate the Zambesi and the Shire, as soon as possible.[45]

However, with revolts simmering in the Massingire and Mang'anja *prazos*, and the Kololo well armed by the British, it was impossible to guarantee the safety of any expedition up the Shire. Furthermore no amount of edicts from Mozambique could drum up porters if they were unavailable on the *prazos*. The four missionaries were stuck in Quelimane. By early October, Lechaptois was desperate enough to be thinking of asking the African Lakes Company to take them to Mponda, the chief selected by the Portuguese as their patron.[46]

At last, on 13 October, the party led by Cardoso himself moved on by boat to Marral, the staging area for caravans to the interior. Amongst the Portuguese it was always Cardoso and Pinto who showed the greatest emotional involvement in the establishment of the mission. They had a stake in Africa and a genuine interest in seeing Portuguese settlement in the Shire Highlands. It was their misfortune that enthusiasm for colonial expansion tended to decrease in proportion to the distance from the Shire river.

For the rest of the month the expedition stayed at the Jesuit mission in Marral while porters were summoned from the neighbouring Mopeia, Makuz, and Marral *prazos*. Marral served as the turn-around point for traders from the interior, and porters could normally be found there waiting for a return journey. Only chiefs such as Matapwiri, who had accepted vassalage to the Portuguese Crown, were permitted to continue into Quelimane itself. The missionaries had been at Marral a week when a large caravan of 500 people, led by Matapwiri himself, brought Cardoso the news that Serpa Pinto's troops were being opposed by Mlauri, a Kololo chief, and his followers. Cardoso immediately set off for the Shire to try to negotiate with Mlauri.[47] But, under pressure from Moir,[48] as eager as ever to see the Portuguese railway venture stillborn, Mlauri attacked the Portuguese and was repulsed with heavy losses, before Cardoso could intervene.

On 5 November a Portuguese Agent set out from Marral with 130 men for Cuirassia's, and two armoured launches were sent up the Shire to reinforce Serpa Pinto. Five weeks later Portuguese troops were at Chiromo and moving north to Katunga. With the Lower Shire effectively under Pinto's military control, the missionaries set off overland for Mponda's village, on the Shire between Lake Nyasa and Lake Malombe. The caravan with its 460 porters, servants, and Portuguese Agent, Mr. Texeira de Sousa, bore the lofty title 'The Henrique Macedo Civilizing Mission', otherwise known as the Portuguese Mission to Mponda's.

The official decree of the mission's foundation had been signed by King Luiz of Portugal on 12 August 1889. The royal approval entailed a number of obligations:

> The obligation of civilizing the tribes in question by means of the propagation of the Catholic Faith among them, by inspiring them with an attachment to labour, by making use of the greatest efforts and exertions with a view to suppressing the Slave Trade, and finally by abolishing their barbarous usages and customs by means of instruction, and especially by teaching them Christian Morality.[49]

Their sphere of evangelization was theoretically the gigantic area north of the Ruo confluence, up to 16° latitude and the Tanganyika border, up to 36° longitude, and to an ill-defined extent westwards. As the caravan moved north along the course of the Luala river, there seemed no immediate reason why the Catholic missionaries should fail to carry out the wishes of the Portuguese Crown to the letter.

On 9 December, after experiencing considerable difficulty in buying provisions along the route, the caravan reached Mount Mulanje and Matapwiri's village. The chief proudly showed the missionaries his shop in the middle of a village of more than 300 huts.[50] Along the rest of the route the priests seem to have been surprised at the sight of heavily armed people in the Yao villages. At Mutomanja's, despite a Portuguese flag flying upside down, the porters refused to continue for fear of ambush, and only personal assurances from the chief got them moving again.[51] The reception at Kabuto's, a well-fortified village on a mountain ridge, was far less cordial than at Matapwiri's; the villagers were 'thievish' and unpleasant.[52] Further rumours reached the missionaries here of a major war going on between Mponda and his relatives. Neither Mutomanja nor Kabuto wanted the priests to leave and they plied them with gloomy tales of Mponda's decline. But on 28 December, when the canoes were taking the porters' loads across the Shire into Mponda's village, the chief himself came to greet the missionaries; he showed them to an unfinished hut in an apparently peaceful and prosperous village.[53] From the heavy fortifications it was clear that the peace was only temporary.

Mponda belonged to a group of Machinga Yao who had peacefully entered the region around the southern end of the lake in the 1860s. They had been pushed from their settlement to the north-east, on the Lujenda river, by pressures from Makua-Lomwe peoples, and by the movements of the Maseko Ngoni.[54] The original Mponda, known as CheMambo, was chief over a large part of the Cape Maclear peninsula between 1866 and 1886, and raided for domestic slaves.[55] He was the son of Msamala, the founding father of the lineage; his mother, Ngala, was a cousin of the chief. When Mponda I died, the legitimate matrilineal heir, Ndile, assumed the rightful title of Msamala II, but was quickly murdered.[56]

When the Livingstonia missionaries began work in 1875, Mponda I's village was already occupied by a number of Arab slavers;[57] its square houses were ornamented in Arab fashion.[58] But, owing to the disputed legitimacy of his chieftancy, Mponda was eager for potential allies and did not allow the Muslim influence to prevail over the advances of the Scots missionaries. A Free Church of Scotland Mission was established, with Mponda's permission, on Cape Maclear, but owing to the unsalubrious conditions moved after six years to Bandawe.

The Swahili influence in the village seems to have increased after the withdrawal of the missionaries. A description of Mponda by an employee of the A.L.C. in 1884 shows the advantages accruing from the coastal slave trade.

> He had sitting around him about 40 of those low-caste Arabs and all were armed with guns . . . Mponda showed the captain a goodly number of Enfield rifles and as he showed them, he boasted that he now had as many guns as the white man.[59]

When the chief died in 1886 he was buried according to Islamic custom, the head pointing towards Mecca.[60] After prolonged exposure to Muslim ideas, he, and a number of his councillors, had decided that conversion to the faith of their business associates was an obvious, and prudent, course of action.

On the death of Mponda I an inevitable succession dispute arose. Nkwate, the son of a slave wife of Mponda I, prevailed. After a brief period of co-existence, Mangamba, a senior wife of the dead chief, with her two sons, Malunda and Chungwarungwaru, were forced to leave the village. They settled further to the south and were joined by an equally discontented faction, consisting of the followers of the murdered Msamala II.[61] When Consul Hawes visited Mponda II in June 1886, the chief had a formidable array of opponents ranged against him. That he 'expressed great friendship for the English, and promised to maintain the same friendly feeling towards the A.L.C. as his predecessor', can be readily understood. Hawes was disappointed to note, though, that: 'On the question of trading with the Lakes Company he was very reserved.'[62]

The friendly sentiments towards the African Lakes Company were, of course, feigned. Company boats had, in the past, been fired on as they went by the village.[63] Mponda was strategically sited at an important crossing of the Shire, and his village was a trading centre where caravans from Mwase Kasungu's to the north-west met with Arab and Swahili traders from Mataka's and Mtarika's on the Lujenda.[64] Large stocks of ivory, an important item in this trade, were stored under the ground in Mponda's cattle pen.[65] Ivory was readily convertible into slaves, powder, or guns. According to Hawes, many of the coastal traders had begun to settle between Lakes Nyasa and Malombe.

> At several of the villages Arabs or coastmen reside, either having permanently established themselves, or waiting until they collect sufficient ivory to start a caravan to the coast.[66]

This slow transformation of trading contact into settlement was similar to the pattern of the earlier invasion of the Machinga themselves, who came initially to trade iron goods made in the Mang'anja ironworks.[67]

Within three years of avowals of allegiance to the British, Mponda had accepted the Portuguese flag from Cardoso. This *volte-face* seems to have been less the fecklessness of a habitual drinker, than an astute piece of diplomacy. The advantages of an alliance with the Portuguese in 1888 were twofold. First, it offered new trade prospects with Quelimane where, it was assumed, there were stocks of gunpowder and guns. Secondly, the activities of the Lakes Company agents, especially the Mlozi War, had begun to frighten slavers at the opposite end of the lake. If Cardoso and Mponda had nothing else in common in December 1888, they shared a strong desire to see the boats of the African Lakes Company, and all who sailed in them, at the bottom of the lake. The Portuguese offered protection from any future attacks by the African Lakes Company, alone, or in alliance with Malunda, Chungwarungwaru, and the rest.

After ambushing a large caravan belonging to Mataka, on the way from Mwembe to Mponda's, in 1888, Mponda's rivals began to make serious attacks on his stockade in the following dry season.[68] Mponda, in difficulties, was ready to swear to anything to gain British support; he gave Johnston solemn assurances that he had not received a Portuguese flag, that he would stay for ever loyal to the British, and that he had no animosity towards the agents of the African Lakes Company. Shortly after Johnston had steamed into the lake to visit the Jumbe's,[69] Mponda's outer stockade was razed by his rivals. The scene was watched by the Rev. W. P. Johnson[70] who was coming down the river from the lake. It is a measure of Mponda's lack of animosity towards the African Lakes Company that he immediately seized one of their barges that was in the area, on the assumption it was supporting Chungwarungwaru.[71] Mponda later burnt over thirty villages belonging to his rivals, in revenge. It was rumours of these repeated skirmishes that reached the missionaries along the route from Mozambique, sometimes inflated according to the demands of the situation, but giving the not unjustifiable impression that Mponda was fighting for his life throughout 1889.

The priests' expectations of a chief fully occupied in self-defence were not, then, too inaccurate. Mponda's corresponding expectations of the Catholic missionaries were doubtless coloured by his earlier experience of Scots and missionaries of the Universities' Mission to Central Africa. The Livingstonia missionaries had repaired his father's musical box, mended the broken leg of one of his wives, and retired to Bandawe. Their presence some way from Mponda's town had caused minor difficulties with Chewa vassals who no longer had wished to pay tribute. W. P. Johnson was even more innocuous, centred on Likoma Island to the north [72] and only occasionally calling in to share a joke. By being housed inside the town stockade the Catholics would have difficulty in contacting Chewa vassals and would be a guarantee of intervention by at least one of the European powers if the town was again in danger of being overrun. The Portuguese were likely to provide a liberal supply of guns and powder to protect them.

The Chief's behaviour on the missionaries' arrival gives a number of clues as to the role he saw them playing in the town. From his persistent demand for presents [73] it is plain that they were thought of as an inexhaustible supply of luxury goods, guns, and powder. The Portuguese Agent only managed to eke out his stock of fifty barrels of powder and fifteen guns for three months. The missionaries were expected to perform in the same way and only managed to convince Mponda that they had no arsenal by asking him to be present when their trunks were opened. [74]

The insistence of Mponda's demands stemmed from his fear of further more devastating attacks. Besides Malunda and Chungwarungwaru, he had also to contend with the enmity of another Yao chief on the corner of land where the Shire river opened into the lake. Chindamba was liable to attack any stray groups from Mponda's town. [75] More serious than such minor Yao chiefs was the enlistment by his enemies of support from raiding parties of Ngoni. Chikusi, the aged paramount of the Maseko Ngoni, [76] had little control over his war divisions. The Blantyre mission and European settlement in the Shire Highlands had reduced raiding there and the Ngoni were looking for fresh territory in which to prove themselves in battle. The lakeshore region was sufficiently profitable for the Maseko to become almost permanent mercenaries of the different Yao factions. Although their reputation certainly exceeded their performance, Mponda was terrified at the prospect of all his enemies attacking with Ngoni support, and needed to improve his firepower.

When the priests reached the town it was under siege conditions.

Around the royal quarters are earthworks a metre high by a metre wide, supported by a sort of reed scaffolding. The two entrances to the royal enclosure have spiny branches in them for extra security. Behind them is a large deep moat in rather poor repair. [77]

In Lechaptois' apt phrase, it was a case of 'manus ejus contra omnes et manum omnium contra eum'.[78] To offset Chikusi's mercenaries, Mponda had hastily recruited 400 Ngoni from the rival Njokozera war division under the command of Chifisi, Chikusi's cousin.[79]

The power of Machinga chiefs such as Mponda was, at this time, almost entirely dependent on two related factors, the possession of heavy fire-power and the control of the coastal slave and ivory trade. Mponda's survival could be attributed to his possession of over 1,000 rifles,[80] and a large band of followers. While the trade routes to the East Coast stayed open – and here it was the commerce more than the Christianity of the Moir brothers and the Blantyre mission that was the threat—Mponda could hold on to his chieftancy. By raiding for slaves, he gained the wherewithal to buy guns and ivory, augment the number of junior slave wives, increase in prestige and stay in power. Any private caravans sent to the coast by dependent headmen required strong military escorts which only Mponda could supply. His monopoly of gunpowder supplies ensured the total dependence of both Chewa and Yao subordinates.

The effect of almost continual warfare on the loosely-knit Yao polity, with its freemen, who could split off to found new villages, and domestic slaves, who ran off on pain of death, was one of consolidation and concentration of population.[81] Outlying villages moved in for the protection afforded by Mponda's fortified town. What the missionaries first saw as they descended from the hills to river level, was a stockaded town about a mile wide, stretching along the banks of the Shire, and with a population of over 5,000 inhabitants.[82] Something very different from today's Machinga village of ten to twenty huts. Apart from the acute problems of providing food for a population this size, the missionaries' observations of daily life at Mponda's indicated that town life was producing new social tensions. The problems of war, overcrowding, disease, and famine, were being dealt with in a number of ritual ways.

Foremost among the social pressures was Mponda's need to assert his authority against the presumptions of headmen, brought into unusually close proximity to the royal stockade. These pressures gave rise to waves of *mwabvi* ordeals.[83] CheChangali, an important and powerful headman was obliged to undergo the ordeal, as was Mponda himself.[84] Conditions in the town were conducive to a high degree of religious innovation. Most striking were two rituals that involved the use of fire, a symbol of chieftancy and transition.[85] Both rituals resolved in symbolic form some of the deeper tensions and anxieties of social existence in the Machinga town.

Once a year Mponda ceremonially doused his fire, and all the fires in the town were extinguished. A new fire, from which the women in the village rekindled the fires in their own hearths, was then lit by the chief with his tinderbox. The ashes from all the old fires were placed outside the town and considered as a powerful medicine against attacks on the stockade, in the belief that they rendered the village invisible to all assailants.[86] In January 1891, before a Ngoni attack, Lechaptois heard that a 'madman', some form of spirit medium, was letting it be known that the ancestral spirits, the *masoca*, were dissatisfied. After the medium's demands, the planting of some beans on the stockade, had been carried out, his mouth was filled with water and a burning brand, made of straw, pushed in front of his face. The man instinctively spat out the water on to the flames and extinguished them. This was taken as a sign that the *masoca* were appeased.[87]

Continual raiding for slaves, and skirmishes with the enemy, had induced a state of permanent anxiety in all the inhabitants of Mponda's town. Apart from the traditional *mwabvi*, which had been modified so that slaves could take the poison on behalf of their masters,[88] an enormous proliferation of magical charms and talismans gave individuals an illusion of security. The priests discovered a royal medicine, *Liconocono*, which the chief hired out for payment, consisting of a large snail's shell filled with powder, that rendered the wearer impervious to attack. Many of the potions came from Lolo[89] recipes, the powder inside the *Kirisi* amulet being one such example. More interesting was that a number of charms showed the influence of imported religions; *Alibadiri*, with verses of the Koran wrapped up in little leather thongs, were commonly worn. They also noticed a charm known as *Mkira* which consisted of a boned buffalo-tail with the horn of a small gazelle inserted, and filled with powder. To gain protection from his enemies the wearer had to make the sign of a cross with it on the forehead;[90] since the powder was black this gave an uncanny resemblance to the penitential ashes on Ash Wednesday. Ritual crosses are known from the *unyago* drawings,[91] and other non-Christian derivations are equally possible.

The town was, then, a centre for an astonishing hotch-potch of religious ideas and practices. Mponda insisted on a full Ramadan, although Lechaptois noted with amusement that, instead of singing the correct Ramadan hymns, a number of common Arab songs were substituted.[92] Alongside a resident *muezzin* there was the official sorcerer in charge of making offerings to the ancestral spirits and protecting the entire population from attack. There was nothing out of the ordinary in a practising Muslim like Mponda welcoming into his town proponents of another religion. The town was already a thriving market-place for religious wares and if the White Fathers wanted to peddle their particular merchandise, alongside the Swahili charm sellers, Mponda did not object. Enough religious eclecticism was practised amongst the Machinga to accommodate the Catholic symbols.

But, just as Mponda maintained a monopoly of gunpowder and war medicines, he immediately made it clear that the White Fathers were to be solely under his patronage. Though they were not residents of the royal stockade itself, the chief made it impossible for them to procure food except as a gift from his own hands. His authority over members of the town did not stop at the door of the mission school. When an Ngoni boy was given one stroke of the cane by Father Heurtebise for bad behaviour, Mponda insisted on receiving a length of cloth as compensation.[93]

As a result of their training in North Africa, the missionaries' expectations of Mponda were not clouded by the romanticism that characterized the first missionaries of the Universities' Mission to Central Africa to follow Livingstone. They were present as slave caravans rested in the town, Ngoni marauders were decapitated in public and their hearts torn out, and Mponda's wives executed for trivial misdemeanours. Not having expected a 'noble savage', they were less inclined to leap to arms when they found the contrary. Despite having read Livingstone and Waller[94] avidly, they did, however, expect to meet with a 'King', or at least a 'Sultan'. They were disappointed to find on arriving that: 'He is an elderly, thinnish man hardly affecting the airs of a mayor's clerk.'[95] They persisted in talking about a 'Machinga nation' who were 'in the process of rallying to the Portuguese'.[96] But, however long they looked, Mponda did not turn into a Kabaka, and the warring Machinga chiefs bore no resemblance to the centralized Buganda state.

Their knowledge of a little Arabic and Swahili meant that the coastal traders held less mystery for them than for their contemporaries at Blantyre. What they did underestimate, at the beginning, was the extent of the Muslim penetration of the town. While nobody at Mponda's could decipher Johnson's Arab characters,[97] and Arab influence was less marked than in the Masininga towns[98] of Mataka and Makanjila, Islam was dominant. Although few of the Machinga could speak Swahili, many of them could understand it.[99] Not appreciating the pervasive syncretism of African Islam, they assumed that the existence of traditional Machinga practices, such as the male circumcision rites of *unyago*, and the veneration of ancestral spirits, meant that Islam had not penetrated society to any great extent.[100] Their first Ramadan came as a shock, and they discovered with amazement towards the end of their stay that there were twelve Koranic schools in the town run by *mwalimus*.[101] Lechaptois wrote back ruefully to Rome in June 1891: 'Nous sommes arrivés ici avec les lunettes absolument noires, ce qui nous a empechés de voir les choses sous leur vrai jour.'[102] After the Portuguese had turned out to be only nominally Catholic, the Machinga proved to be strongly Muslim. Lavigerie had made his Nyasa mission the victim of his own rhetoric.

For the first few months after their arrival Mponda appears to have been undecided what to do with the missionaries and their agent. His attitude changed with the balance of power around the lake. Mponda had been much impressed by his first contact with Johnston, and had asked the Anglican missionary, Johnson, who was 'the little man who spoke with authority?'[103] The second meeting, as Johnston was returning to Blantyre in January 1890, resulted in his signing a treaty with the British. The priests had barely been at Mponda's a fortnight when the chief accepted British vassalage, and, according to Johnston, were 'practically prisoners in their own hired compound'.[104] Johnston's literary talents were running wild on this occasion. According to his account, for consumption in London by Salisbury: 'After signing this treaty he proceeded to hoist the British flag on his beach just in front of the house where the Portuguese were residing.'[105] The station diary tells a different story. A steamer arrived on 7 January 1890 and Mponda went on board to look at a machine gun—doubtless part of the inducement to sign on the dotted line.[106] There was no mention of a British flag being raised. The missionaries would not have failed to mention a change of flags; seven months later when the British flag was raised for the first time they comment on it with some alarm.[107] Flags were, after all, symbolic.

It was on this second visit from Johnston that Mponda's behaviour towards the Catholics changed for the worse. His demands became more imperious, and he began abusing the priests for not providing him with adequate supplies of gunpowder.[108] He had winkled most of the powder out of de Sousa by the end of the month with threats of handing back the Portuguese flag. Mponda had decided to throw in his lot with the British. And his evaluation of political realities was surprisingly accurate. As he was signing Johnston's treaty the Portuguese Council of State in Lisbon were stepping down before an ultimatum from Salisbury to evacuate the Shire Highlands. It was a crushing humiliation for Portugal, that brought down the Gomes government. Serpa Pinto's troops were withdrawn from Katunga.[109] As a weather-vane responding to the contending colonial forces around the lake, Mponda could not be bettered.

News of Serpa Pinto's withdrawal first reached the White Fathers in May 1890 by way of the Anglican Bishop, Chauncy Maples,[110] who was returning to England for a holiday on board the steamer *Charles Janson* of the Universities' Mission to Central Africa.[111] Three weeks later the *Domira* anchored off Mponda's with Moir on board, his arm still broken from the Mlozi War, together with Buchanan and his wife *en route* for Tanganyika.[112] They confirmed the news. The same evening, 'Mr. de Sousa abruptly declined to dine with us over some question about servants.'[113] A few weeks later Mponda made his preferences public; the missionaries wrote: 'A surprise. The English flag is flying by the Nyasa.'[114] By the time the flag was taken down, a day later, de Sousa had decided to leave. Father Mercui accompanied him to Quelimane in the hope of getting instructions from his own superiors.

Mercui's journey to the coast was forced upon the mission by an unbroken silence from Maison-Carrée. Their last contact with the Mother-House was a letter from Deguerry, dated 8 October 1889. Since that date Lechaptois had written fourteen successive letters giving details of the mission's progress.[115] They are an amazing testimony to Lechaptois' self-discipline; even in the last letters hardly a sign of desperation is allowed to appear. Instead, there is the plaintive, and faintly ludicrous demand, repeated in each letter, to know exactly the limits of the canonical powers held by the Mponda missionaries.

Lechaptois and his fellow missionaries had taken with them to Africa the full canonical structure of nineteenth-century European Catholicism. At Mponda's nothing was allowed to be altered in the laws of the Church. Through the most alienating events, the missionaries found comfort in strict adherence to the rules of their missionary society.

Towards noon, an Angoni in the prime of life had his throat slit. His heart was torn out and given to the medicine-man. It will be reduced to ashes and then mixed with flour. From this mixture a clear soup will be made, and all the warriors will drink this concoction to protect themselves from musket balls and arrows in the next campaign. A mix-up in our trunks led us to believe that we had a statue of Our Lady. But the box only contained broken vials with ingredients for the pharmacy. We do the month's spiritual exercises before a picture of Our Lady that we have found'.[116]

In the last few months of their stay, as they ran out of communion wine, all three priests gave up saying mass, their greatest spiritual support. There was a plentiful supply of palm wine, but since the rubrics demanded pure grape wine, they did not make use of it. To have used palm wine would have brought crashing down the ordered world of Church Law, and the specific regulations for the religious life.

By defining their existence in terms of the highly-regulated life of a monk, the missionaries were able to survive almost constant sickness, and total isolation from their Religious Superiors, for over a year. It was precisely this legalism, which today seems as grotesque as Johnston's dinner jacket in the bush, that structured their daily lives, and made their existence at Mponda's less stark. The daily pattern of prayer and spiritual reading went on as Englishmen drank tea on board the Company boats anchored in the Shire, and Ngoni troops were slaughtered within yards of their hut. Some measure of the psychological importance of routine in this alien environment can be judged from the time it took before the priests dared to venture far from their stockade.

> After Vespers, which we always sing on Sundays, we went out with our little box of medicines to care for the sick. This is the first time that we have ventured forth like this.[117]

It was after a year, and within a few months of leaving, that the priests undertook an overland march of several hours, which took them some distance from the town.[118]

Coupled with this isolation, tantalizingly broken at intervals by the passage of the lake steamers, and the numerous small kindnesses of Johnson,[119] was their uncertainty as to the fate of the mission. In the course of 1890, Mponda gained the upper hand in battles with his rivals, and much of the immediate danger to the mission disappeared. Malunda was captured and killed and Chungwarungwaru put to flight.[120] On 22 January 1891, a decisive engagement was fought with Chikusi's mercenaries during which they turned tail and fled under withering fire from Mponda's guns.[121] But this respite from local pressures did not alter their precarious political situation as a Portuguese mission in British territory.

A combination of military success and Texeira de Sousa's departure changed Mponda's attitude to the White Fathers.[122] His friendship with Johnston had only been motivated by the fear that the British might attack his town. And he was well aware of the animosity between the Portuguese and British. When Sharpe refused to talk with him in July 1890; 'Great anxiety. He has now come to ask if this meant that war was imminent'.[123] In Mponda's mind the Portuguese Agent's return to Quelimane greatly reduced the probability of a British attack, and opened the possibility of trading with the African Lakes Company to gain British favour.

None the less, on 6 December 1890, when the *Domira* came to anchor at 8 a.m., the captain had the unpleasant surprise of seeing the Portuguese flag flying on the beach next to the British.[124] Mponda, coming home from a beer party at his brother's, Matavere's, arrived to find the British demanding that the

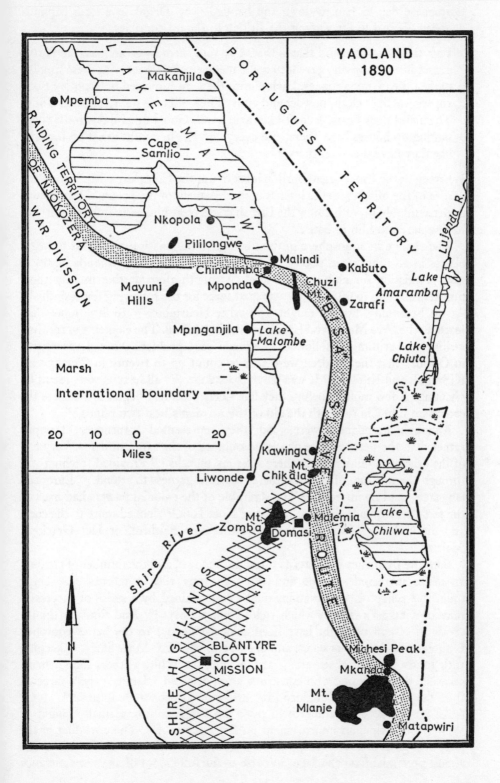

YAOLAND
1890

LAKE MALAWI

PORTUGUESE TERRITORY

RAIDING TERRITORY OF NJOKOZERA

WAR DIVISION

Lujenda R.

Mpemba

Makanjila

Cape Samlio

Nkopola

Pililongwe

Chindamba

Malindi

Kabuto

Lake Amaramba

Mayuni Hills

Mponda

Chuzi Mt.

Zarafi

Mpinganjila

Lake Malombe

Lake Chiuta

Marsh

International boundary

20 10 0   20
Miles

Kawinga

Liwonde

Mt. Chikala

Malemia

Lake Chilwa

Mt. Zomba

Domasi

Shire River

SHIRE HIGHLANDS

BISA SLAVE ROUTE

N

Michesi Peak

BLANTYRE
SCOTS
MISSION

Mkanda

Mt. Mlanje

Matapwiri

Portuguese flag be hauled down and handed over. Drunk as a lord, Mponda confided his real feelings about the British to the missionaries.

I am the King here and that is that. I've told them to go and see the Portuguese; it was they who gave it to me. I made an agreement with these English to the tune of 3,000 rupees. Each month they are supposed to bring me 1,000 rupees worth of cloth, powder and guns. They still owe me 1,000 rupees of it. Them and their boats, I don't like them at all. Going up and down the river, putting up houses here, there, and everywhere. They want to eat up my land like they have done to others.[125]

Whereupon the Chief began hurling invective at the Company officials from the garden of the mission, to the intense embarrassment of the priests. Mponda was understandably mystified how the British could treat him as an inferior, without having defeated him in battle.

The change in atmosphere in the town gave the missionaries heart to begin classes in an improvised school.[126] After de Sousa had left, Mponda began to give permission for children to attend. A month after starting in July 1890, numbers shot up to fifty,[127] and averaged forty for the following few months.[128] At the beginning, lessons taught by Father Heurtebise were little more than learning the 'Ave Maria' and Lord's prayer in ChiYao. The elements of reading, writing, and arithmetic, followed. Language was a problem. Mercui was writing in October that the children were able to count up to twenty in 'Portuguese, KiSwahili and KiYao'.[129] It was 'kuyimba sukulu',[130] all lessons were learnt by chanting. A few months before they left Lechaptois had begun to translate the catechism into ChiYao with the aid of the mission's best two pupils.[131]

Although attendances were good, they represented a turnover of pupils rather than the perseverance of a large number of the same students. Very few of the original attenders were there after six months.[132] Provided teaching was through the medium of Swahili, there was an eagerness to attend.[133] European languages held no interest.[134] The scramble of the colonial powers had masked the fact that Mponda, like the Jumbe of Kota-kota,[135] looked more to the coast and the Sultan of Zanzibar than to either His Faithful, or Her Gracious, Majesty.

Both the frequency of caravans through the town, and the number of resident *mwalimus* increased in 1890 and 1891; in June 1891 a mosque was being built.[136] Lechaptois' observations might be explained by a series of successful raids on Chikusi's villages which yielded many slaves.[137] And similarly the increase in *mwalimus* might have been a local response to the better-equipped Catholic school, with its slates, and one or two books.[138] More likely, in keeping with Johnson's own observations at the time, the White Fathers found themselves at the beginning of a conscious attempt at an Islamic revival, directed from the coast against European pressure on the major trade routes.[139]

An advantage the Fathers held over the *mwalimu* was a small amount of Western medicine, an improvement on Swahili amulets. The crowding of the population into stockades had produced an unprecedented level of squalor. The almost perennial food shortage gave rise to the full gamut of vitamin deficiency diseases; scabies was rife, and attacks of smallpox reached epidemic proportions.[140] Most cases of serious illness were isolated outside the town in special huts. Treatment of smallpox involved a slight degree of ritualization of behaviour so that the patient was virtually in quarantine. Only a single man was allowed care for to the smallpox case and all women were obliged to leave. The male nurse was not allowed to shave or cut his hair until the patient died, or recovered, and treated the case in a hut outside the stockade. The spots were pierced and then washed on alternate days with hot and cold water. Any smallpox patients in slave caravans were obliged to stay outside the town, as were troops wounded in war until they were declared fully recovered.[141] Whenever the priests left the town on medical visits they attracted huge crowds.

The White Fathers' isolation and uncertainty came to an end on 15 May 1891. The *Domira* anchored opposite the town during the night, carrying a letter from Mercui with their marching orders. Lavigerie's instructions on where to withdraw to had arrived in January at Quelimane, but the vagaries of the mail to the interior had held up Mercui's vital letter. It was high time. Portuguese supplies and communications to the interior had broken down, and there was no contact between the Portuguese stations in the Shire Highlands.[142] When Mercui arrived at Matapwiri's, on his way to the coast in August 1890, the Jesuits, newly installed there, were amazed to discover that the White Fathers were still alive at Mponda's.[143] Very few letters ever reached Mponda's from the other station at Cuirassia's;[144] in September, the resident there, Leal, had been obliged to sell his clothes to buy food before he could leave.[145]

The orders were to go north but this did not surprise the Fathers. They had heard about the Anglo-Portuguese treaty of 20 August 1890[146] in a letter from Mercui. They had seen the Portuguese flag hauled down, and listened with some amusement as agents of the African Lakes Company informed them that, since the region north of the Ruo confluence was under British jurisdiction, their safety had become a British responsibility.[147]

For fifteen months, almost completely unknown to the missionaries, the Catholic mission of San Luiz de Mponda had been at the centre of a diplomatic storm. Heurtebise's phlegmatic assessment of the complicated international politics, involving the mission, had a simplicity that defied denial.

Nous sommes partis sous le couvert du drapeau portugais; à peine étions-nous arrivés ici que le Portugal était supplanté sur les rives du Nyasa par l'Angleterre. C'était la réponse de Dieu.'[148]

On 16 June 1891, Lechaptois, Heurtebise, and Antoine, joined four Moravian Brethren and four Free Church of Scotland missionaries on board the *Domira*.[149] They had left behind Dominique Corogado, an ex-slave bought in the Sahara and trained in the Malta Institute whom they brought with them from Marseilles.[150] He had married a domestic slave and did not want to leave. They took with them three children whom they had bought at Mponda's during their stay.[151] Three weeks later, after a visit to the Jumbe, who seems to have impressed them greatly,[152] they left Karonga for Tanganyika and Bembaland where they founded a mission at Mambwe, within striking distance of the White

Fathers' missions in the Upper Congo and the Karema mission in Tanganyika.[153]

With a certain historical appositeness, it was finally British shells that flattened the San Luiz mission, on 19 October 1891; as the Fathers' improvised chapel and school went up in flames the last traces of Lavigerie's missions in nineteenth-century Nyasaland were erased.[154] Heurtebise, debilitated by fever, and returning to North Africa, made a pilgrimage to the mission and was present when Mponda's was attacked by Johnston's troops. A preliminary British sortie against Chindamba had driven a large number of captives into Mponda's hands. With almost 2,000 guns and a good supply of powder, Mponda tried Johnston's strength and refused to send off all the captives by boat. In the subsequent bombardment, Mponda fled to his villages in the Mayuni hills, to the west, whence he sent a peace offering of ivory. A peace treaty was signed on 27 October 1891, and the circular redoubt used by the British forces was fortified to become Fort Johnston.[155] Mponda, with typical aplomb, continued slaving from the hills until 1896 when the key links in the slave routes were finally broken by British punitive expeditions against the Machinga.

For ten years Mponda II had lied, pleaded, fought, and bluffed, to keep open the slave trade and stay in power. His diplomatic juggling had included keeping the British, Portuguese, Chikusi's mercenaries, Malunda, Chungwarungwaru, and Chindamba, in the air simultaneously. His skill earned him the somewhat inadequate reference from the much-manipulated Johnston of 'a very repellent type of Yao robber, alternately cringing and insolent'[156] and from Duff, 'dirty, ignorant, and uncouth'.[157] Inasmuch as the Catholic missionaries did not get in the way of this remarkable performance, and aided it, their presence in the village was tolerated. Some sort of genuine affection grew up between Lechaptois and Mponda during their stay. The chief consulted them on the issue of flags, enquired from them about 'Victoria and her son', used them as his amanuenses, and seems finally to have been very sorry to see them go.[158] Over the months the mission house became the meeting place for people, with queues of sick at the door. But both in the international politics surrounding them, and the local vendettas around the shore of the lake, the White Fathers were innocents abroad. They tried bravely to piece together the details of succession disputes, and the fragmented news from Quelimane, Lisbon, and London, but in vain. Only in the end did they see things 'in their true light';[159] they had been used and abandoned by the Portuguese.

As the Mponda mission was failing, the Portuguese made a second attempt to gain a foothold amongst the Yao through the use of Catholic missions and negotiated with the Jesuits for a settlement at Matapwiri's village. With the increasing effectiveness of the British coastal blockade in the 1880s, the old slave routes to Kilwa and Lindi took less and less traffic. The old Bisa trade route to Quelimane, Ingorde, and Angoche, was used with greater frequency so caravans increasingly passed through Matapwiri's village as they moved south from Mponda's, Zarafi's, and Kawinga's.[160] As a result Matapwiri came to assume an importance in the ivory and slave trade second only to Mponda. And since the rest of the route passed through Portuguese-controlled territory he was willing to fall in with Portuguese requests for a mission station—at least temporarily.

The problems confronting the Jesuits at Matapwiri's arose from the same factors that had bedevilled the White Fathers at Mponda's: Islamic slave-traders, Portuguese patronage, and poor communications. Their stay at Matapwiri's was short-lived.[161] With the Portuguese in full retreat, Matapwiri was anxious lest their presence cause trouble with the British. He complained bitterly to the Governors in Quelimane and Mozambique that the priests were causing difficulties in his village by attacking Islam. The Fathers were equally adamant that the chief's allegations were fabricated; he had been alienated by the too fulsome welcome accorded the missionaries by his Chewa vassals. Unable to obtain food, and with the Governor-General of Mozambique fearing for their safety, they moved nearer the Portuguese settlement at Milanje.[162]

Their second settlement on the slopes of Mount Tumbini put them in Portuguese territory after the 1891 frontier settlement. They had taken with them two Chewa chiefs who were glad to escape from Yao rule, and had the protection of a Portuguese garrison of fifty troops with a fort and cannons.[163] The arrival of troops had impressed Matapwiri, and the Father-Superior of the mission, Father Pierre Dupeyron, called for two further priests to serve a population he estimated at over 40,000 in the neighbourhood.[164] At the beginning of 1891 he seemed optimistic that the change of site would lead to a successful mission field.

It is true that there are a lot of superstitions in the country, and rough types who would slit your throat on a word from the King; but the people are intelligent, very keen to learn Portuguese, and the King is being careful not to do anything against the people sent by the government.[165]

The interest in Portuguese contrasted strongly with the apathy at Mponda's. It was a product of the different trade connections between the two towns, Mponda linked principally to Mtarika and the Swahili coastmen, Matapwiri with the prazos and Indian traders near Quelimane and Angoche. By the beginning of 1893, Matapwiri was a protégé of the Portuguese, a Capitao-Mor, with a colonel's uniform.[166]

On the other hand, the missionaries began to feel the pressure of Islamic mwalimu. Converts to Islam were called 'children of light and sons of the Most High', while anyone else belonged to 'a race of dogs'.[167] This aggressive Islam, of which there had been intimations at Mponda's two years previously, was a response to increasing European, Christian, control of the Shire Highlands. On the feast of St. Francis Xavier the first twenty-three children were baptized but by Christmas 1893 attendance at school had dropped off and only five people attended the Christmas mass.[168]

Part of Matapwiri's hostility to the mission came from the missionaries' association with the Chewa who were considered to be vassals. Nharuso had, in fact, held out against Matapwiri with the aid of thirty to forty old flintlock rifles and a well-fortified village for several years.[169] Chewa immediately under Matapwiri's jurisdiction were banned from attending the mission and from the end of 1893 threats were being made against the missionaries and the garrison.

Dupeyron lost both his reinforcements with malaria on the way from Quelimane and the Bishop of Mozambique, who visited the station for three weeks, suggested that the Jesuits give up.[170]

Despite the deteriorating situation Dupeyron stayed on, though without any illusions about the danger involved.

> These chiefs are all hostile to us because of Islam; all of them are polygamous and involved in the evil slave trade. For these reasons, deep in their hearts, they are badly disposed towards all Europeans. However, since there is a Portuguese commander at Milanje, and an English military post nearby, the power of the chiefs seems to diminish little by little, and after a short while, will be gone, unless of course there is a plot amongst all the chiefs and a universal rebellion takes place, something we very much fear.[171]

His fears were not unfounded. In August 1894, as part of more general Yao resistance to Johnston's raids, Matapwiri began to put his threats against Europeans into practice. Since raiding into the Shire Highlands had become increasingly dangerous he began seizing catechumens from the mission and selling them as slaves. The priests' association with the Portuguese had become a liability. On 15 and 16 October Matapwiri attacked the Portuguese, razed the mission and nearly succeeded in taking Milanje fort.[172] The Jesuits barely escaped with their lives to find refuge in the garrison, and the commander of the Portuguese troops had shamefacedly to send runners to Fort Lister to ask for support from the British.[173] Matapwiri was finally forced to retreat by the combined European forces, and a year later was obliged to surrender.[174]

The history of the Catholic missions in Yaoland was written eloquently in the rubble of Matapwiri's village, razed by the British.

> Besides a Koran was found a book entitled 'Défense du Christianisme', a Gospel according to St. Mark, a manual of polite correspondence in Portuguese and a number of account books.[175]

The mission crucifix later found its way back to Dupeyron at the Jesuit mission of Boroma near Tete.

The setback to Catholic missionary efforts in the area was total. As a result of Portuguese patronage the missionaries had found themselves astraddle the main trade routes to the coast for ivory and slaves. At Mponda's conditions had improved when the Portuguese Resident had left but their isolation was in no way alleviated. At Matapwiri's the need to rely on Portuguese armed support almost proved fatal when the chief finally turned against all Europeans.

In Mercui's words, the Catholic missions in Yaoland were sitting from 1889 to 1894 'sur un point d'interrogation'.[176] Far from 'making use of the greatest efforts and exertions with a view to the suppression of the Slave Trade', they had been obliged to co-exist with its main proponents. Unable and unwilling to resort to arms, the Catholic missionaries were helpless bystanders at the slow demise of slavery under British economic and military pressures. They left behind them the 'Yambo Maria',[177] the memory of 'some Fathers whom Matapwiri and Mtiramanja chased out'[178] and a few bricks on the slopes of

Mount Tumbini. The Catholic missions had to await the end of slavery and the *Pax Britannica* of the twentieth century before they could return to Nyasaland.

REFERENCES TO CHAPTER I

[1] Deguerry to Lavigerie 5 April 1889 Lavigerie Correspondence C.20.23 White Fathers' Archives Rome. Trans. from French. All quotations from Catholic sources are from the French with a few exceptions.

[2] Chirnside A. *The Blantyre Missionaries: Discreditable Disclosures* London 1880. Taken from the bibliography of Axelson E. A. *Portugal and the Scramble for Africa: 1875-1891* Johannesburg 1967.

[3] The Portuguese colonies were used as a place of exile for convicts and other undesirables

[4] Axelson E. A. 'Portugal's attitude to "Nyasaland" during the period of the partition of Africa' in *The Early History of Malawi* ed. Pachai B. Longmans 1972, 252. Background material for Anglo-Portuguese relations has been taken from Prof. E. A. Axelson's exhaustive studies on this topic.

[5] The African Lakes Company was a trading company which, with the Blantyre and Livingstonia missionaries, was, in theory at least, putting into practice Livingstone's ideas of Christianity and Commerce. The trading up the Shire and on the lake was supposed to stop the slave trade and open up the lakes region. The company had been founded in 1878 by James Stevenson to supply the missions. See a doctoral dissertation by H. W. Macmillan University of Edinburgh, 1970.

[6] Cardoso had been First Lieutenant of the Portuguese boat *Mindello*. He later became Governor of Quelimane and Inhambane for a period of three years. He was an indefatigable traveller and a staunch believer in Portuguese colonialism.

[7] Axelson *Portugal and the Scramble* 184

[8] ibid. The Masininga were a sub-group of the Yao who at the beginning of the nineteenth century had lived in the Lisininga hills. Their leading chiefs, Mataka, Mtarika, and Makanjila were the most powerful Yao in East-central Africa.

[9] Ross to Smith 4 April 1889 CP 5970 Quoted in Axelson *Portugal and the Scramble* 185

[10] Mponda Mission Diary 5 June 1891 'One thing is certain, the Negro Kings do not understand the obligations that they are supposed to accept with the national flag.' From a bound collection of cuttings from *Rapports annuels* and *Chroniques trimestrielles* for the Nyasa vicariate. 1941. Maison Carrée.

[11] Serpa Pinto had met Coillard in Barotseland and was a well-known figure in East-central Africa. He was a major in the Portuguese army with twenty years' experience in the Mozambique area. Like Cardoso he was a fervent imperialist.

[12] Schebesta *Portugals Konquestamission*, 295. Trans. from German. Original in *Boletim da Sociedade de Geografia de Lisboa IX/6*.

[13] Schebesta *op. cit.*, 298. Trans. from German Original B.S.G.L. Ser. 14 No. 7-8, 1895

[14] M. Desprez to de Freycinet 6 February 1882 Foreign Office Archives, Paris, Vol. 1072 Jan. to April 1882. Fol. 103-6 quoted in Roeykens Aug. *La Politique Religieuse de l'État Indépendant du Congo* (Documents I: Leopold II, le Saint-Siège et les missions catholiques dans l'Afrique Equatoriale 1876-1855) Acad. Roy. Sci. d'Outre-Mer Brussels 1965 NS XXXII 1, 372.

[15] The two missionary bodies concerned were the Holy Ghost Fathers and White Fathers. Cardinal Lavigerie experienced much the same difficulties with the Belgians as with the Portuguese. Neither were happy about having non-national missionaries in their territory, see Perraudin J. *Le Cardinal Lavigerie et Léopold II*. Editions C.I.P.A. Rome 1959.

[16] Note du Père Ch. Duparquet 7 August 1881 Holy Ghost Archives, Paris 658 V, 4 in Roeykens *L'État* 316

[17] Gomes to Martens 10 November 1888, Negocios externos: Documentos apresentados as Cortes 1890 No. 2 243

[18] The Kabaka, Mwanga, was deposed by Muslims on 10 September 1888 and his elder brother, Kiwewa, enthroned. Kiwewa's supporters attacked both Protestants and Catholics. The missionaries were driven out to the southern end of Lake Victoria. It was only in April 1889 that Mwanga regained his throne and reinstated the Christians at court.

[19] Abushiri bin Salim attacked Pangani in September 1888 in a wave of popular resistance to German occupation of coastal Tanganyika. There was heavy fighting at Bagamoyo. Abushiri was finally hanged in December 1889.

[20] Kimambo I. N. and Temu A. J. *A History of Tanzania* Nairobi 1969, 11

[21] Père Duchene *Les Pères Blancs: 1868–1892* Maison-Carrée, Algiers 1902 Appendix I

[22] Renault F. *Lavigerie L'Esclavage Africain et L'Europe, Tome II* Paris 1971, 167

[23] Renault *Lavigerie, Tome II* 166

[24] Martens to Lavigerie 14 December 1888 Negocios No. 8 250

[25] Gomes to Lavigerie 27 May 1889 Negocios No. 16 256 (9,000 milreis with 3,600 milreis per annum)

[26] Lavigerie to Gomes 1 June 1889 Negocios No. 19 261

[27] Gomes to Lavigerie 10 June 1889 Negocios No. 20 261

[28] The Portuguese Prime Minister whose government was shortly to fall over the issue of the Shire Highlands.

[29] *Missions Catholiques* 30 June 1889 568 White Fathers' Archives, Rome

[30] Deguerry to Lavigerie 5 April 1889 C.20.23

[31] Maison-Carrée, near Algiers overlooking the sea, provided the first of the White Fathers' orphanages for Arab children. The site was later built on in 1870 and became the Mother-House for the Society of Our Lady of Africa.

[32] Mponda Mission Diary 23 June 1889 White Fathers' Archives, Lilongwe. The Basilica was taken over in 1873 from the Premonstratensians, a Religious Order who were heavily in debt at the time. It was in the Archdiocese of Algiers.

[33] Duchene *Les pères* 293 Full text: Negocios externos No. 22 'Extracto do Jornal "Les Missions Catholiques" 6 July 1889

[34] ibid. Francis Xavier S.J. spent a few months on Mozambique Island in 1542 before going to Goa.

[35] Axelson *Portugal and the Scramble* 199

[36] The third Marquess of Salisbury (born Lord Robert Cecil, 1830; Lord Cranborne 1865–1881), was responsible for the direction of British Foreign policy for much of the time between 1885 and 1900. From 1886 to 1892 Salisbury acted, for most of the period, as both Prime Minister and Foreign Secretary. In 1892–5 Rosebery, and then Kimberley, served as Gladstone's Foreign Secretaries, until Salisbury was returned again. For his influence on Africa see Robinson R., Gallagher J. and Denny A. *Africa and the Victorians* London 1961, 254–7.

[37] Oliver R. *Sir Harry Johnston and the Scramble for Africa* London 1959, 150

[38] Cecil Rhodes came to London in March 1889 to found his British South Africa Company with a Royal Charter. In May he offered to pay for the cost of controlling the region of Lake Nyasa. Rhodes' money was a convenient answer to Salisbury's problem of saving the Scots missionaries from the Portuguese.

[39] Axelson *op. cit.*, 201–8

[40] Ribeiro to Ross 22 August 1889. F.O. 403.111

[41] Unsigned note C.20.295 and Axelson op. cit., 210

[42] *Rapports et Chroniques* Quelimane 1 September 1889. For *machila* see note 76 chapter II.

[43] Mponda Diary 3 August 1889

[44] Lechaptois to Livinhac 23 September 1890 C.20.280

[45] Minister of Marine to Governor of Mozambique 2 September 1889 No. 114 66. Trans. Portuguese

[46] Lechaptois to Livinhac 10 October 1889 C.20.274

[47] *Rapports et Chroniques* 21 October 1889 Report from Quelimane

[48] Two Scots brothers, John and Frederick Moir, sons of an Edinburgh doctor, ran the African Lakes Company at this time. The nominal capital of the company, £20,000, had completely disappeared in the Mlozi war, and the trading company was in serious difficulties.

[49] Petre to Salisbury 20 August 1889 F.O. 403.111 Enclosure

[50] Mponda Diary 9 December 1889

[51] ibid. 16 December 1889

[52] ibid. 26 December 1889

[53] ibid. 28 December 1889

[54] Alpers E. 'The Yao in Malawi: the importance of local research' in *The Early History* 170

[55] Waller H. *The Last Journals of David Livingstone in Central Africa* Vol. I London 1874, 103

[56] Rangeley W. H. J. 'The Amacinga Ayao' *Nyasaland Journal* Vol. xv No. 2 1962, 54

[57] Jack J. W. *Daybreak at Livingstonia* Perth 1899, Chapter IV, 7

[58] Young E. D. *Nyassa* London 1877, 61

[59] Quoted in Ross *Origins and Development*, 124

[60] Hawes to Rosebery 3 June 1886. F.O. 541.50

[61] Mponda Diary 19 March 1890

[62] Hawes to Rosebery ibid.

[63] Hanna A. J. *The Beginnings of Nyasaland and N.E. Rhodesia: 1859-1895* Oxford 1969, 74

[64] Mponda Diary 13 February 1891 and 19 March 1890 (Mwase Kasungu was a Chewa chief to the north of Lilongwe)

[65] ibid. 16 August 1890

[66] Hawes to Rosebery ibid.

[67] Oral Testimony G. Mitawa ex-chief Machinga Yao, Likoswe village Limbe area. May 1970.

[68] Mponda Diary 20 February 1890 and 19 March 1890

[69] The Jumbe of Kota-kota dominated the lake north of Cape Rifu. In 1891 his town was the most Arab of all African settlements on the lakeshore, with a well-frequented mosque. The Catholic missionaries described him as 'much cultivated by the English and cultivating them' Mponda Diary 18 June 1891. See Shepperson G. 'The Jumbe of Kota Kota and some aspects of the history of Islam in British Central Africa' in *Islam in Tropical Africa* ed. Lewis I. M. Oxford 1966, 193-207.

[70] Rev. W. P. Johnson was born in 1854 and first arrived in Africa in 1876, in which year he was ordained deacon at the station of the Universities' Mission to Central Africa at Masasi. In September 1878 he was ordained priest in Zanzibar, and two years later started work at Mataka's whence he was driven out in October 1882. By October 1886 he was centred on Likoma Island and using the U.M.C.A. steamer *Charles Janson* on the lake and river. He died at Liuli on 11 October 1928. Throughout the Catholic missionaries' stay at Mponda's he was their friend and helper. The one occasion when he seems to have ignored them may only have been a result of his very poor eyesight. See Barnes B. H. *Johnson of Nyasaland* U.M.C.A., 1933.

[71] Johnson W. P. *My African Reminiscences: 1875-95* U.M.C.A. 1924, 164 and Hanna *The Beginnings* 150

[72] Likoma was a small island in Lake Malawi where the missionaries of the Universities'

Mission to Central Africa under Bishop Chauncy Maples made their headquarters in the 1880s

73 Mponda Diary 31 December 1889, 11 January 1890, 13 February 1890, 23 February 1890

74 ibid. 29 December 1889, 31 January 1890

75 ibid. 11 March 1890. Chindamba was also known as Makandanji and was an ally of Makanjila and a relative of Kabuto.

76 The paramount chief of the Maseko Ngoni c. 1870–1891. Head of the Lizulu war division.

77 Mponda Diary 1 January 1890

78 'His hand against everyone and everyone's hands against him' ibid.

79 ibid. 22 February 1890 and Inkosi Willard Gomani III to Linden I. 15 June 1970.

80 ibid. 22 January 1891

81 Mitchell J. C. *The Yao Village* Manchester 1966, 35–37

82 This process of town formation was more striking amongst the Masininga Yao: see Alpers E. A. 'Trade, State and Society among the Yao in the 19th century' *J. African History* X No. 3 1969, 417

83 Any person accused of witchcraft, eating the flesh of corpses, was required to drink an infusion of the pounded-up bark of a tree, *Crossopteryx febrifuga*. The alkaloids contained within the infusion were lethal unless the poison was vomited, proving innocence. The art of the *mapondera*, or administrator of the ordeal, was to judge the quantities of bark to achieve the desired result: death and guilt, or vomiting and innocence.

84 Mponda Diary 3 October 1890 and 7 March 1891. Mponda was accused of having murdered his predecessor, her former husband, by witchcraft.

85 Schoffeleers *The Meaning and use of the name 'Malawi'* 97–100

86 Mponda Diary 13 December 1890

87 *Rapports et Chroniques* 21 January 1891

88 Mponda Diary 6 March 1891

89 A tribe living to the south-east of the Yao, occupying what Portuguese documents refer to as the lands of Bororo.

90 *Rapports et Chroniques* 21 January 1891

91 'Unyago' is a term including the three Yao initiation ceremonies of Lupanda, the male circumcision rites, and the two female rites of Chiputu and Litiwo. The drawing 'Chiuta' is in the form of a cross. See Stannus H. S. 'The Wayao of Nyasaland' Varia Africana III *Harvard African Studies* ed. E. A. Hooton and N. I. Bates, Cambridge, Mass. 1922, 268.

92 *Rapports et Chroniques* 22 April 1890

93 Mponda Diary 21 July 1890

94 They seem to have read Waller H. *The Last Journals of David Livingstone in Central Africa* London, 1874

95 Mponda Diary 28 December 1889

96 ibid. 24 February 1890

97 ibid. 28 October 1890

98 Alpers *Trade, State and Society*, 416–20

99 Mponda Diary 4 February 1890

100 For a discussion of Islamic eclecticism see Alpers E. A. 'Towards a History of the expansion of Islam in East Africa: the matrilineal peoples of the southern interior' in *The Historical Study* 172–202

101 Swahili teachers

102 *Rapports et Chroniques* 3 June 1891 'We came here with dark glasses which stopped us from seeing things in their true light'

103 Johnson *My African Reminiscences* 202

104 Johnson H. H. *British Central Africa* London 1897, 90, and Hanna *The Beginnings* 150

105 Johnston to Salisbury 1 February 1890 F.O. 84.2051

[106] Mponda Diary 7 January 1890
[107] ibid. 25 July 1890
[108] ibid. 31 January 1890
[109] Axelson *Portugal and the Scramble* 231
[110] Chauncy Maples, born in 1852, first arrived in Nyasaland in 1876, but proceeded immediately to Masasi. Ordained by Bishop Steere, he was put in charge of the U.M.C.A. mission on Likoma in 1886. He was, tragically, drowned in Lake Malawi on 2 September 1895. See Maples E. *The Life of Chauncy Maples* London 1898.
[111] Mponda Diary 4 May 1890
[112] *Rapports et Chroniques* 29 May 1890. Buchanan, a Zomba coffee planter, had been made Acting-Consul by Johnston in 1889 and proclaimed the establishment of the Protectorate.
[113] Mponda Diary 29 May 1890
[114] ibid. 25 July 1890
[115] Lechaptois to Livinhac 23 September 1890
[116] Mponda Diary 1 May 1890
[117] ibid. 17 August 1890
[118] ibid. 9 April 1891
[119] ibid. 17 November 1890. 'Two excellent bottles of wine, jam, tea, a box of Corinth raisins, and a box of Lagon with a box of Bouillon.' Johnson also gave them a Yao Grammar and Dictionary. An impressive piece of ecumenism. Even the Fathers were forced to admit that the Rev. Mr. Johnson 'was in the best of possible faith'.
[120] ibid. 10 May 1890
[121] ibid. 22 January 1891
[122] Heurtebise to Livinhac 1 April 1891 C.20.291 and Lechaptois to Mercui 17 August 1890 C.20.279
[123] Mponda Diary 24 July 1890
[124] ibid. 6 December 1890
[125] ibid.
[126] ibid. 4 July 1890
[127] ibid. 3 August 1890
[128] ibid. 31 October 1890
[129] ibid. 19 October 1890. Scarcely any Chewa children attended the school. Whether this was the result of indifference, language difficulties, or an outright ban by Mponda on their attending, is impossible to know. See Mponda Diary 28 February 1891. The Jesuits at Matapwiri's did find that the Chewa villagers were banned from the school by the chief.
[130] 'To sing school' i.e. chanted lessons
[131] *Rapports et Chroniques* 28 February 1891
[132] Mponda Diary 19 October 1890
[133] *Rapports et Chroniques* 10 June 1890
[134] Mponda Diary 31 May 1890
[135] Shepperson *The Jumbe* 195–207
[136] *Rapports et Chroniques* 12 March 1891 and Mponda Diary 10 January 1891, 13 February 1891, 29 March 1891, and 12 June 1891
[137] Mponda Diary 1 May 1891
[138] *Rapports et Chroniques* 30 April 1891
[139] Johnson *My African Reminiscences* 202 'It seemed as if the slavers, checked by the government, were determined to extend their moral force.' This combination of Islam and the slave trade was not necessarily directed consciously to the development of Islamic states, any more than the Christianity and commerce of the Scots was a *conscious* prelude to British colonization of Nyasaland.
[140] Mponda Diary 17 August 1890
[141] *Rapports et Chroniques* 28 February 1891

[142] ibid. 22 July 1890

[143] Mercui J. 'Missions du Nyasa' MS Handwritten. 'Retour à Quelimane' 6 August 1890. White Fathers' Archives Rome.

[144] *Rapports et Chroniques* 22 July 1890

[145] Mponda Diary 1 October 1890

[146] Axelson *Portugal and the Scramble* 239 The treaty defined the borders of present-day Malawi. North of the Ruo confluence was British, as were the western slopes of Mount Mulanje. The White Fathers were therefore over 25 miles inside British territory. The treaty was only finally ratified on 11 June 1891.

[147] Mponda Diary 6 December 1890

[148] Heurtebise to Livinhac 1 April 1891 C.20.291 'We left under the protection of the Portuguese flag. No sooner had we arrived here than Portugal was superseded on the shores of Lake Nyasa by England. It was the reply of God.'

[149] Mponda Diary 16 June 1891

[150] The early policy of the White Fathers was to buy slaves to form the nucleus of Christian communities. The Malta Institute was used as a training school for bought slaves. For the way this policy was put into practice by the Holy Ghost Fathers see Kieran J. A. 'Christian Villages and Politics in North-Eastern Tanzania' *U.S.S.C. Conference* Kampala 1969–70.

[151] Mponda Diary 16 June 1891

[152] *Rapports annuels et chroniques* 18 June 1891

[153] Pineau H. *Évêque Roi des Brigands* Montreal 1937, 65

[154] Johnston *B.C.A.*, 90

[155] Heurtebise to Livinhac 29 October 1891 C.20.292. Fort Johnston is now called Mangochi.

[156] Johnston *B.C.A.* 90

[157] Duff H. *Nyasaland under the Foreign Office* London 1903, 21

[158] Mponda Diary 15 January 1891, 11 November 1890, and *Rapports et chroniques* 3 June 1891

[159] See reference 102 above

[160] Rangeley W. H. J. 'The Ayao' *Nyasaland Journal* Vol. 16 1963, 21

[161] They left Quelimane on 2 May 1890 and had moved to Mount Tumbini when Mercui passed through in August 1890. Their stay could only have been about one month.

[162] Pr. Lusit. Litt. ann. et Hist. dom. 1877–92, 659–61 Jesuit Archives, Rome. Milanje is the Portuguese town over the border from Malawi's Mulanje.

[163] Schebesta *op. cit.*, 331, and *British Central African Gazette* 30 April 1894

[164] Father L. Loubière and Father I. Perrodin both died *en route*. Schebesta op. cit.

[165] Pr. Lusit. Miss. Goa-Macao-Zambesi. Dupeyron to Aloy quoted in Aloy to *Patrem-Generalem* 6 January 1891. Jesuit Archives, Rome

[166] Hanna *Beginnings* 119

[167] Dupeyron to Editor 22 May 1894. Letter columns of B.C.A.G. 4 June 1894

[168] Schebesta *Portugals Konquistamission* 332

[169] See reference 160 above

[170] Schebesta op. cit.

[171] Pr. Lusit. Miss. Goa-Macao-Zambesi Vol. I Dupeyron to Patrem-Generalem 27 January 1893. I am grateful to Rev. J. A. G. Hautvast *S.M.M.* for correcting our Latin translation of this document. 'Chiefs' is given as a translation of the latin 'reguli' (French *roitelets*).

[172] *B.C.A.G.* 21 October 1894 and 14 December 1894.

[173] Fort Lister, placed strategically between Mchesa and Mulanje mountain in the 'Lister Gap' commanded an important route south to Matapwiri's. The sending of a runner to Sir William Manning, later Governor of Nyasaland from November 1910 to May 1913, is

still remembered in oral traditions though confused with an earlier war against the Songea
Ngoni.

[174] Sharpe to Kimberley 14 August 1894 F.O. 2.67 and B.C.A.G. 15 October 1895

[175] B.C.A.G. 24 September 1895

[176] Personal Communication. Rev. J. Lamey W. F. Archivist, Rome. I have been unable
to find this quotation in print.

[177] ChiYao for 'Ave Maria'

[178] Oral testimony. Pio Samikwa, Alomwe of Mulanje, interviewed in December 1969 by
a Kachebere seminarian, Valens Khoriyo, to whom we are indebted for this information.

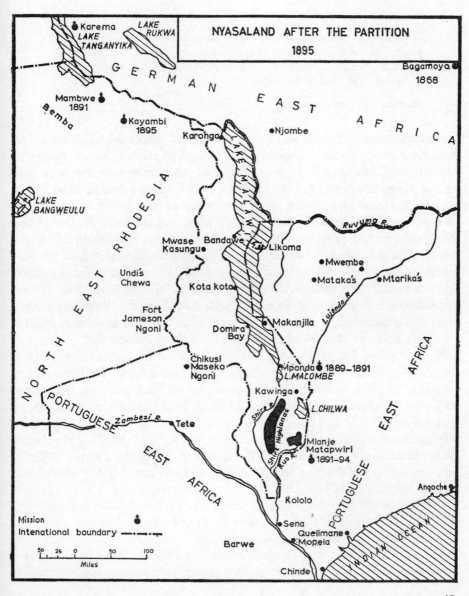

NYASALAND AFTER THE PARTITION
1895

CHAPTER II

The First Permanent Settlement: Disputes, Rivalries, and Misunderstandings

> Experience has shown that it is highly undesirable that Churches whose
> tenets differ so widely as those of the Roman Catholic and Reformed Pres-
> byterian Churches should labour in close proximity, as their teachings tend
> to bewilder the mind of the native.
>
> du Plessis to Lansdowne[1]

Johnston's policy of 'Divide and Rule'[2] had proved successful. With the aid of
mercenary troops he had subdued the leading Yao slavers, Zarafi, Kawinga,
Mponda, and Matapwiri. On the slightest of provocations, troops were sent
against Mpezeni's Ngoni at Fort Jameson, after Chikusi's son, Gomani I, had
been tricked into surrendering, and subsequently executed. The last resistance
of the Maseko Ngoni took place in 1898 when the surviving leaders of the
Phungwako clan, the keepers of the royal medicines, reassembled the Mfundeni
war division at Domwe and attempted to revolt. Msekandiwana, whose brother,
Kachere was shot in 1896, suffered a similar fate.[3] The northern Ngoni avoided
an open military confrontation. Amongst the Yao, Makanjila survived to continue slaving into the twentieth century, collecting slaves by dhow from a sanctuary in Portuguese East Africa. These were often recalcitrant subjects sold off
by their chiefs along the lakeshore from Cape Rifu to Ntaka-taka.[4]

By the end of Johnston's tour of duty, British Administration was firmly
established; Bomas[5] were built as far north as Karonga, and permanent army
barracks, hospital, and Government headquarters, had gone up in Zomba.
Although the Government kept a tight rein on land speculation, the trickle of
planters into the Shire Highlands increased during the 1890s. The powerful
African Lakes Company was cut down to 55,000 acres in the Shire Highlands,
with a prize of 2·7 million acres in the distant North Nyasa District.[6] All the
rest, the territory of defeated chiefs, was Crown Land under Government jurisdiction. The region in which tax was collected spread outwards from Blantyre
and Zomba in the wake of Johnston's punitive raids. By 1896, £5,000 was being
brought in, a little more than ten per cent of the Protectorate's total budget.[7]

If the region of Lake Nyasa under Scots missionary rule was on the way to
becoming a theocracy, in Nyasaland under the Foreign Office the Protestant
missionaries were limited to forming the nagging conscience of the Protectorate

government.[8] This change of role from kings to prophets did little to diminish their hold over the religious affairs of the country. At the beginning of the twentieth century Nyasaland was, in every sense of the word, a Protestant Protectorate. The enlightened ideas of churchmen such as Scott had been given free rein for two decades, and were well on the way to being translated into bricks and mortar. In 1897, the Livingstonia mission, now at the north end of the lake, had seventy-eight bush schools plus the well-equipped Overtoun Institute which taught English and Theology to advanced students. The Church of Scotland ran fourteen schools from their Blantyre mission, and eight from Domasi mission near Zomba.[9] They could boast the most impressive 'cathedral' in Central Africa.[10]

The Scots and the Universities' Mission to Central Africa were joined in 1889 by Dutch Reformed missionaries from the Cape. In the next decade the Shire Highlands and Central Region began to fill up with smaller Protestant missions. In 1892 Joseph Booth[11] founded the Zambesi Industrial Mission. Three years later Baptist missionaries from Glasgow began another Industrial Mission at Ncheu. After the fitful but effective pacification of the Yao and Ngoni, a second wave of larger, better-endowed, missions was attracted, the South Africa General Mission in 1900, and a year later, the 'Plainsfield' Seventh-Day Adventist Mission. The first United Missionary Conference took place at Livingstonia in 1900, a year before the Catholics appeared on the scene. The cake was divided up in their absence.

For the White Fathers, 'Nyasa' remained a staging post into the more important territories of Bembaland and Tanganyika. Caravans came up from Quelimane to pass through the Protestant hinterland into Catholic territory. They rarely went unnoticed amongst the tiny European population,[12] either producing a vague sense of disquiet among the Scots, or viewed with typical warmth by the Universities' Mission to Central Africa. The comment of one Anglican priest in 1894 was:

> I always rather regret that we do not come across any of their missions out here. A party of eleven—six men including a Bishop and five Sisters—went up the other day, but I did not see them. Their station is on the high plateau between Nyasa and Tanganyika.[13]

Although a Nyasa pro-vicariate existed on paper, dating from the days of Lechaptois, no move had been made to occupy the lake region.

When Dupont[14] began missions in Bembaland in 1896 he inherited a pro-vicariate which covered 300,000 square miles, between the Anglo-German border in the north, the lake in the east, 30° longitude (Lake Bangwelo) in the west, and the Anglo-Portuguese frontier at the Ruo confluence in the south.[15] When he was made Apostolic Vicar of this vast territory on 16 February 1897, he had only three priests and Brother Antoine at his disposal. The upgrading of the region into a Vicariate, and Dupont's consecration as Bishop at Lechaptois' hands, changed nothing in the situation; there were not enough personnel to evangelize the area beyond the north-west tip. Not that Dupont ever wanted to. From the beginning, he developed a touchingly intimate relationship with 'his'

Bemba. On 26 October 1898 Dupont wrote to 'the Governor of British Central Africa':

> He (Mwamba)[16] died yesterday. All his people have rallied around me. They recognize truly me as their chief and have been coming from all the villages for instructions.[17]

This profoundly satisfying psychological relationship with the Bemba, reminiscent of Livingstone's unshakable affection for the Kololo, which led to Dupont's becoming temporarily the Bemba chief, coupled with an acute shortage of priests, resulted in the Nyasaland part of Dupont's Vicariate being treated as nothing more than a north-bound highway for Bembaland.

Father Mathurin Guillemé, a qualified doctor with experience in Tanganyika, and Dupont's second in command, travelled into Nyasaland in November 1897 and October 1899. On the first occasion, he had been summoned to help Dupont in Bembaland, and took the opportunity of visiting Mponda's which, by then, had been handed over with good grace to the Universities' Mission to Central Africa. The purpose of the second journey was to accompany an ailing Dupont back to Quelimane, and so to France.[18] The Bishop, who depended a good deal on Guillemé, wanted him to sound out the possibility of starting a station in Nyasaland, to cut down the distances caravans had to cover on their way north, and oppose Protestant influence in the area.[19]

On 17 August 1900, Dupont was at the Mother-House of the Montfort Fathers at St. Laurent-sur-Sèvre, Nantes, and wrote to an old friend of his from seminary days, Pierre Bourget S.M.M., that he might not be able to counter 'the Protestant menace' in Nyasaland, through lack of personnel.[20] Pious story has it that Dupont had decided to become a missionary at the age of four years, on hearing the retreat sermon of two Montfort priests. He had met Bourget while at college in Beaupré and followed him to the Major Seminary at Angers, whence they had pursued different careers, Bourget becoming a Montfortian, Dupont joining the White Fathers and going to Maison-Carrée. They met again in Algiers when Bourget became head of the Montfort scholasticate at El-Biar.[21]

The Montfort Order already had missions in Haiti that dated from 1871 and were looking outwards from France, where the future for Religious Orders under the Waldeck–Rousseau government was gloomy.[22] Preliminary discussions, with a view to sending Montfort missionaries as auxiliaries to Dupont, were begun between the Superior-General of the Montforts, Father Maurille, when he returned from Canada, and Father Livinhac, head of the White Fathers. The final contract was signed on 12 January 1901 by Dupont, Livinhac, and Maurille. The Montforts agreed to send three missionaries to staff a station in the south of the Nyasa Vicariate. They were to pay for the foundation and upkeep and send half-yearly reports to Dupont on the progress of the mission. In exchange the White Fathers contracted to stay out of the Shire district, with the long-term aim of making the Montfort missions into a separate Shire Vicariate.[23]

The three priests chosen were Pierre Bourget as leader of the expedition, Antoine Winnen, a highly-educated Dutchman with a gift for languages, and Auguste Prézeau, a French Father who had spent some time at Kingston,

Ontario, and had the invaluable advantage in Montfort circles of speaking English. Although Winnen had been Professor at Schimmert Seminary in Holland, he had all the qualities of a lay Brother. He was a good carpenter and stone-mason.[24] They passed through Rome at the beginning of May 1901 to meet Pope Leo XIII and Cardinal Ledochowski, the Prefect of the Propaganda,[25] and on 24 May left Naples on board the German ship, 'General', to land almost a month later at Chinde.[26] They left behind them an ecclesiastical muddle that took two years to disentangle.

The unsuspecting Company of Mary found themselves in the midst of a canonical dispute between two powerful clerical personalities. Joseph Dupont, born in 1850 at Geste, near Nantes, France, ordained White Father in February 1881 and chosen chief of the Bemba in 1898, had a penchant for assuming powers, both secular and ecclesiastical, that were not readily conceded by his contemporaries. His assumption of the Mwamba chieftancy had raised the ghost of a French Catholic state, and produced palpitations in the hearts of the administration of the British South Africa Company.[27] Miecislaus Holka, Count of Ledochowski, born in 1822 in Poland, ordained priest in 1845, had acted as chief negotiator with William I, King of Prussia, to enlist his good offices in the withdrawal of Victor Emmanuel's troops from Rome. He was imprisoned in 1873 for refusing to resign during the *Kulturkampf* and was made a cardinal by Pius IX. He had been made Prefect of the Propaganda in 1894 and was, by any standards, a formidable opponent.[28]

It was the misfortune of the Montfort missionaries that Dupont, through ill health, only found time to see Ledochowski about the contract in June 1901. The White Fathers' representative in Rome, Burtin, also forgot to inform the Propaganda of the negotiations. Meanwhile the Montforts had been warmly received in Rome and articles had appeared about the new Shire Mission in 'Missions Catholiques' and 'La Verité Francaise', magazines widely read in clerical circles of the day.[29] It was, of course, illegal for Vicars-Apostolic to create new missions and recruit different missionary societies into their areas without Propaganda's permission.

The Shire had first come to Ledochowski's notice in 1896 when Harry Johnston, on his honeymoon in Rome, had paid him a goodwill visit to smooth over the issue of the Mponda mission. At the time, the Cardinal Prefect's acquaintance with Africa was such that he thought the Shire was the Shari affluent of Lake Chad. A tactful correction from Johnston clarified the matter.[30] When Dupont arrived in Rome, Ledochowski not only knew where the Shire was located, he was very much aware that three Montfort missionaries were illegally beginning a mission there. In a heated interview in June 1901 he insisted on their immediate recall.[31] Within a few months the Propaganda was circulating a reminder of Leo XIII's constitution on missions of 8 May 1881, *Romanos pontifices*:

All Ordinaries under the authority of the Propaganda will abstain from this time forth from permitting Religious Institutes to open houses in their territories, without prior authorization from this Congregation.[32]

On 21 June Winnen, Prézeau, and Bourget boarded a steamer of the African Lakes Company for the journey up the Shire into Nyasaland. They were at Nsanje three days later, where Bourget disembarked to put a 'Miraculous Medal'[33] at the foot of a baobab tree, 'so that she can take possession of the land consecrated to her (Mary)'.[34] It was, of course, an accident that Bourget chose a baobab tree at whose foot religious offerings were traditionally made by the Chewa peoples. In retrospect there is a certain irony that Bourget chose a tree that had evoked the religious sense of generations of Chewa. For the Montforts it meant the claiming of Nyasaland for Catholicism. For the people watching it must have looked like a European making an offering to the spirits of the land. In the ambivalence of this first act was contained both the similarity of Catholicism to traditional religion, and the gulf that separated priests and people in their understanding of the world.

On arriving in Blantyre the Catholic missionaries received a favourable press.

> Admiration has been expressed of the methods of the White Fathers by those who have had the opportunity of judging. They endeavour to inculcate into the Native a gospel of work and in that regard they may be found useful in the undeveloped districts of Southern Angoniland.[35]

This anonymous attempt to gain the planters' favour was the work of the chief judicial officer of Nyasaland, Judge Joseph J. Nunan. Young, good-looking, and something of a stage-Irishman, Nunan had a 'naturally excitable' temperament, and was 'hasty, obstinate, and tactless'. On the credit side, his contemporaries in the colonial service were willing to concede that he was 'very energetic, enthusiastic and most honourable and upright in character'.[36] His faults dwindled to insignificance for the priests beside the consideration that he was a staunch Roman Catholic, and more, wanted to help them find a site for a mission.

Nunan first directed the Montforts to the Chiradzulu district and the Melotta estates, but the owner, Martin, was unwilling to sell any land. There was another offer of land near Lunzu, free of charge, from a Catholic coffee planter, Besseling, but Bourget finally decided on a site near the border of Portuguese East Africa in the district of Njobvualema, a sub-chief of the old Maseko paramount, Gomani I.[37] One advantage of this site was that the French planter who had occupied it, had been deported, leaving behind a sizeable two-roomed hut occupied only by an African policeman, so that the missionaries would have a roof over their heads immediately.[38]

While it would not be true to say that the Montforts were chased out of the Shire Highlands, they were given a number of indications that their presence was not wanted. They were invited to the Blantyre Mission and, over the celebrated tea at the manse[39] served by the minister's wife, the Scots pointedly brought up the question of spheres of influence and schools.[40] It was blandly suggested that Chiromo might be a good spot for a mission.[41] Prézeau politely replied that missions had a right to evangelize anywhere, given the permission of the local chief. The head of the Blantyre Mission's suggestion to get the Catholics off the Highlands, into the sweltering heat of the Lower Shire, was taken a hundred miles further by an 'onlooker' in the *Central African Times* who thought the priests would be better in Portuguese East Africa.

> Surely then with such a vast area unoccupied the White Fathers cannot possibly be consulting the best interests of Christianity if they establish themselves in the Shire Highlands where they can only encroach on the work of others; with the probable result that instead of doing good, chaos and confusion will result à la Uganda.[42]

It was not to be the last time that the spectre of the 'Bafransa'[43] was to be raised over Catholic missions.[44]

When the Montforts reached Njobvualema's on 25 July 1901 their gaining of a first foothold in Nyasaland had been entirely due to resident lay Catholics. They had been provided with a cook and interpreter by Nunan, and one of the employees of the African Lakes Company, whose wife was a Catholic, had gone so far as to offer to build them a brick house at Njobvualema's and a church at Mpimbi.[45] There were even possibilities for new missions at Lunzu on Besseling's estate, and of a hundred acres near the Melotta estates.

After the local Ngoni headmen were reassured that the priests had not come to steal their wives, and Njobvualema was given a necklace and eighty metres of calico, the Ngoni at Nzama were no less co-operative. Njobvualema had lived through the Johnston era almost unscathed. In 1896 his village remained, while many other Ngoni fled eastwards. After Gomani's execution, Njobvualema joined another sub-chief, Nkwaila, in a revolt against Mandala, who had in the past tried to usurp the paramountcy. Frustrated ambition had not improved Mandala's character[46] for he proceeded to abduct Njobvualema's and Nkwaila's villagers and sell them to Kunda slavers on the Zambesi.[47] Njobvualema, embroiled with Mandala, was prevented from assisting Msekandiwana in the 1898 revolt so that he avoided the severe treatment meted out to other Ngoni by Johnston.

When the Fathers arrived, the area was highly Ngonized[48] with good herds of cattle browsing on the hills along the border of Portuguese East Africa. Njobvualema had kept most of his old authority, much to the missionaries' relief.

> The King presides over the mustering of 150 labourers and gives them orders to collect their implements. What a pleasure it is to see these people subservient to the authority of their chief. May we also be equally subservient to the Divine Will.[49]

He was not, however, well liked by his people,[50] and engaged in a massive *mwabvi*-taking orgy in 1905.[51] With a strong authoritarian figure on which they could lean, an equable climate, plenty of fresh milk, and a ready-built hut, the territory to the west of Ncheu seemed to the inexperienced Montforts an ideal spot for their first mission.

News of their recall mercifully did not reach the missionaries before Ledochowski had been successfully placated. By careful lobbying in Rome, the Montfort representative at the Vatican, Jouet, managed to get the issue brought before a session of the *Congresso*, the executive body of the Propaganda.[52] Acknowledging the enormous costs of getting the priests back to Europe again,[53] the *Congresso* relented. On 30 November 1901, Bourget received a letter telling him that, although Ledochowski was still annoyed, the storm had abated.[54] A visit to Ledochowski by Nunan, at the beginning of 1902, poured more oil on what had been very troubled waters.

Before the arrival of the White Fathers in Nyasaland in 1902, the Montforts had a year to themselves to evangelize Nzama. They built a brick house, opened their first school on 2 February 1902, punished a Portuguese soldier who had stolen money from one of their pupils, and translated the Lord's prayer into ChiChewa. Like their predecessors at Mponda's, they suffered from a degree of isolation not made any easier by uncertainty. The news that all congregations unauthorized by the French government were banned in France reached them at the end of August. The Company of Mary was disbanded and the scholasticate at El-Biar dispersed, drawing from Bourget the bitter words: 'The men who preside over the destiny of France are more savage than our wild Ngoni.'[55] Their Order was in exile and their own position still in doubt.

In April 1902, the White Fathers had enough priests in training to consider extending their work into the region of Central Angoniland. Guyard, a new priest who had arrived in Bembaland in 1899, was selected to be the Superior of a Nyasaland mission. On 28 April 1902, Guillemé left Chilubula[56] for Blantyre to discuss the project with Griffin, another Catholic who was Acting Judge in Nunan's absence. The Catholic network even extended to Dowa where MacDonald, the collector, suggested to Guillemé a number of possible sites for the new mission. First choice was Chiwamba, on the Dowa–Dedza road, significantly midway between two well-established Dutch Reformed stations. A second possibility suggested by MacDonald was Kachindamoto's by the Lake at Ntaka-taka, but the Collector accurately forecast that the missionaries would not be allowed in immediately. As a compromise, Mua, at the foot of the escarpment leading down to the lakeside plain, was selected.[57]

Guillemé returned to Chilubula in early August, choosing a third site, Kachebere on the Bua river, on the way. Meanwhile, Guyard and another newly ordained priest, Perrot, had arrived at Chiwamba from Chilubula. MacDonald allowed them to stay in the Government rest house until they had built their own accommodation. In September new missionaries began to arrive from Algiers. The first was Alfred Honoré[58] who left a large caravan heading for Bangwelo, at Domira Bay. On the same evening the southbound boat brought down two more missionaries from Bangwelo, Father Louveau and Brother Wilfrid, who joined Honoré at Chiwamba. On 11 September 1901, Louveau, Perrot and Wilfrid set out from Chiwamba to found the station at Mua.[59] A second caravan, reaching Nzama on 29 September, brought Fathers Bellière and Dequeker, and Brother Sebastian. They were reinforced a year later by Fathers Braire, Tellegen, and Ter Maat, and Brother Willibrord, providing adequate manpower for a mission to be started at Kachebere on 11 May 1903.[60]

This sudden influx of over a dozen Catholic missionaries into the Central Region in the space of two years seemed to the Dutch Reformed ministers a

Popish Plot. If the Scots had been glad to see the backs of the Montforts, their Dutch Reformed colleagues further north were doubly keen to be rid of the White Fathers. For the past thirteen years they had dominated the Central Region and could claim over eighty schools with almost four hundred baptized Church members. Between 1899 and 1903 the number of Afrikaner missionaries had risen from fourteen to twenty-eight, and two new stations had been started at Mlanda and Mphunzi.[61] The Dutch Reformed ministers were understandably perturbed by the Catholic invasion. A month after the foundation of Mua mission, Du Plessis[62] was petitioning the Secretary of State for Foreign Affairs in London, Lansdowne.[63]

> From a political point of view too, we cannot but think it unwise to permit the White Fathers who have wrought mischief elsewhere to settle in Nyasaland. For your information I enclose an extract from last month's 'Church Missionary Gleaner', which will show how these same 'White Fathers' were a source of trouble and danger in Uganda.[64]

A number of factors conspired to make it unlikely that the Dutch Reformed bid for a monopoly of the Central Region would be heeded by either the Protectorate Government, or the Foreign Office. After the Anglo-Boer War which only ended that year, 1902, all things Afrikaner were viewed with some suspicion. Anglo-French relations, on the other hand, were moving towards the *Entente Cordiale*.[65] More immediately, the Dutch Reformed Church in the person of the Rev. Robert Blake had been charged the previous year with inciting Africans to refuse to pay taxes, or go off to work in the south. Complaints about Government abuses sounded less well in the thick accents of the Transvaal, than in the more homely dialects of Glasgow and Aberdeen. As Sharpe pointedly noted in his report to Lansdowne:

> I should be sorry to say that any missions in the Protectorate are a cause of trouble to Government officials, but it is certainly a fact that the White Fathers are working in more complete harmony with district officials of this Protectorate than the members of any other mission in it. They confine themselves entirely to their mission operations and have been so far noticeable for their refusal to enter into any questions with natives which in any way touch on administrative or judicial work. This cannot be said of all the other Mission Societies in British Central Africa.[66]

In compiling his report, Sharpe had talked to—of all people—Nunan and MacDonald, the prime movers in settling the White Fathers in the Central Region. Sharpe himself had met Deguerry and the Mponda missionaries on a number of occasions between 1889 and 1891. After having talked to three rather sick missionaries in a thatched hut by the side of the Shire, brought there under a Portuguese flag, he was unlikely to heed the dire warnings of the *Church Missionary Gleaner*[67] that the White Fathers were the vanguard of French imperialism.

Far from being cowed by the Afrikaner attempts to oust them, the White Fathers continued to try to evangelize as much territory around their three

49

stations as their stamina and resources allowed. The exchanges between Cape Colony and London had been a hopeless attempt to foreclose a religious scramble for Nyasaland that was to last some fifty years, engender much bitterness, and drive the Colonial Government to distraction.

On 1 July 1903, Bellière was called to Lilongwe and the decision was taken to abandon Chiwamba. The Protestants had moved into the region west of Lilongwe, so a new mission was to be founded at the confluence of the Likuni and Lilongwe rivers. Eight days later, preceded by a crowd of catechumens from Chiwamba, the White Fathers pitched their tents at the chosen site and Bellière, with a Brother who had accompanied Guillemé from the north, founded Likuni mission.[68]

The Catholic missions suffered far more initially from Montfort–White Father rivalry than from disputes with the Protestants. Despite a letter from Dupont saying all was well, the Montforts were still in a state of canonical limbo. Ledochowski's death in July 1902 had removed one obstacle from their path, and his replacement by the Cardinal Protector of the Montforts, Cardinal Gotti, as Prefect of the Propaganda, was equally providential. However, Bourget, who had left Nzama for Europe in February 1903, had had a very disquieting interview with Dupont in Marseilles. The Bishop, who was refusing to reply to Gotti's letters, heaped all the blame for the difficulties with the Propaganda on to the Company of Mary. Livinhac made some deprecating noises about Dupont's ill health but seemed unable to restrain him.[69]

After his censure from the Propaganda, Dupont had petulantly decided to occupy the Shire himself. Although he would consider augmenting their numbers at a later date, the Montforts were to be limited to Nzama mission. Livinhac begged Bourget not to push Dupont too hard until after the White Fathers' General Chapter [70] was finished that year. Guillemé, faithful to the instructions from his Religious Superior, went down to Blantyre to find a site for the White Fathers' Shire mission. A part of the Melotta estates was up for auction so Guillemé promptly bought it.[71]

It can be imagined with what surprise Winnen and Prézeau read in the *Central African Times* [72] that a Monsignor Guillemé had taken possession of land at Nguludi bought from Mr. W. P. Martin.[73] Guillemé had formerly been on very good terms with Nzama, giving the Montforts tips on how to make soap, vinegar, and oil, teaching them how to cure common tropical ailments, and advising them on missionary techniques. His underhand purchase of Nguludi was out of character, and must have been carried out dutifully on Dupont's orders; the Bishop was convinced that all his troubles, from rheumatism to Montfortian Cardinals, came from his association with the Company of Mary. News of Nguludi was immediately sent to Bourget who then broke off all relations with Dupont. So much for the Romish monolith.

With Cardinal Gotti presiding over the *Congresso*, and Jouet lobbying its members skilfully, the White Fathers' days in the Shire Vicariate were numbered. On 3 December 1903, the region south of the Rivelezi river was declared an Apostolic Prefecture solely under the jurisdiction of the Company of Mary.[74] The telegram was lost *en route* to Nzama and the unfortunate missionaries had to wait for January of the following year to hear the news.[75] Guillemé stayed on at Nguludi to await Dupont's return and was found there, in obvious embarrass-ment, when the Montforts came to claim the mission in June 1904. Five new missionaries, Fathers Gachassin, Déau, and Cadoret, and Brothers Odilon and Cléophas, who had started their journey to Nyasaland when it was clear the canonical situation would soon be resolved, were shared between Nzama and the new Montfort station of Nguludi.

Dupont bypassed both the Montfort missions on his return, in a show of un-usual tact, and proceeded directly to Mua. He was given a good reception.

> They surprised us all today at 2.30 p.m. About twenty minutes previously, the school children began whispering that a *machila* was coming; they could hear the songs of the bearers in the distance. We were still wondering whether it was only the songs of porters when the news came that a *machila* had been sighted. We quickly finished the lesson, and everyone rushed out to conduct our good father and his companions to the mission.[76]

By the end of 1904, with the Bishop back in Africa, the Catholic missions had survived the worst they could do to each other, an outright bid to oust them by the Dutch Reformed, and the death of the first White Father Superior at Nguludi, Father Guyard. They had founded five stations in all: Likuni, Kachebere, and Mua, staffed by White Fathers, and closer to Blantyre, Nguludi, and Nzama in the hands of the Montforts. Besides nuns, there were twenty Catholic missionaries working in these stations, thirteen of these White Fathers and seven Montforts.[77]

In their second attempt to evangelize Nyasaland the White Fathers, as a Society, had brought to the country twenty-five years' experience in Equatorial Africa. Founded in the plague and famine-ridden Algiers of 1867, the Society of Our Lady of Africa was still stamped with the personality of its founder, Cardinal Charles Lavigerie. The spirituality brought by the priests from North Africa was Ignatian.[78] Lavigerie's first novice-masters were Jesuits and the emphasis on obedience remained. There was an equal insistence that the high demands of poverty and obedience, required of the priests, could only be ful-filled if they had a strong community life. Each station was to have a minimum of three missionaries and its daily life should be centred on prayer, spiritual reading, and meditation. In Lavigerie's words: 'You will convert nobody nor sanctify anyone unless you, yourselves, first undertake to work steadfastly at your own sanctification.'[79]

Techniques of evangelization were specified in as much detail as the routine of the mission house. The policy of adaptation to local culture and conditions, which had characterized the White Fathers' missions amongst the Arabs, was not practised to the same extent in Central Africa. The directive was cautious.

> The spirit that must prevail in everything is that we must draw as near as is prudently possible to the African way of life; that is to say, in everything com-patible with Christian and priestly life.[80]

Fewer elements compatible with priestly life were found in pagan than in

Muslim societies, but an educated interest in local culture continued. The first White Fathers recorded details of the religious, political, and economic life around them, and learnt the local language as quickly as possible.

Before baptism there was a four-year catechumenate, two years as a postulant and two years as full catechumen. During this period the central truths of Christianity contained in the catechism had to be learnt by heart, and the norms of Christian conduct observed. To avoid any possibility of idolatry, devotion to individual saints was treated with circumspection. Similarly Christian ethics were taught in the light of local conditions. Lavigerie felt that:

> To put the people in a position in which they would have to carry obligations which you could be sure they would soon throw off, would be the extreme of imprudence and would retard, perhaps for centuries, the hour of transformation.[81]

His thoughts on the matter, however, did not always reach the missionaries in the field. Finally, each station was to have a small library with facilities for reading and writing; the theological formation of the priests was not to be neglected.

On Lavigerie's death in 1892 Livinhac inherited an almost overprecise rule for a Society dedicated solely to the evangelization of the African continent. It had grown by accretion in response to specific queries from the missionaries in the field. This central direction from Maison-Carrée was a mixed blessing in the early days, priests being left for long periods without instructions, usually as a result of poor communications. It seems likely that in the case of the Mponda Mission the Mother-House was at a loss to know what to do. After the formation of prefectures and vicariates under their respective bishops, who stayed within a hundred miles or so of their stations, centralization became a little less intense. Yet this did nothing to reduce the military regulation of the White Fathers' lives.

The White Fathers in the Nyasa Vicariate used to receive from Dupont sheets of instructions, copied by hand and circulated to every mission. Regulations ranged from the relations that were to be maintained with Africans and colonial officials to categories of people ineligible for baptism.[82] The regulations were to be read, furthermore, at regular intervals by the missionaries. Each station was inspected by a 'visitor', appointed by the Bishop, whose job it was to comment on any irregularities in the affairs of the mission, from an unhygienic kitchen to lack of books for spiritual reading. The mission diary was read, and checked for *lèse-majesté* and omissions; extracts were sent to the Bishop, who forwarded them to Algiers as part of his annual report. There was a Father-Superior for each station who was held responsible for the progress of evangelization and the general spirit of the house. In theory, at least, he commanded the respectful obedience of his confrères at the station.

The advantage of this tight control over the mission stations was that it went a long way to reducing the worst effects of personal tensions that were inevitable in small, isolated, communities of celibates. Mission policy was consistent, and relatively immune from the idiosyncrasies of individual missionaries. In a Society that brought together a number of different nationalities at a time of fanatical European nationalism, men of different educational level and personalities, this close structuring of mission life kept rivalries to a minimum. The martial qualities of the White Fathers were the envy of those who, while reaping the benefits of clever and individualistic thinkers, often had to suffer from the dissensions they caused. The rather wistful reflection of the Livingstonia Mission magazine, in 1901, was:

> As we are now coming into touch with the Roman Catholic Missions in this land, nothing we find so striking in connection with them as the clearcut definiteness of their policy and the ready subordination which is rendered in carrying it out.[83]

In comparison to the White Fathers, the Montfortians[84] seemed singularly unadapted to mission work in Nyasaland. Their founder,[85] St. Louis-Marie Grignon de Montfort, received the title of 'Apostolic Missionary' from Pope Clement XI in 1706, but for work within France, preaching against Jansenism[86] and leading great revivalist campaigns. De Montfort's methods were unorthodox; besides the usual fiery sermon, he staged dramatic presentations of the Gospel stories and wrote numerous hymns[87] in simple language set to popular tunes. The Christianity he preached stressed suffering for the sake of Christ,[88] faith in Divine Providence,[89] and Devotion to the Blessed Virgin Mary, all themes well within Catholic orthodoxy but cast by De Montfort in hyperbolic terms, which evoked in his hearers strong feelings of attraction or revulsion.

'The Treatise on True Devotion to the Blessed Virgin Mary'[90] is considered to be the finest example of his spiritual writings. While preparing this book de Montfort read every piece of published material on the Blessed Virgin he could find,[91] but characteristically produced not a manual of Marian theology but a tract exhorting its readers to embrace 'slavery to Mary'. L'esclavage de Marie was becoming a common devotional practice in the seventeenth century. The devout Catholic made an offering of his thoughts, words, and deeds, to Mary, and placed himself entirely under her protection and guidance. The formula supplied at the end of the treatise is quite restrained compared with many in circulation at the time.[92] Yet the language of such declarations, if understood literally rather than symbolically, verged on the heretical.[93] Many of the Montfort Fathers, while practising this devotion themselves,[94] did not consider it the stuff of sermons to catechumens with no knowledge of Christianity.

On the other hand, lacking a well-formulated missiology, and with practical mission experience only from Haiti, some of the early Montforts did try to introduce their converts to these peripheral Marian practices. Their neophytes were consecrated as esclaves, were obliged to join the brotherhood of Mary, Queen of Hearts, and belonged to the Archconfraternity of the Rosary.[95] Only gradually did these missionaries come to realize that such pious practices caused confusion. The neophytes at Nzama, when told to approach a relic of the 'True Cross',[96] at Easter 1906, 'as you would for communion' came to the altar rail prepared to eat the Holy Relic.[97] Their grasp of the Mariology surrounding concepts such as esclavage must have been equally slight. When Father Martin produced a ChiChewa translation of 'The True Devotion' in 1921, many

Fathers felt that the time was not yet ripe; the uniquely Montfortian ideas were considered to be 'too advanced'[98] for ordinary Christians, and only survived, with a few exceptions,[99] into the 1920s in the training at the Minor Seminary at Nankhunda, and in the noviciate for African Sisters at Nguludi.[100]

But the central core of Christianity preached by the Montforts was the same as that of the White Fathers, who also encouraged the saying of the Rosary and devotion to the Blessed Virgin. However, there were also differences in missionary techniques. The Montfort emphasis on revivalism meant that even postulants were allowed to attend mass and hear the sermon, while the White Fathers expected catechumens to leave before the offertory. While the White Fathers attempted to give three to four hours a day of instruction, the Montforts were content with fifteen- to twenty-minute catechism lessons, morning and evening.[101] More important, the Montforts were always willing to expand whatever the personal hardships and difficulties.

It is probably true to say that the two orders had different notions of conversion. For the White Fathers, formed in the Jesuit mould, conversion was primarily an intellectual assent to the basic Christian truths. The candidate for baptism was given an examination, and the catechism answers to such questions as 'who is God?', 'who is Christ?', were expected. The four-year catechumenate was seen as a simple training in Christian Doctrine and Ethics. Examinations were far from being a mere formality; at Mua in 1909 only thirteen out of 139 catechumens were allowed through for the special six-week preparation for baptism.[102] The Montforts, who had been reinforced in their evangelism by the nineteenth-century 'Missions de France',[103] brought a more Wesleyan idea of conversion to Nyasaland. Conversion was primarily a personal assent to Christ. The catechumenate was only three years.

Common to both Orders was the primacy of the Eucharist in the devotional life of the mission. It was the *terminus ad quem* and the *terminus a quo* of all missionary activity. Official Papal directives about frequent communion[104] meant that any Jansenist tendencies were shunned. Benediction of the Blessed Sacrament and its reception in Holy Communion were the central acts of worship. But the mass itself was in Latin, said quietly by a priest at the end of the church. However much the different parts of the Roman Catholic liturgy were explained during the catechumenate,[105] mass on Sunday was a partly hidden ritual, performed by a European in an esoteric language. More than any other aspect of Church life, it was the Catholic mass, with its Latin, vestments, incense, and strangely occult character, that made both White Fathers and Montforts, *priests*, not ministers, and distinguished their congregations as the 'Aroma'.

While it is possible to discuss with some assurance the idea of conversion of the two Missionary Societies and their theology, the same is not true of the African reaction to these ideas. African conversion to Christianity was an amalgam of religious, psychological and intellectual, needs, social and political considerations, and personal inclination. It was instrumental, spiritual, and sometimes magical in motivation. Information about the psychology and religious needs of Africans in Central Malawi is scanty and an emphasis on the political

54

and social parameters of relations with missionaries is forced on the researcher. However, missionaries were distinguished from planters and colonial administrators; they were taken seriously both as powerful Europeans and as religious leaders; Christianity was seen as an intrusive religious system in its own right as well as an aspect of European rule. The interaction was complex and varied and its political aspect only one dimension of a much more complicated process. With this *caveat* it is possible to talk about patterns of interaction in Malawi.

The immediate response of African people to the two missions varied from station to station. At Nzama, Njobvualema, who had married into the Ngoni aristocracy, ruled a conservative, Ngonized, community.[106] His chief wife, Manga, was the daughter of Mlangeni and the aunt of the future paramount, Gomani II.[107] The European invasion in the Dedza district had first made itself felt, not by planters, who were thin on the ground, but by the exactions of tax collectors. Tax defaulters were obliged to work in the Shire Highlands for a period of three months, and villagers were hounded for money.[108] At the mildest the Collector would leave behind him a trail of burning huts; after the passage of the Collector through Mua the priests 'soon saw columns of black smoke drifting over the woods from Mankhamba'.[109] At the worst there were cases of serious violence. A Dutch Reformed minister reported from Mvera in 1900:

> Because men refuse to pay taxes (on account of the hardships entailed in going to work 200 miles away from their homes, where there is a great scarcity of food), women and little children have been ruthlessly shot down by native policemen . . .[110]

Under Njobvualema's personal supervision 350 workers were recruited in two days to begin building at the mission. Judging by the speed with which labourers appeared, the mission was first seen as a source of work within the district. Rather than leaving the village for long periods, tax money could be earned at the Fathers'; for 95,000 bricks, baked in crude kilns, the payment from the mission was £7.10s. At the current Hut Tax of 3/-, if the villager had been in the employment of a European, this provided fifty villagers with their annual Hut Tax and allowed them to stay on in their villages. While building continued, Njobvualema was a loyal patron of the mission, occupying the only chair in the temporary chapel each Sunday.[111] It was when the first wave of construction ended in 1908 that the priests remarked for the first time: 'Now that work of buildings has finished Njobvualema is on very bad terms with us.'[112] But the bad relations did not last long.

Even when not directly providing work, the missionaries' presence was felt to be some protection against the worst excesses of the Boma soldiers and Collector. The arrival of anyone connected with Government invariably caused a panic. On at least one occasion intervention from the priests resulted in compensation for a catechumen whose hut had been wrongfully burnt down by the Collector. The fact that the priest's mediation between people and colonial officials was somewhat equivocal, and limited to catechumens and baptized Christians, did not go unnoticed. In 1909, with the main mission complex finished, Njobvualema brought in nine of his children for baptism, stimulating a rush for baptism that produced 400 neophytes that year alone, treble the number in the previous year or any subsequent years. Families moved increasingly into the neighbourhood of the mission until it became the centre of a sizeable village.

If priests were required to act as mediators between the people and their colonial rulers, they were also expected to play this part in relation to indigenous agents of social disruption, witches and sorcerers. Here their religious claims were taken with the utmost seriousness. But perversely, it was when their priestly expertise, in the African sense, was being acknowledged that the Fathers were least likely to do what was expected of them.

As a result of a bad drought in 1903 Njobvualema carried out the traditional rain-sacrifice[113] of a black bull at Nzama.[114] A month later, with still no rain, an explanation for the failure of the sacrifice was sought, and found in the person of Nsitamwali, a sorcerer from Nchenga at the foot of Dzunje mountain. Accused of withholding rain from Njobvualema's by magical means, the sorcerer was brought for trial at the mission, bound hand and foot, and loaded down with beads, gourds, and a hartebeest horn. It is obvious, in retrospect, that the priests had been cast in the role of witchfinders. The performance of the Father-Superior left a lot to be desired.

> The Father said that only God controlled the rain and that no mortal man could stop the rain coming, even with sorcery, which was complete nonsense anyway. He told them that they should take the case to the Boma, but Njobvualema was unwilling to do this. He wanted the sorcerer to hand over all his equipment to the Father.[115]

After the priest had reluctantly taken all the sorcerer's stock-in-trade, 'it then rained confirming their belief in the sorcerer's powers'.

With a little prompting from the chief, the Catholic priest had finally done the right thing and behaved as a witchfinder should. Njobvualema had been trying to define the missionaries' tasks and roles in the villages. And the Montforts, themselves, were in their turn trying to initiate the Africans around them into Western institutional Catholicism. European missionary and African villager were trying painfully to fit each other into their separate world-views, finding equal distress in the fact that the task was impossible. They were separated by a mutual incomprehension that remained a feature of the interaction between Catholic missions and the villages surrounding them, for many years.

At Mua, the White Fathers were also in an area controlled by the Maseko Ngoni. Throughout the 1880s Chifisi's Njokozera war division had tried to detach itself from the paramountcy of Chikusi. Caught between the powerful Mangoche Yao chiefs, Tambala and Mpemba, the European-dominated Shire Highlands and the Lake, Chifisi's segment was unable to break away completely. The heirs of Chikusi and Chifisi, Gomani I and Kachindamoto I, became embroiled in serious clashes in the 1890s, until Kachindamoto, deserted by his allies Mandala and Bvumbwe Maseko,[116] was defeated and forced down into the plain overlooking the Lake.[117] Kachindamoto, eighteen years old and wounded in the legs by Gomani's Yao mercenaries, sent runners for help to Fort Johnston.[118] In a scene of high colonial farce, the leaders of the two war divisions, under the eyes of their troops and the approving gaze of two local missionaries, were made to shake hands and declare a truce in the best public school tradition.[119] Kachindamoto returned to settle on the Nadzipulu river.

The weakness of this branch of the Maseko on their arrival in the plain resulted in far less Ngonization of villages around Ntaka-taka compared with those at Nzama. Kachindamoto had inadvertently chosen a site within a few miles of the old capital of the Maravi Karonga, Mankhamba. When the plain was safe from Ngoni and Yao raids, the Chewa began to return and settle under the Maseko to form a very dense population. When the White Fathers arrived in 1902 they found that: 'Kachindamoto's consists of a large number of villages; at the very least there is a population of 12,000 to 15,000 souls. There are a large number of subsidiary villages connected to the town, making altogether the highest population density that we have come across in Africa.'[120] The numerical preponderance of Chewa-speaking peoples and the strong sense of Maravi identity engendered by the continued existence of important Chewa shrines and nyau societies in the area, limited the impact of Ngoni culture.

The Catholic Mission at Mua was, then, operating in a more complex society than at Nzama. Under the thin Ngoni veneer was a culture of great antiquity. The station was on the edge of the main Ngoni centre of Ntaka-taka. Their initial reception was hostile, although it was apparent that Nyathei, the regentess was merely voicing the sentiments of her sub-chiefs, and would have been more willing to accept the priests herself. The greatest opposition seems to have come from the Chewa section of the community.[121] The principal Ngoni objection was that the Christian ban on polygamy would disrupt traditional society.[122]

Ntaka-taka was still quite prosperous and isolated at the beginning of the twentieth century, with the nearest Boma the other side of a mountain range at Dedza.[123] Pressure from government tax collectors seems to have been less intense than at Nzama. Interest in working for the mission was correspondingly slight until the missionaries began recording regular visits from soldiers on labour-recruitment drives in 1909.[124] The response to the mission schools, which soon fanned out around the station, depended almost entirely on the ethnic composition of the village. The greater the Chewa influence, the worse the attendances at class.[125] It was a pattern that was to last until the present day.

The third station in Angoniland was at Kachebere on the North-East Rhodesian border. The priests had arrived there barely six years after the defeat of the Fort Jameson Ngoni under the leadership of Mpezeni's son, Nsingu, and his chief *nduna*, Mlonyeni.[126] Nsingu had been shot, Mlonyeni fled to seek refuge amongst the Mbelwa Ngoni, and Mpezeni himself died a natural death in September 1900. The large Ngoni villages[127] were destroyed. The missionaries arrived, therefore, in a somewhat demoralized society, shortly after the appointment of a new paramount, Mpezeni II.[128] Although, as at Kachindamoto's, a number of Chewa villages began to move back with the ending of Ngoni raids, the Fort Jameson Ngoni had a far greater number of Swazi-clan aristocracy to call on, and the area was more Ngonized than any under the Maseko.

The account of the priests' arrival, retained in oral traditions, captures the Dutch Reformed/Roman Catholic rivalry of the time in a simple, but effective literary device.

> The first missionaries who came to teach us were protestants. So we said, 'Let us give them a chance'. They began 'Let us pray', and told us all to shut our eyes. We thought that this was very impolite and Chief Mshawa asked them to go away. On the afternoon of the same day the Catholic Fathers arrived with their tents. They were very polite and cheerful. They rested for a while then asked us to kneel down and showed us how to make the sign of the cross. They did not ask us to shut our eyes. Then they said, 'You will hear the rest tomorrow'. They talked to us and ate African food. So Chief Mshawa allowed them to stay.[129]

Chief Mshawa was a sub-chief of Mlonyeni and was not directly involved in the 1898 fighting. He seems to have accepted the Catholic Mission as an in-evitable product of British Rule. He was genuinely friendly with the priests, eating with them and spending a considerable amount of time in their company. His ready acceptance of the European missionaries must have appeared to his villagers as a further piece of collaboration, for three weeks after the Fathers had pitched their tents, on 31 May 1903, Mshawa was stabbed to death during the night. He had been lured out of his hut by someone interfering with his pigeon coop. The missionaries assumed that he had been killed accidentally while apprehending a robber. He had, it is said, been deliberately murdered. A sorcerer was employed to discover the culprit but, being bribed, failed to produce any names.[130]

The Fort Jameson Ngoni, an offshoot of the Mbelwa Ngoni of northern Nyasaland, assimilated captives more successfully than their Maseko contemporaries. None the less, Chewa culture had made some impact. A belief in 'Chisumphi',[131] a messenger of the Rain-God in the form of a python, was wide-spread, but frowned on by the true Ngoni. Wandering groups of dancers, the *Avirombo-a-Chisumphi*,[132] moved freely in the area, inducing in villagers spirit-possession by Chisumphi. The Chewa wives of the Ngoni would become possessed and ceremonies at local pools were required to free the victim of the spirit.[133] While important chieftancies were handed down in the leading Ngoni families, four being held by relatives of Mpezeni, the Chewa maintained many headmanships over small villages and were allowed a greater degree of autonomy under British Rule than they would have enjoyed formerly. Much of the land bought by the priests for Kachebere mission was sold to them by a Chewa village headman, Mkhumbi, who owned it in his own right. On his death in December 1903, two of his wives were ritually killed to join him in the grave, a custom usually reserved for important chiefs.[134] But whatever the exact balance of power between Ngoni and Chewa at village level, the Catholic Mission was, once again, welcomed as a potential ally by the leading Ngoni. The first baptisms in November 1907 were '8 young men and 5 girls from the best Angoni families'.[135] The Chewa, on the other hand, were tending to frequent the Dutch Reformed Mission at Magwero some fifteen miles away.

The Ngoni attempt to maintain their identity and position in relation to their subject Chewa is seen very clearly at Kachebere, where the pre-European Ngoni domination, though checked, continued in a modified form into the colonial period. Ngoni soldiers refused to work alongside Chewa, and the priests remarked on the Ngoni 'prejudice' against Achipeta.[136] Contacts between Fort Jameson and the Mbelwa Ngoni, where Mlonyeni lived away from the English eye until his death in August 1906, were maintained. When there were strong rumours that the Fort Jameson Ngoni were to be moved across the border into the Luangwa valley, the young Mpezeni, although '12 years old, timid and shy', gathered together the leading *ndunas* to discuss a site in Nyasaland where the North-East Rhodesian and Protectorate Ngoni could live united. It is interesting that the two sites chosen were in the Maseko areas of Mua, and further south, along the banks of the Rivelezi.[137] Some Ngoni consciousness that transcended the differences between the separate Ngoni groups still remained to be called on in times of pressure from British or Chewa.

The response to the Catholic missions in the three Ngoni areas was, then, fundamentally the same. To differing degrees Mpezeni, Kachindamoto, and Njobvualema, saw the Catholic priests as potential supporters in the political and cultural infighting in which they had to engage to keep a hold on their Chewa villages. Neither the Fort Jameson nor the Maseko Ngoni had finished the task of assimilating their subject villages; the formation of potentially centralized Ngoni states had been finally terminated by the European invasion. Catholic missionaries were potential allies against British and Chewa alike. And the priests were delighted whenever Ngoni chiefs helped them to eradicate 'pagan practices'.[138] That these practices were always parts of Chewa village life, rather than Ngoni culture, was not at first noticed.

Reared in an authoritarian environment themselves, the early Fathers were at home in the precise hierarchy of Ngoni society. They believed, not without reason, that a society in which orders came from the top and authority was universally acknowledged was one in which Catholicism could thrive. They were therefore happier in Ngoniland, where the chiefs were willing to comply with most of their wishes, than amongst the small Chewa villages where authority was diffuse, society lacking centralization, and the missionaries regarded as a threat. Kachebere proved to be numerically the most successful of any of the Catholic stations in the Central Region.

The very difficult first five years of Likuni Mission, in a predominantly Chewa area, confirmed this preference. Only in 1909 were the first Chewa baptized, and for the entire period the Fathers had been forced to rely on catechists imported from another station. A strong resistance was put up to the mission and its Ngoni catechists, some having to go for over two days before finding a welcoming village that would provide them with food.[139] Although there were important chiefs like Dzoole and Matanda recognized in the district, there was nothing comparable to the central authority of the Ngoni paramounts. Authority over wide areas was held only by rain-shrine officials and was, by the beginning of the twentieth century, of a purely religious nature.[140] Mission influence was opposed strongly by old people and village headmen.

In all stations the simple medical treatment provided by nuns and priests was an immediate lure for villagers of all tribes. At Nguludi, where the local Yao were at first reluctant to enter the catechumenate, the mission was inundated with patients.[141] Proximity to Blantyre and contact with the coast had produced a confidence in Western medicine. The provision of medical services, even if it were only a vaccination against smallpox, brought countless villagers into the orbit of the five Catholic mission stations. Characteristically, at Likuni, headmen made attempts to stop villagers from visiting the mission for treatment.[142] Their continued visits were a tacit admission that the mission did have something to offer, for certain classes of ailments.[143] And since disease was always assumed to be caused by some human, usually magical, agency this was an important step. Medicine provided many occasions for misunderstanding between missionary and Africans. For both, curing the sick was related to religion but the relationship was, of course, very different for each party. The Catholic missionary saw his dispensary work as one of the 'corporal works of mercy', an act of Charity expressing Christ's redemptive victory over suffering. The religious aspect of the work was the human caring, rather than the medical technology. For the Africans it was the opposite. The supernatural qualities of the missionary were demonstrated by his effective ritual use of needles and glass vials. The religious power of the dispensary lay in its medical technology, and if the priest did not give 'injectioni' he was failing in his religious duties to his flock. A compromise was sometimes reached by injecting distilled water to avoid the idea that the Father did not care. Even though Western medicine might be effective, the relationship of patient and doctor could often be one leading to mutual frustration and anxiety.

The African response to the second attempt of the Catholic missionaries to enter Nyasaland was entirely different from the apathy and hostility of Mponda's and Matapwiri's, a decade earlier. The Fathers had steered clear of the main Islamic areas and wisely so; as late as 1914 the station of the Universities' Mission to Central Africa at Mponda's was their worst in Nyasaland.[144] Amongst the Ngoni they had found, for a while, natural allies. If not avid for education, most villagers in Ngoniland wanted to learn the elements of reading, writing, and arithmetic, to equip themselves for jobs in the European cash economy. But the Catholic missions had certainly not taken up with the most progressive chiefs in the area; these were already in Protestant schools.[145] Njobvualema was a habitual beer-drinker who was reputed to consume three to four calabashes of the strong *jejuru* beer[146] at a sitting; he was fat, illiterate, and usually drunk. Nyathei, regentess at Ntaka-taka, vied with Njobvualema for girth; like him she drank to excess and only accepted baptism on her death-bed. All three of the Ngoni chiefs lived polygamously, and since polygamy was integral to the older Ngoni society, were unwilling to put away their wives for a monogamous Church-blessed union. Their neighbouring chiefs already had Protestant Missions. At the lowest level of motivation, the Catholic Fathers could be relied on not to fuss about drunkenness.

By 1905, the first two-storeyed buildings were being constructed with local labour, catechists were being trained and catechumens being examined for baptism. The priests were beginning to move out of temporary thatched huts into the brick mission stations, with their long verandahs and catwalks, rooms for bishops, Apostolic Delegates, countless missionaries, and catechumens. Much to the disgust of their Protestant rivals, the Roman Catholic Missions—the Society of Our Lady of Africa and the Company of Mary—had pushed their way into Protestant Nyasaland.

REFERENCES TO CHAPTER II

[1] Du Plessis to Lansdowne 14 October 1902 F.O. 2.615

[2] See Reference 55 of the Introduction

[3] Pearce to Manning 15 May 1898, Brogden to Manning 17 May F.O. 2.147 Personal Communication. Inkosi Willard Gomani III, Lizulu.

[4] Oral Testimony. Pio Kupempha. Nyanja, Catholic Catechist. Mua. May 1969.

[5] 'Boma' was originally the name for a fortified stockade. It came to be used for the local government headquarters as many of them started off as military posts in the nineteenth century.

[6] Palmer R. H. 'Johnston and Jameson: A comparative study in the imposition of colonial rule' in *The Early History* 312. The North Nyasa district, 4,334 square miles, extended from the South Rukuru River up to the River Songwe and the Tanganyika border.

[7] *British Central African Gazette* 1 June 1896

[8] For example Hetherwick led the protests against rapes committed by Nyasaland troops sent for the Somali campaign in 1903

[9] MacDonald R. J. *A History of African Education in Nyasaland: 1875–1945* Doctoral Dissertation, University of Edinburgh 1969, 43

[10] Blantyre Church was built between 1888 and 1891 by David Buchanan and David Clement Scott. It was dedicated on 10 May 1891, see Hetherwick A. *The Building of Blantyre Church: 1888–1891* Blantyre 1962 (1st. edition 1926).

[11] Born in Derby, England, in 1851, he left for New Zealand in 1880 to become a sheep farmer. From 1887 to 1891 Deacon at North Brighton Baptist Church in Melbourne. He arrived in the Shire Highlands in August 1892 to found the Zambesi Industrial Mission at Mitsidi. One of the most important formative influences on John Chilembwe, see Shepperson G. and Price T. *Independent African* Edinburgh 1958, 18–63.

[12] See Murray S. S. *A Handbook of Nyasaland* Zomba 1922, 25. Population was 314 in 1901.

[13] *The Life and Letters of Arthur Fraser Sim, Priest of the U.M.C.A.* U.M.C.A. 1897, 138. Letter of 14 October 1894. The party was led, in fact, by Lechaptois on his way to Tanganyika from Algiers where he had been ordained bishop and attended the General Chapter.

[14] See later in Chapter II and Pineau H. *Évêque Roi des Brigands* Montreal 1937

[15] Pineau *Évêque* 114

[16] Mwamba died on 24 October 1898. He was senior chief but not the Chitimukula, or Bemba paramount.

[17] Rea W. F. 'The Bemba's White Chief' Unpublished paper, University of Rhodesia

[18] Pineau *Évêque* 166

[19] Paradis E. 'Notes on White Fathers' Missions' MS White Fathers' Archives Lilongwe

[20] Frissen J. 'Vers une Histoire des Missions Montfortaines'. MS Montfort Archives, Rome 1969.

[21] Pineau op. cit. 16, 202

[22] It was finally the Émile Combes government that drove many Religious into exile in 1903. In Brittany, Montfort territory, the Government's action caused serious riots.

[23] The original contract can be found in the Montfort Archives, Rome.

[24] Querel L. 'Historie du Vicariat du Shire' Cahier I MS Orleans. Handwritten 1960, Montfort Archives, Rome.

[25] The Sacred Congregation of the Propaganda Fidei, founded in the first great wave of missionary expansion of the sixteenth and seventeenth centuries, had, by the twentieth century, full control over the activities of Catholic missionaries in every part of the world. The appointment of Prefect of the Propaganda was an important Vatican position but bore little relation to the Cardinal's knowledge of, or interest in, the missions. Even today, the heads of Missionary Congregations have little say in Vatican decisions on the missions, it still being the preserve of cardinals, many of whom have not been outside Europe.

[26] Nzama Mission Diary 24 May 1901, 19 June 1901 Montfort Archives, Rome.

[27] Pineau op. cit., 174–84

[28] Frissen ibid.

[29] It is not certain, however, whether Ledochowski ever read the issues in which the Shire was said to belong to the Montforts.

[30] Oliver *Sir Harry Johnston* 275

[31] Frissen ibid.

[32] Propaganda Fide 'Illme ac Rme Domine' 7 December 1901 Montfort Archives, Rome Trans. Latin.

[33] A popular name for a medal depicting the Blessed Virgin with the inscription 'Mary, conceived without sin, pray for us who have recourse to thee.' The devotion was started by the visions of a French nun, Catherine Labouré in 1830, and the wearer of the medal was considered to be under the special protection of the Blessed Virgin.

[34] Nzama Diary 24 May 1901

[35] *Central African Times* 6 July 1901

[36] References to Nunan in a B.C.A. Chamber of Agriculture and Commerce petition to Lansdowne, enclosure 8 April 1903 F.O. 2.754

[37] Nzama Diary 8 July 1903, 20 July 1903

[38] Querel ibid.

[39] The Rev. Clement Scott used to have regular teas at the manse for his African staff, for which everyone would dress up in their best suits. The occasion was probably no less terrifying for the three Montforts, though it must have been another 'Rev. Scott' in attendance on this occasion, Clement Scott having left Nyasaland.

[40] Nzama Diary 12 July 1903

[41] ibid. Chiromo was a village on the Lower Shire through which the Montforts would have already passed. At that time of the year the heat would have been moderate.

[42] *Central African Times* 13 July 1901

[43] The name given the Catholic adherents at the Kabaka's court in Buganda after the French White Fathers, Lourdel, Livinhac *et al*.

[44] From subsequent troubles with the Dutch Reformed, the letter was almost certainly from a Dutch Reformed minister, or sympathizer.

[45] Nzama Diary 13–25 July 1901

[46] Mandala, who was said to be older than Gomani I, was passed over, it is said, for reasons of character. It was customary for the *ndunas* to have the right to reject a candidate for the paramountcy if they felt his character would be damaging to the Ngoni.

[47] Manning to Salisbury 22 April 1898, F.O. 2.147

[48] The terms 'Ngonized' and 'Ngonization' are used to denote the imposition of Ngoni social, political, and cultural patterns on their subject peoples. e.g. patrilineal, patrilocal villages with the payment of bride-price, cattle-herding, etc. see Read M. *The Ngoni of Nyasaland* London 1956 and Read M. *Children of their Fathers* London 1959.

[49] Nzama Diary 19 August 1901

[50] Ncheu District Book Vol. I. The chief was described as 'overbearing' and 'disliked'. National Archives, Zomba.

[51] *Chiefs and Headmen of Nyasaland* A guide for District Commissioners published at Zomba c. 1914 after the District Administration Ordinance of 1912. Society of Malawi Library. Blantyre, see under Ncheu Headmen.

[52] Frissen ibid.

[53] The cost of the journey of one missionary from Europe to Nyasaland was 2,600 francs in 1906. The fixed budget for the White Fathers' Vicariate was 13,333 francs. *Chroniques Trimestrielles de la Societé des missionaires de Notre-Dame d'Afrique* July 1906 No. 129.

[54] Nzama Diary 30 November 1901

[55] Nzama Diary 30 August 1902, and Bourget to Maurille 10 January 1902. Correspondence for Shire Vicariate. Montfort Archives, Rome.

[56] Chilubula Mission to the north of Lake Bangwelo was founded in 1899 in the Bemba capital. The name means 'Deliverance'.

[57] Bishop Joseph Fady 'Notes on Mathurin Guillemé' MS Undated White Fathers' Archives, Lilongwe, and Personal Diary of Alfred Honoré. w.f. 63–9 in possession of Rev. J. Heymans, w.f. Regional Superior, Lilongwe.

[58] Alfred Honoré, born on 10 February 1876, at Tourcoing, was ordained on 8 September 1899. After a short period as a seminary teacher, he sailed for Central Africa on 18 June 1902. He wrote a French–ChiChewa Grammar and had a passion for astronomy. He was the first of the White Fathers to use a bicycle in the bush. He suffered from leprosy between 1935 and 1941 and died on 25 March 1950. Except for two short stays in Europe, in 1910 and 1924, he spent all his missionary life in Nyasaland.

[59] Fady ibid.

[60] Nzama Diary 29 September 1902, and Kachebere Mission Diary 11 May 1903, Kachebere Seminary

[61] Pretorius J. L. 'An introduction to the history of the Dutch Reformed Church Missions in Malawi: 1889–1914' in *The Early History* 1973, 370

[62] Rev. Jan Du Plessis was head of the Ministers' Mission Union at Sea Point, Cape Colony, and supervisor of Dutch Reformed missions in Nyasaland. Author of *A History of Christian Missions in South Africa* (first published 1911) republished Cape Town 1965.

[63] The fifth Marquess of Lansdowne was the Liberal-Unionist War Minister in Salisbury's third cabinet, in 1895, before becoming Foreign Secretary. He was intimately involved, therefore, in the opening stages of the Boer War.

[64] Duplessis to Lansdowne 14 October 1902. F.O. 2.615

[65] When Lansdowne became Foreign Minister England's period of 'splendid isolation' came to an end. In 1903 Edward VII paid a very successful visit to Paris, which was returned by a visit from President Loubet to London. Formal agreements between England and France were drawn up in 1904, of little substance, but known as the *Entente Cordiale*. See Brogan D. W. *The Development of Modern France* London 1963, 391–403.

[66] Sharpe to Lansdowne 14 January 1903 F.O. 2.746

[67] Mullins J. D. 'The Wonderful Story of Uganda' *Church Missionary Gleaner* 1 September 1902, 130

[68] *Chroniques* July 1904 No. 108 381

[69] Nzama Diary 1 August 1902, 11 February 1903, 3 June 1903

[70] General Chapters were attended by representatives from all the White Fathers' missions. Mission policy was formulated, Superior-Generals were elected, and new regulations to fit the changing circumstances of the missions were drawn up.

[71] *Central African Times* 23 September 1903

[72] Originally *The Central African Planter*, begun in 1895, it became a fortnightly paper published in Blantyre and then a weekly before becoming the *Nyasaland Times* in January 1909.

[73] As Reference 71

[74] *A Catholic Directory of East Africa* Dublin 1950, 126

[75] Nzama Diary 9 January 1904

[76] A *machila* was a litter carried by runners. Each machila had a team of runners who took it in turns to carry the passenger. The bearers kept up the rhythm by singing. It was most uncomfortable over long distances. Mua Mission Diary 28 May 1904.

[77] White Fathers: Guillemé, Louveau, Perrot, Honoré, Tellegen, Ter Maat, Braire, Bellierè, Dequeker, Schenk, and Brothers Lucien, Willibrord, and Sebastian. Montfort Fathers: Bourget, Winnen, Prézeau, Cadoret, Déau, and Brothers Odilon, Cléophas, not counting ten nuns—see Chapter VII.

[78] Based on the Spiritual Exercises of St. Ignatius Loyola, founder of the Society of Jesus. The exercises were something of a spiritual ordeal through which the priest achieved a purity of spirit and clarity of spiritual insight through contemplation of death and damnation, etc.

[79] Burridge W. *Destiny Africa* 1966 London. White Fathers' Rule 45

[80] ibid. 104

[81] ibid. 118

[82] *Règlements et Instructions pour les missionaires du Nyassa* D. Roy. MS 10 February 1919, 'confirmed drunkards, those who have caused scandal several times, those who do not know, according to their intelligence, the Faith: and those who know it but are unwilling to carry out its precepts'. White Fathers' Archives, Lilongwe.

[83] *Aurora* 1 April 1901. An article on 'Union of the Churches'.

[84] There are two Montfortian societies, one for priests and one for nuns. The 'Filles de La Sagesse' were founded in 1713 for work amongst the poor, as nurses and teachers.

[85] Louis-Marie Grignon de Montfort was born in 1673 at St. Malo, the son of minor nobility. He entered the seminary at St. Sulpice in 1693 and was ordained in 1700, after which he engaged in itinerant preaching in the north-west of France. He died in 1716 and was canonized by Pope Pius XII in 1947, see Lamoot J. *Un nouveau saint français: Louis-Marie Grignon de Montfort* Lille c. 1948.

[86] The doctrines of Cornelius Otto Jansenius (1585–1638) which emphasized supernatural determinism and moral rigorism. One of his disciples, Antoine Arnauld, published 'De la fréquente communion' in 1643 condemning frequent communion. Jansenism was officially condemned by Innocent X in 1653.

[87] These were published as a collected volume of 'Cantiques'

[88] De Montfort's New Year greeting to *Les filles de la Sagesse* in 1716 was; 'I wish you a year full of struggles and victories, of poverty and humiliations.' A Daughter of Wisdom *The Wisdom of Folly* Ottawa 1950, 165.

[89] De Montfort was probably influenced by Henry Suzo's *Le livre de la Sagesse*, a famous seventeenth-century mystical work. The idea of Providence strongly affected his life-style, almost no concern for material welfare, and indirectly resulted in his early death.

[90] Written in 1714 but not published until 1842, it was recommended spiritual reading by the nineteenth-century Popes, as well as Pius X, XI, and XII

[91] The late seventeenth century had seen a flowering of Marian theology as luxuriant as the court of Louis XIV against whose courtesans it was something of a reaction.

[92] For the way Marian devotion recurrently tended towards excesses see Graef H. *Mary: A History of Doctrine and Devotion.* Vol. I and II London, 1963, 1965

[93] For example 'They (the saints) cry out . . . that the length of her power which she exercises even over God Himself, is incomprehensible; and finally that the depth of her humility, and of all her virtues and graces, is an abyss which can never be sounded. O height incomprehensible! O breadth unspeakable! O length immeasurable! O abyss impenetrable!' from *True Devotion to Mary* New York 1954 (trans. F. W. Faber) 6. De Montfort's works were what Rahner calls 'cryptogamic heresy', inasmuch as they were certainly understood popularly in an heretical fashion, see Rahner K. *Theological Investigations Vol. V* London 1966, 468–512. On the other hand Pius XII, speaking at the canoniza-

tion of De Montfort said: 'He strenuously opposed all who popularized erroneous pious practices or who upheld doctrines contrary to the teaching of the Church. As a result of his labours the integrity of Catholic doctrine was safeguarded'.

94 The formula of the consecration was: 'In the presence of the heavenly court I choose thee this day for My Mother and Mistress. I deliver and consecrate to thee as thy slave my body, my goods, both interior, and exterior and even the value of all my good actions, past, present and future, leaving to thee the entire and full right of disposing of me . . .' *True Devotion* 228. All the Montfort Fathers renewed this vow annually after their retreat.

95 *Messager de Marie Reine des Coeurs* September 1907, 215 Cadoret M. 'Une dimanche aux pays des noirs'. An Archconfraternity is simply a pious association of lay people.

96 After the Middle Ages Western Christendom was flooded with spurious relics, there were thousands of such pieces of the 'True Cross'. The devotion was practised in both Vicariates.

97 *Bulletins trimestrieles* September 1906, 7–9

98 Interview with Auguste Baslé S.M.M. Arrived in Nyasaland 1908. Pirimiti mission, October 1970.

99 For example at Utale, where there was a Grotto to the Blessed Virgin, neophytes underwent the consecration ceremony as late as June 1924. *Bulletins trimestriels* June 1924, 14. Father Martin, who arrived in Nyasaland in 1914, finished the translation of the 'True devotion' into ChiChewa in 1921, see Nsanje Mission Diary 30 November 1921, when a packet of copies of his translation arrived at the mission.

100 *Bulletins trimestriels* December 1926, 9

101 Nzama Diary 16 December 1902

102 Mua Diary 28 February 1909

103 The 'Missions de France' attempted to reconvert France from Republicanism and Atheism during the period of the Restoration. The movement began in 1814 under the direction of Abbé Rauzan and was strongly royalist. See Dansette A. *Religious History of Modern France Vol. 1.* Freiburg and Edinburgh 1961, 194–6.

104 In a Decree in 1905, Pius X recommended frequent communion and the communion of children

105 In the six-week preparation for baptism given by the White Fathers the catechumen was given a 'dry run' through the mass so that he knew what to do at communion. In this simulated mass the hosts were not consecrated.

106 Ncheu District Book Vol. I. National Archives, Zomba.

107 Philip Gomani was a young child when his father was 'executed' by the British and was looked after at Maganga, the principal village of the Ndau clan, until old enough to become paramount. In the interim period Chakumbira Ndau was recognized as regent. Mlangeni had been a very powerful figure at Chikusi's court. Personal Communication. Inkosi Willard Gomani III Lizulu.

108 Ncheu Boma was founded in 1902. By 1905 the revenue had risen from £1,200 to £2,311 as tax collecting became more efficient. Ncheu District Book Vol. I.

109 Mua Diary 14 January 1909

110 Pretorius *An introduction* 371

111 Nzama Diary 19 August 1901, 3 July 1903, and *Messager de Marie Reine des Coeurs* September 1907, 215

112 Nzama Diary 6 February 1908. At Mua the priests paid the workers' tax and received their tax slips from the Collector. Personal Diary, Alfred Honoré, W.F. This was the usual European practice and allowed pressure to be brought to bear to make Africans work for them at times when the men would have preferred to till their fields.

113 Rain sacrifices were common to both Ngoni and Chewa. The animal had to be black to signify the heavy rain clouds. The sacrifice of a white calf was used by the Ngoni to stop excessive rain. Unlike the Chewa they used cattle, and skin of the dead animal was not put

on a rain-shrine. Although the Ngoni had a hut for the worship of ancestral spirits, this was their only religious shrine and not connected with the rain cult. Kachebere Diary 21 January 1909.

[114] Nzama Diary 22 February 1903

[115] ibid. 7 March 1903

[116] The heads of the Liwiswini and Namba war divisions, respectively. Personal Communication. Inkosi Willard Gomani III.

[117] Linden I. 'The Maseko Ngoni at Domwe: 1870–1900' in *The Early History* 237–52 for details.

[118] Edwards to Acting-Consul 31 October 1894, F.O. 2.68

[119] *British Central African Gazette* 21 November 1894

[120] Mua Diary 14 September 1902

[121] ibid. 25 April 1903

[122] *Rapports annuels de la Societé des missionaires de Notre Dame d'Afrique* 1912–13 Ntakataka. Kachindamoto's idea of renouncing his wives was strongly criticized by his *nduna*.

[123] There was a steep path from Bembeke on the other side of the escarpment.

[124] Mua Diary 10 May 1909

[125] See Chapters VI and IX where the point is taken up in detail.

[126] Brake to Manning 20 January 1898 F.O. 2.147. Fort Jameson is now Chipata in Zambia.

[127] Barnes J. A. *Politics in a Changing Society* Manchester 1967, 102–6. There were at least 1,000 huts in the capital, Loangeni, and several other villages of comparable size.

[128] Ciloa, the eldest son of Nsingu, was made paramount in September 1901 but was opposed by Madzimawi, a son of Mpezeni I. Barnes *Politics* 111.

[129] Oral Testimony, Salina Mshawa Jere, Ngoni, Mchinji; August 1969

[130] Kachebere Diary 31 May 1903, and Mshawa Jere. It was impossible to confirm, or disprove this testimony. From a daughter of the chief, there may have been grounds for distortion, but it is difficult to understand why such a story should be fabricated.

[131] Kachebere Diary 23 August 1903. See Gamitto A.C.P. *King Kazembe* Lisbon Vol. I 76–7.

[132] 'The Beasts of Chisumphi' literally

[133] Interview with Alusio Tembo, born 1898, Chief Catechist Kachebere Mission, October 1971

[134] Kachebere Diary 20 December 1903

[135] ibid. 1 October 1907

[136] ibid. 8 March 1904

[137] ibid. 11 August 1906 and 6 March 1906 a number of Swazi-clan Ngoni like Nkwaila and Nkwerere lived along the Rivelezi river.

[138] See Chapter IX for details

[139] Notes made by Bishop J. Fady and kindly lent us.

[140] In 1969 at Msinja, a simple villager, a shrine official, was able to summon other officials from a radius of over forty miles on the arrival of Rev. Dr. J. M. Schoffeleers. Personal Communication.

[141] *Messager de Marie Reine des Coeurs* October 1907 Bourget P. 'Nouvelles des missions', 245, and *Chroniques* August 1907 No. 140 467

[142] *Chroniques* March 1908 No. 159 226

[143] This did not mean, of course, that the *sing'anga* was being rejected. The missionaries could not compete with *sing'angas* if the ailment had a psychosomatic cause. In most cases both African and European medicines would be tried.

[144] Blood A. G. *The History of the Universities' Mission to Central Africa Vol. II 1907–1932* London 1957, 63

[145] For example Chiefs Makwangwala and Philip Gomani

[146] A particularly strong maize beer reserved for the chief

CHAPTER III

Catholicism as a Religious Option

> These people lacked the material and emotional support afforded by tradi-
> tional social groups; their kinship-groups had disintegrated and they were
> not effectively organised in village communities or in guilds; for them there
> existed no regular, institutionalised methods of voicing their grievances or
> pressing their claims. Instead they waited for a *propheta* to bind them together
> in a group of their own—which would then emerge as a movement of a
> peculiar kind, driven on by a wild enthusiasm born of desperation.[1]
>
> Norman Cohn: *The Pursuit of the Millenium.*

Kupita ku missioni[2] was to enter an extensive European settlement. When construction was complete there were a large church, a private chapel for the convent, a mission school, offices, workshops, stores, stables, and a granary, all on
mission grounds. If the station took in boarders, the majority of whom were the
illegitimate children of planters and Government officials, an orphanage was
added to the complex. The rural Catholic mission was an oasis of two-storey
brick buildings amongst wattle and daub huts. The North African style houses
of the White Fathers at Mua, Ntaka-taka, and Bembeke, with their long
verandahs, were, and still are, impressive sights. The Montfort stations, with
their thick timber beams, were reminiscent of large Dutch farmhouses. Only
they separated the missionaries, emphatically and glaringly, from their
parishioners.

The problem of buying land for the mission was more acute in the White
Fathers' districts than in the south, where there were many plantations. In the
Central Region, the Fathers were buying Crown Trust land from a Government
that saw itself *in loco parentis* for the Africans in the Protectorate.[3] Permission
from the local chief was required, but not always forthcoming. At Mua, the land
was bought under a 'Mission Site Agreement',[4] which allowed missionaries to
buy land at sixpence an acre, provided prior consent had been given by the
chief. Buildings erected on it had to be concerned with some aspect of mission
work and not occupy more than one acre. Further land around the mission was
usually leased at a later date, giving the typical appearance of a central complex
surrounded by gardens and outbuildings.

At the beginning, there was sometimes fear amongst villagers that the priests
might have come to steal the land from the people. Once Nyathei and her *ndunas*
were convinced that the White Fathers wanted neither to annoy her people, nor
to occupy their gardens, permission was given to build in the capital, Ntaka-

taka. The Montforts had an easier time in the Shire Vicariate, as they could usually persuade a planter to sell a small portion of his estates, in a transaction that was not directly controlled by the Government. Chikwawa, Blantyre, and Nguludi Missions were built on private land of this type. The land was relatively cheap, furthermore; 300 acres at Nzama went for £52.10s, one of the highest sums ever paid by the Catholics for a mission site in the early days.[5] The moment the ink was dry in the Lands Registry Office the priests would move in, sleeping on anything from cotton bales to drying tobacco leaves, or if there was no barn, in their own tents. Only rarely, as in the extension of the leprosarium grounds at Mua to provide the lepers with gardens, did land become a point of friction between the mission and the local population.[6]

It was always Lavigerie's intention to make the White Fathers' stations self-contained. Shortage of funds from abroad made it a necessity for both mission societies. Money came into the vicariates from both official and unofficial sources. For the White Fathers who had to rely on funds from the Propaganda and their Mother-House, the official sources were hopelessly inadequate. Relatives and benefactors of the missionaries, often prosperous farmers, or bourgeois families from small towns in France, Holland, and Canada, supplemented the budget on a personal basis.[7] Although the White Fathers were a missionary society, rather than a Religious Order like the Montforts, and had no formal vow of poverty, such money was distributed throughout the vicariate, to avoid any one station's becoming inordinately well-endowed. The bulk of correspondence from the first Vicars-Apostolic consisted of begging letters replete with pious anecdotes for the eyes of benefactors. Stringent economy was practised. Bricks were made, rarely bought; wood for the kilns and for building was purchased, begged, or occasionally cut without permission, from plantations and Government forest reserves.[8]

An important task of Brothers in each vicariate, of whom there were usually one per mission, was to develop a good vegetable garden and produce one or more cash crops around the station. Returns from the sale of coffee, tobacco, and cotton, became important items on the income side of the budget. Most of the missionaries had grown up in rural areas and were used to living off the land. The Brothers mainly came from farming families in Brittany, East and Central France, Quebec, and Limburg in the south of Holland.[9] Brother Willibrord at Kachebere supplied Fort Jameson with 3,500 francs worth of vegetables in 1905,[10] and in the famine year of 1909 had 12,500 lb of wheat hoarded in bags.[11] Their home background in Republican France, as the persecuted Church, provided a rich soil for the growth of the capitalist ethic; Dupont himself had fought against the Paris Commune of 1871.[12] Brother Willibrord had equally little respect for socialism, primitive or otherwise: 'The famine is partly the natives' fault. Because of this communistic life of theirs no-one gets the fruits of his own labour.'[13]

By 1906 at Nzama, there were 44 cows, 29 sheep, 49 goats, 2 asses, a mule, and 115 doves.[14] The White Fathers had a large herd of cattle, too, which they had brought up with them from Nguludi[15] to Kachebere. At the beginning of the First World War, Guimard caused some consternation amongst the Blantyre

Town Council by asking permission to sell meat on the African market.[16] This pressure to raise money was not lessened by flamboyant gestures by some of the early missionaries towards chiefs and people. The climax to important days in the religious calendar was often the giving out of presents from the mission house. Game, caught in the Fathers' frequent hunting trips,[17] and *nsima*,[18] were handed out to large crowds of people.

The common practice of distributing presents had the unwanted effect of consecrating an attitude of dependence on the mission; it defined the relationship between mission and people as one of giver and receiver. The gifts were not usually given with any ulterior motive. Some Montfort nuns, though, distributed small presents and salt to entice children to come to school, or to pray at the Holy Grotto at Utale.[19] It was often the new missionary, shocked by the disparity in material welfare between the station and the villages he visited, who felt an overwhelming need to give in a tangible fashion. Guillemé, with his long experience,[20] was quick to sound a warning. In a letter to the Nyasa missionaries shortly after the foundation of Mua, he wrote: 'The giving of presents can perhaps be useful, even necessary, but it is a two-edged sword that often wounds he who gives and he who takes.'[21] He insisted that gifts should be the prerogative of the Father-Superior only, and that they should be given sparingly. Although some largess was to be exercised at the foundation of a mission, particularly towards chiefs, it had to be reduced as rapidly as possible. Like other directives from the bishops, this rule was not always adhered to strictly.

While it is true that the mission stations appeared to be astonishingly rich by local village standards, they were no better endowed than any poor French farm-house of the time. The budget at Mua in 1908, where there were five priests and one brother working, was made up as follows: Running costs—£148, Catechists' pay (38 catechists)—£63, Upkeep of Schools (36)—£32: Income— Government Grant—£62, Donations—£38, Vicar-Apostolic—£35, Sale of Crops—£4. Deficit—£104.[22] To quote from Dupont's report to Maison-Carrée that year:

> Our missionaries live in great poverty. After imposing on themselves severe personal sacrifices to get their work under way, I am obliged to my chagrin to reproach them for having overspent their budget. It is not very encouraging either for me or for them.[23]

The priests had no luxuries beyond a pipe, in which they would smoke their home-grown tobacco, and were still lucky if they got through a year without a serious bout of malaria or dysentery.

Yet, however poor by European standards, and despite the fact that they ate, talked, and mixed freely with everyone in the village, the priest remained 'Abambo',[24] set apart, and above the poverty of village life. This was neither the individual missionary's, nor the Mission Societies', wish. The Fathers at Mua deliberately stopped using the *machila* for journeys to the villages to distinguish themselves from other Europeans.[25] Their contact with lepers was so casual that Father Honoré contracted leprosy.[26] But their buildings, gardens, livestock, the black boots and white cassocks they wore, defined their position in society. Even

69

if it had occurred to them to be anything other than paternalist, it would have been inconceivable in the conditions of village life in the bush.

A scene recorded by the diarist at Mua, of the distribution of prizes after a religious feast, captures the relationship between priests and people better than any lengthy catalogue of events. The Fathers, standing on the verandah of the mission are looking out over the crowd in the courtyard.

> Everybody was dressed in their Sunday best, some were wearing white cloths with brilliantly contrasting full-length red skirts, others had on hard-earned leather jerkins, and finally, some enamoured with European civilization had risen to a pair of trousers and a shirt, alas, somewhat dilapidated. Groups soon began to form in the courtyard . . . In the middle were the children surrounded by two groups of adolescents, with around them numerous smaller groups of women. Then, most imposing of all, the chiefs and old people . . . Fr. Louveau distributed the prizes by throwing the 'balle'[27] into the crowd for the most agile to catch. They competed for beads, cloth, knives, mirrors, and trinkets. After the sport came the beer.[28]

If the comparison may be made, the priests were seen on the same level as an Ngoni paramount, who was expected to entertain his sub-chiefs, judge cases in his district, and command respect and allegiance. In a limited way, the early Fathers did all these things.

After gaining their initial foothold in the Central Region the Catholic missions were quick to consolidate their position by the addition of new contingents of missionaries. In December 1904, five nuns, four French and one Arab, belonging to the Daughters of Wisdom, were escorted to Nguludi from Chiromo by Father Winnen, and to Nzama, by Njobvualema himself.[29] Nine months later five more sisters arrived at Nguludi, which was to become their permanent base.[30] Although their principal efforts were to be made in the sphere of women's education, they were given special medical training at Marseilles, which they were able to put to good use at the two Montfort stations.[31] After a cloistered existence in French convents and the difficult boat journey up the Shire, the shock of mission life found them 'saddened and ill at ease'.[32] They were, after all, exiles. But they soon learnt to milk cows, look after the half-caste children who were put in their charge,[33] and teach women in ChiChewa at the mission school. Their main contact with the village was medical visits. Sister Marie-Reine, remembered as 'Mai Maria', travelled a great deal around the villages by *machila*, and had a reputation for baptizing the sick children she cared for, with or without their parents' permission.[34]

The policy of the two societies towards expansion was surprisingly only partly influenced by their financial limitations. Lavigerie's missionary philosophy laid great weight on the slow, patient evangelization of a small area, a long catechumenate, and heavy concentration of manpower in a small region. The missions in Central Angoniland remained peripheral to Dupont's main interests in the Luangwa valley and Bembaland. Only two new stations were opened, both previously outstations of Mua: Ntaka-taka in 1908, after a prolonged exercise in public relations had reduced opposition in the town, and, in 1910,

Bembeke in the Dedza plain, formerly a sanatorium where priests could rest from the heat of the lakeshore. The arrival of the first White Sisters in Nyasaland, in October 1911, coincided with an abortive attempt to start a station in the village of the Mangoche Yao chief, Tambala.[35] Their policy of fighting every inch of territory with the Dutch Reformed had overcome common sense; the Catholics had moved into a strongly Muslim area. Tambala's was originally an outstation of Ntaka-taka, and returned to that status a year later on instructions from the Government. Its proximity to the well-established Dutch Reformed station at Nkhoma resulted in endless disputes of which the District Commissioner rapidly tired.[36]

By 1914, the number of Montfort priests and Brothers had increased to twenty with almost as many Sisters to help them. Not having any rigid policy of evangelizing one area in depth, and without such widespread commitments in the mission field as the White Fathers, the Montforts began to spread out from Nzama and Nguludi. They seemed to have viewed the introduction of Catholicism in the typically ecclesial sense of establishing the institutional structures of the Church over as wide an area as possible. While the quality and degree of commitment of their Christians was considered important, they were marginally more willing to accept large numbers of semi-converts than the White Fathers. The revivalist tradition of de Montfort was most applicable to a situation in which there were large numbers of nominal church members. They excelled at the retreat sermon. And once the churches were packed they felt sure that the quality would come later.

Likewise their interest in local conditions around their missions was not motivated by the scholarly interest that marked the early White Fathers. They produced nothing comparable to the works of Braire, Denis, Roy, and Hovington, which are still today of interest to social anthropologists.[37] The policy of the Montforts was to retain their cleverest members in Europe. They did all learn the language, though; Father Ryo undertook a translation of the catechism into ChiChewa, ChiLomwe, and ChiYao,[38] and Winnen and Prézeau both took a lively interest in village culture.[39] But, on the whole, the Montforts saw their task as introducing the Church to Nyasaland. And as exiles they tended, more than the White Fathers, to want a European Church with not one devotion or pious Association missing.[40]

St. Armand de Neno was founded in 1906. The station was in the district of Chief Chikalema, a Matengo *nduna* of Gomani II, who appears to have favoured the Catholics as a result of a dispute with a neighbouring Yao chief, Che-Kucheku, who had accepted the recently arrived Seventh-Day Adventist missionaries.[41] In 1912, orange pips were imported from Madagascar and Neno became one of the richest of the Montfort stations, supporting itself entirely on the proceeds of its extensive citrus orchards.[42] In May 1908, St. Pierre d'Utale was founded near the Rivirivi river by the future Bishop, Auneau.[43] It was situated in a large plain, full of game, and was later the site of the Montfort leprosarium. Both stations were in thickly populated and ethnically mixed areas which later suffered badly from soil erosion[44] and subsequent depopulation. The disadvantage of the large permanent Catholic settlements was that they could easily be left high and dry as the population moved on from exhausted soils.

Throughout these years mortality remained high. Dequeker died in July 1906 of what seems to have been rabies, and in the same year Louveau, the founder of Mua, died of trypanosomiasis after returning ill to France. A year later Father Tellegen died at Mua.[45] In 1908, the Montforts also lost three of their missionaries. Prézeau died only a year after being named first Vicar-Apostolic of the Shire, Father Gachassin after four, and Father Marmogeot after two years of missionary work in the country.[46] Amongst the Daughters of Wisdom, Sister Charité de Montfort died of malaria within five months of arriving, in 1906, and Sisters Thérèsine and Marie-Thérèse de St. Yves died in the same year after returning sick to France. While it was not the dreadful mortality of the nineteenth century, this still represented fifteen per cent of all the Catholic missionaries in Nyasaland.

Dupont, suffering from rheumatism and the effects of repeated malarial attacks, returned to Europe in 1911.[47] His letter to the Nyasa missionaries, announcing his departure and so typical of that peculiar mixture of tenderness, humility, and authoritarianism, that characterized the White Fathers under Lavigerie, spoke reams on his past direction of the Nyasa vicariate.

> However, to separate myself from you and from the Nyasa Vicariate is very hard for me. Willingly I offer to God this sacrifice which utterly breaks my heart. May it bring down on the missionaries and on the missions of Nyasaland some Graces . . . I ask your pardon for the mistakes that I may have made in my administration, and if anyone of you have failed me in anything whatsoever, I pardon him from the bottom of my heart.[48]

It was the letter of a sad man whose panache and personal involvement with Africa had been unsuited to the colonial period.

The next Bishop, Guillemé, brought to Nyasaland less emotional intensity but a self-discipline and ability to say the right thing at the right time, that proved invaluable in relations with Government.[49] If Dupont was the Catholic adventurer, Guillemé was the Catholic gentleman, a not unimportant quality for survival in the subtle class distinctions of a British colony. Dupont's resignation led to a division of the Nyasa Vicariate. It was long overdue. Father Larue[50] was put in charge of a separate vicariate which included Bangwelo. Guillemé kept the Central and Northern Region of Nyasaland. The station at Kachebere, with outstations in the two colonies, linked the two Vicariates. Although the Protectorate Government would have liked to see the White Fathers extend into the North Nyasa District shortage of staff was still a brake on expansion.

The second Montfort Vicar-Apostolic, Louis Auneau, was born at Messanger, in France, on 11 February 1876, a day of great significance for the Montforts, the first apparition of the Virgin Mary at Lourdes. His first pastoral experience was to be tending his mother's sheep. He was admirably suited to lead a peasant Church. Despite an education in Canada, experience in Algeria at El-Biar, and several years as Principal of the Minor Seminary at Schimmert in Holland, his French peasant instincts never left him. His manner of buying large tracts of land impressed even the Nyasaland planters who knew him as 'the landlord',[51] and a rustic capacity for food coupled with short stature, earned him the nickname of 'le petit tonneau' from his fellow French Montforts.[52] Auneau was a faithful servant of the Church and brought to his job all the astuteness, almost cunning, of his rural background. Every last penny legally available for the vicariate was shaken out of a surprised colonial Government. After long struggles the Montforts escaped both poll and income tax. To gain the exemption from poll tax each Montfort missionary was required to prove annually that he was in a state of complete poverty. An amazed administration discovered that Auneau was prepared to do exactly that for every nun, priest, and Brother in his Vicariate:

It would almost appear as though they intended to appeal every year, which in view of the reasons for refusal already given does not seem proper.[53]

The Zomba Secretariat soon realized, though, that propriety did not figure prominently in the Bishop's dealings with the colonial administration.

Auneau became second Vicar-Apostolic of the Shire, consecrated at Dupont's hands in 1910. After ordination he saw his first task as breaking into the Scots' enclave around Blantyre and Zomba. This did nothing to lessen his popularity amongst his fellow Montforts, who were equally game for combat. Nankhaunda, founded in 1912, cost him only £28 for an enormous piece of property on the side of Zomba mountain,[54] but getting in close to Blantyre took more time and met with more resistance.

A Mr. Josselin de Jong of the British South Africa Charter Company[55] visited Auneau in 1911. The Bishop asked him to enquire from his Company head, Wallace, if there was any land for sale in the Blantyre area. Wallace's wife was a Catholic. Auneau received an offer of four acres along the Chikwawa–Katunga road on the edge of a property owned by Mandala.[56] Once the news of the prospective purchase reached the ears of the Town Council, it was suddenly remembered that one acre of the land bought by Auneau had been officially selected as a site for the town abattoir.[57] Not to be outdone, Auneau had the site surveyed immediately, paid £25, and staked his claim. Without any bill of sale the Town Council were obliged to look elsewhere for a site for the abattoir, and the Catholics gained their foothold in Blantyre.

On 10 June 1913, a procession of twenty-seven labourers led by Auneau with Fathers Régent and Guimard wound their way down into town from Nguludi to pitch their tents on the site of the future Blantyre mission. Schools were radiating out from the mission within half a year and Hetherwick, who had until then restrained himself, gave vent to his feelings in *Life and Work*.

The Marist Brothers of the Roman Catholic Church whose headquarters are at Nguludi, 14 miles from Blantyre, with an unwonted zeal, are planting schools in our neighbourhood.[58]

Although the Church of Scotland mission was on the other side of the town from the Catholics, the two missions were evangelizing the same population.

The Catholic move was seen by Hetherwick, and with good reason, as a thoroughly aggressive gesture on Auneau's part.

When the Protestant citadel of Blantyre fell to Auneau, Nyasaland was already one of the most heavily missionized countries in Central Africa; out of about eight hundred Europeans in the protectorate almost a quarter were associated with some aspect of mission work. To differing degrees all missionary bodies had increased their personnel and were showing results. As the figures on Catholic baptismal roles moved into hundreds, the final products of Protestant mission education began looking for their place in colonial Nyasaland. The Overtoun Institute at Livingstonia, with its semi-secondary school education, and the Church of Scotland school in Blantyre, had produced a small African élite. The positions open to these 'new men' in Government service or as Protestant ministers, shopkeepers, or businessmen, brought them daily into situations charged with racial tension in which only the thickest skinned would not experience personal humiliation. Having produced an élite, the Protestant missions, and more so the Government, were loathe to treat them as such.

Men of exceptional ability such as Domingo,[59] Kamwana,[60] and Chilembwe[61] looked for alternative positions of leadership in society, and found them in becoming pastors of their own Independent Churches. Their ability to gain a following was very much a product of conditions in pre-war Nyasaland. African society was suffering from the effects of emigration. Despite legislation by the Governor, Sir Alfred Sharpe, to stop the flow of labour from villages in Nyasaland to mines in Rhodesia and South Africa, there were estimated, in 1910, to be 20,000 Nyasaland workers in Rhodesia alone.[62] A conservative estimate in 1913 put the total number of workers out of the country as 25,000.[63] Pressure from a British Liberal Government had resulted in recruitment within the Protectorate being officially stopped in 1907, but recruiting posts had merely moved over the border to resume business as usual.[64] The exodus was particularly severe from the Central Region. Small-time operators for the Portuguese were still allowed to recruit within the Protectorate. From one of the Fathers' descriptions it was a lucrative trade.

> Mr. Wenham arrived from Ntaka-taka today. He's recruiting labour for the sugar plantations at Chimbwe and Mopeia where they employ about a thousand workers annually. He certainly travels in greater style than we do, machila, bicycle, and 30 porters to carry all his trunks.[65]

Like the Protestant missionaries, the Catholics were opposed to this migration of labour. They found that it disrupted village life, and hardened attitudes towards Europeans in the men that went.

The mines became centres for the exchange of radical ideas, whether religious or political. When the workers got back to their villages the ideas of trade unionists, like Clemens Kadalie,[66] were passed on. The docility of African villagers, which had been the early experience of the priests, gave way imperceptibly before the World War to sullenness and resentment. Missionaries like the Catholics, in close contact with feeling in the villages, were fully aware how effective the spread of radical ideas could be, both before and after the War.

The day that a native who has been in contact with those in the south wants to 'serve the cause' and provoke an anti-social, anti-moral, xenophobic movement, he will find a well prepared ground waiting for him.[67]

Despite their awareness of the dangers of emigration Catholic complaints never got beyond the level of private grumbles.

Contact with religious radicalism, particularly Russellite ideas of Armageddon and the End of the World, culminated in the Watchtower movement of Eliot Kamwana.[68] Before his deportation in mid-1909, it is estimated that he baptized over 10,000 people in Tongaland in the space of half a year. Kamwana preached the coming of the parousia in October 1914, when all opposition, particularly the exactions of tax collectors, would end.[69] Instead of the long catechumenate of the institutional Churches he offered immediate baptism. For those who found the White Fathers' four-year period of postulancy and catechumenate an unnecessarily long preparation for baptism, Kamwana offered a solution. For the many who found release from poverty and oppression in apocalyptic dreams, Kamwana presented a post-parousial Nyasaland free of Whites. Even after his deportation he managed to maintain links with the Ncheu area where Watchtower ideas had also made a profound impact.[70]

Behind the discontent and emigration lay the Hut Tax, and behind that the demand of European planters for labour. The efficiency of tax collection, or rather the punishment of defaulters, had increased so that in the fiscal year 1907–8, 18,000 Africans in Central Angoniland were registered as defaulters.[71] The Catholic Mission diaries only rarely bothered to record what had become so common a scene as to hardly warrant mention.

The tax-collector is going through the villages near us. There are columns of smoke going up everywhere from the huts of the people who did not pay up.[72]

A technique used by the Boma soldiers was to tie up the women in a village in order to lure their husbands from the bush where they had hidden to avoid payment.[73]

Against this background of unrest within the country, troops returned from fighting revolts against the British in Somaliland and the Gold Coast. News and discussion of the Maji-Maji war[74] in Tanganyika were current amongst the European population, and would not have passed unheeded by educated Nyasaland Africans. Yet despite an undercurrent of resentment against European rule there was an overriding dependence on its agents. The desire to enter the new alien colonial superstructure guaranteed the continuing success of the missions. At Livingstonia in 1909, revivalist style[75] meetings were held in which 2,000 people applied for baptism and 683 were baptized in one day.[76] In both Vicariates the Catholics felt the impact of the religious enthusiasm. At Nzama there was a record crop of 400 baptisms,[77] while the Mua diary was recording encouraging signs such as 'good school attendances, perfect knowledge of the catechism and things really humming everywhere'.[78]

This rush for baptism was evidence that Western religious institutions and solutions were still seen at this time as an answer to religious needs and to the problems of colonial rule. Kamwana was taking up an overflow from the Institutional Churches as well as offering a more Africanized, eschatologica Christianity. The *prophetae* of Mediaeval Europe and colonial Nyasaland: had this much in common that they were responding to a sense of crisis induced by a period of social dislocation and legitimizing their movements within a Christian framework.[79] But Christian symbols were not the only ones to which Africans turned; alongside a renaissance in Islam around the Lake there were other prophets whose claims owed as much to the traditional African religion of the lake region as to the new world religions.

In June 1907, the Fathers at Nzama remarked on the many people passing the station, loaded down with maize, flour, sweet potatoes, chickens, and goats. Their destination was Maia, a village in Portuguese East Africa to which a Kunda prophetess, Chanjiri, known as 'Daughter of God', had fled to continue prophesying the imminent end of European Rule in Nyasaland. The tenor of her prophecies was anti-European rather than anti-Christian; Nzama and Blantyre missions would be saved from the final destruction since 'they honoured God'. Blantyre township, though, was to be wiped from the face of the earth in a holocaust.[80] She elicited a favourable response from the Ngoni around Nzama. After a few months, mounting pressure from Zomba obliged the Portuguese to remove her to Tete. She had meanwhile managed to accumulate thirty-four goats, a sheep, and a large quantity of maize.[81]

Such prophetesses possessed by a messenger of the High God appear recurrently in Chewa history and seem to have been an important element in the traditional religious system. While Chanjiri was collecting tribute around Nzama, by the mission of Ntaka-taka the followers of the leading Chewa prophetess at Msinja, near Lilongwe, were parading her statue and attempting to collect tribute for her shrine.[82] The name 'Chanjiri', meaning wart-hog, was an ancient name for the Deity and would have immediately alerted villagers to her claims. Although as a Kunda she may have had some contact with the *prazos* and Catholicism, her claim of relationship to the High God probably owed nothing to Christianity.[83] The widespread response to Christian prophets who dwelt on the advent of the millennium would suggest that such eschatological themes were not unknown to Chewa prophets in the past. Chanjiri, in short, represented the traditional end of a spectrum of religious response that included increased interest in the Catholic Church.

While Catholic missionaries continued to preach Christianity as a demand for total commitment to Christ, it must have been obvious to Africans from the conduct of Europeans, all of whom were assumed to be Christians, that in practice it meant nothing of the sort. Traditional religion permeated every aspect of an African villager's life and it must have come as quite a shock to discover that Christianity did not bear the same relation to European society.[84] The success of Chanjiri's and Kamwana's movements must, in large measure, also have depended on their ability to evoke scenarios in which their followers were completely involved. The parousia was total, imminent, and existentially engaging; baptism was by total immersion and laws of religious life extended to particular food taboos. All history, past, present, and future, was explained. Blantyre was simply to disappear.

If Western Institutional Christianity did not provide Africans with European wealth and power, there was something wrong. A long catechumenate began to seem like a deliberate attempt to keep Africans from salvation. For baptized Protestants, the failure of the Bible alone to transform a hut in a maize patch into an impressive manse set in mission gardens was easily interpreted as European trickery. The minister was clearly withholding some esoteric knowledge from which he derived his own power and prestige. The Watchtower gloss was perhaps this key to the Bible's hidden power. Kamwana might have the secret. Or perhaps it was better to return to the old religion.

The Western Churches easily engendered a profound sense of disappointment, or the more aggressive feeling that Africans in them were 'kept down'. More important, they provided no solace for the type of pervasive anxiety that sent hundreds of villagers fleeing to the bush to confess their sins and prepare for the end of the world when Halley's comet passed over Mua in 1910.[85] Traditional prophets like Chanjiri could articulate these feelings in terms of the Chewa religious beliefs, the anger of the High God, the need for sacrifice, tribute to the inspired religious leader, and so on. Kamwana had at his disposal the powerful Christian symbols of Revelation and the Apocalypse, and was able to conjure up a time without suffering whose appeal was immediate.

Islam, like Catholicism, had more mundane expectations. At the material level, it was undeniable, as Shepperson points out, that: 'Western culture had obviously much more to offer in the way of technical improvements and creature comforts than the traditional ways of life of the Mohammedan countries. . . .'[86] None the less, by 1913 the missionaries of the Universities' Mission to Central Africa around the Lake were noticing a 'certain quickening of the forces of Islam'.[87] *Mwalimus* in Tambala's villages had responded to the foundation of the Catholic mission in 1911 by demanding from all headmen that mosques be built in the principal villages. Their hold on Tambala's district, to the north of Ntaka-taka, can be gauged by the fact that in 1912 priests visiting the area found new mosques in all the villages.[88] By 1914, Auneau was getting reports of rumours about an Islamic rising from the Zomba area, and from around Utale.[89] This ability of Islam to engage dissidents in the pre-war period was limited to the Yao districts; it could neither offer a thorough-going chiliasm, nor a ticket to the European cash economy.

Once it was found with disappointment that the Western Churches could not offer the immediate satisfactions of the Watchtower movement, the 1909 boom dwindled away. It was the Dutch Reformed and Roman Catholic Missions which registered the slump first. By 1911, the honeymoon with Njobvualema was over; the Chief wrote to the Assistant Resident at Ncheu, Cardew, complaining that the Catholics were disturbing the customs of the people, forcing children to be baptized, performing Christian instead of traditional burials, and worst of all, preaching against polygamy.[90] There was the lowest number of baptisms that year since the early beginnings of the mission.

Since religious interest had never been very great in the Chewa areas, the downswing was most apparent in the Maseko Ngoni areas. At Mua catechists' school it began with difficulties with the students. They were 'insolent', only wanted to learn English in order to leave and find good jobs, and were not interested in the religious side of their instruction.[91] Even at Kachebere, the catechists could 'barely do more than write the names of the children in their classes',[92] and the number of Easter baptisms dropped.[93] In all stations, the belief that baptism *in articulo mortis*[94] magically resulted in death of the recipient still had common currency, and was being used against the missionaries. Passive resistance by villagers is apparent from the difficulty experienced by the caravan that brought the first White Sisters in recruiting porters for the rest of its journey to Bembaland. The caravan was obliged finally to move off with a reduced number of porters, in the hope of recruiting more at Likuni and Kachebere.[95]

If there was any doubt in 1911 that Catholic missions in Maseko areas had entered a period of decline, this was dispelled in subsequent years. The following table shows the fall-off in baptisms, that preceded the First World War, in five stations within a thirty-five mile radius of Ncheu Boma.

TABLE I[96]

Adult Baptisms

Mission Station	1911	1912	1913	1914
Mua WF	415	154	108	60
Ntaka-taka WF	445	193	151	113
Nzama SMM	134	100	66	112
Utale SMM	4	98	41	23
Neno SMM	171	100	80	80
TOTAL	1,169	645	446	388

The high figures in 1911 in the two White Fathers' stations can be accounted for as the remains of the earlier boom, coming through the catechumenate for baptism. Since Utale mission was only founded in 1908, it took some time for it to begin producing its first adult baptisms.

That this was not only a reaction to the Catholics, but represented a more general spirit of disenchantment with the Institutional Churches in Central Angoniland, is clear from the similar experience of the Dutch Reformed Missions. Retief wrote:

In 1912 more Christians and members of the confirmation class had to be forbidden the Sacraments or to be censured than ever before viz. 220 out of a membership of 10,300, or 1 in 47. . . . At the end of the year a spiritual deterioration was plainly visible, and Mr. Murray wrote that the position demanded much prayer.[97]

The Dutch Reformed stations at Mlanda, Mvera, Malembo, and Nkhoma were, of course, dealing with much the same population as the White Fathers.

The 'spiritual deterioration' of 1912 was partly the product of a material deterioration in the lot of Africans living in the Protectorate, that year. Not only was a severe famine raging in most districts, but the Hut Tax was increased from six to eight shillings per annum. At the same time, a District Administration Ordinance was enacted which gave District Commissioners *carte blanche* to appoint their own 'puppets' to headmanships in troublesome districts.[98] The increase in Hut Tax resulted in another massive exodus from the Central Region. One-third of all the men in 300 families visited by the Fathers from Mua, were away from home that entire year.[99] The priests were shocked by how few Christians came in from the major villages for their Easter instruction.[100] They were well aware of the immediate reason why the church attendance had diminished.

Half of them have gone off to Zomba and Blantyre to find work. The four rupees tax has simply terrified them.[101]

Government attempts at getting villagers to grow cash crops, such as cotton, had proved a failure around Mua. For almost everyone, earning money meant leaving the village.

The social disruption and uncertainty engendered by famine and stepped-up emigration had begun to be resolved in a number of different ways by villagers, none of which now included recourse to the European Institutional Churches. At one end of the spectrum there was a positive rejection of Western Christianity, as it had been taught, and a return to polygamy. Priests at Nzama and Mua noticed an increase in polygamous marriages in their areas,[102] which, while possibly a pragmatic response to the shortage of men in the villages, was equally an open repudiation of Christian teaching on marriage. Attendance at church dropped off as the population was depleted. In August 1914, before the outbreak of war had become general knowledge,[103] there was a rash of 'mfiti'[104] accusations around Utale that was only ended when a witchfinder from a neighbouring village, Mbalaze, was called in.[105]

On the other hand, the smaller Independent Churches had begun to thrive in the Ncheu district. African pastors such as Bennet Gospel Siyasiya,[106] Jordan Njirajaffa,[107] and Philipo Chinyama[108] built up networks of schools and preached to full churches. Kamwana was far from being a spent force after his deportation and maintained contact with Watchtower adherents through his brother, Eliot Yohan,[109] who was able to circulate freely in the Protectorate with his cousin, Lot Collection Chimwembe.[110] There were also contacts between the Ncheu pastors and John Chilembwe's Providence Industrial Mission at Chiradzulu. Wilson Kusita, an Ngoni teacher of the Providence Industrial Mission, looked after one of Chilembwe's schools near Ncheu[111] and another prominent elder of the Providence Industrial Mission, Duncan Njilima, owned a store in the district.[112]

The educated Protestant mission élite formed a closely-knit community through which ideas moved with great rapidity. The Scots emphasis on the link between Christianity and commerce was a common denominator; pastors owned stores and business men were preoccupied with religious ideas. A desire for independence embraced both the need for capital to open businesses and the search for autonomy in Church life and education. The frustration of these hopes left educated Protestants particularly vulnerable to the apocalyptic teaching of Kamwana and his Watchtower followers. Two of Chilembwe's teachers, Kusita and Damson Boloweza, temporarily deserted him to preach Watchtower doctrine in the Central Region,[113] and moderately successful business men like Duncan Njilima and H. E. Peters were interested in the creed.[114]

As many villagers were moving in the direction of reaffirming their old way of life, men such as John Gray Kufa[115] and Chilembwe's close associates were dressing with great elegance in almost a caricature of the European gentleman of the day. Dress, shoes, and a hat, had become a symbol of equality and independence. The grievances of the Protestant élite and those of the mass of villagers were different and the solutions they chose to redress them were opposed. Where the two met was in the continuing belief in an imminent crisis. For the simple villager it was an unformulated idea that things had fallen apart and a catastrophe was about to occur, played on by prophets like Chanjiri; for the fervent Watchtower supporters an expectation that 'Babylon and Branches will be broken',[116] while for Chilembwe a more sophisticated Biblical idea of a final conflict between the Elect and the Damned, in which the Elect had an active role, even to the point of engaging German support.[117]

When the prophesied date for the parousia of October 1914 had come and gone the pacifist doctrines of Watchtower suffered a setback. The more militant line of Chilembwe's associates, that advocated armed defence against the forces of evil and expected salvation from Black Americans coming from Karonga,[118] seemed to offer the only hope. As the more ardent pacifists amongst Watchtower tried to hold on to their followers, waverers like Kusita returned to the Providence Industrial Mission[119] to join in a rising against the British. Although Kamwana had moved up to Mulanje to be close to Nyasaland, when the end came he refused at all times to be lured into complicity with the small inner circle around Chilembwe who had begun to plan the details of a rebellion.[120]

Where Chilembwe and the mission élite differed from the majority of the Protectorate Africans was in their preoccupation with the Bible. They were further isolated by the 1912 District Administration Ordinance that guaranteed that the élite would be unable to assume positions of traditional authority in village life. The product of long debates in the Legislative Council, the Ordinance showed the marks of conflicting interests. While its ostensible aim was 'the gradual formation of subsidiary local government by means of sectional councils of headmen chosen as far as possible by the Natives themselves', it was supposed at the same time to do away with the 'archaic system of tribal rule'.[121] It pleased no one. The older chiefs saw themselves even more at the mercy of District Commissioners while educated Protestants could count on the mistrust of colonial officials for 'mission boys'. The Ordinance only came into force in May 1914; and then only in the Kota-kota and Ncheu districts where there was no pressure from planters, who were frightened that it would adversely affect their chances of recruiting labour.[122]

On the eve of the First World War all sections of the Protectorate population had reason to dislike the Protectorate Administration and its Institutional

Churches. As late as 1913 Dutch Reformed missionaries had gone as far as locking up an important chief, Msakambewa, when he tried to oust them from his village, while the Catholics periodically irritated their neighbour Njobvualema. More educated chiefs who were part of the mission community were under surveillance from their local District Commissioner. Makwangwala, trained at the Baptist Industrial Mission and a frequent visitor to the Providence Industrial Mission, was described by the Ncheu District Commissioner as 'of some education . . . has hitherto spent the greater part of his time in Blantyre', and, as a necessary corollary, 'requires watching'.

The cleavage in the Protectorate Africans was not so much between 'new' and 'old' men as between those formed politically in the harsh realities of Johnston's punitive raids and those for whom politics grew out of the Bible. Chiefs like Njobvualema had lived through two Ngoni rebellions in 1896 and 1898 and knew well enough that wars were won by Maxim guns rather than by the intervention of Heavenly Hosts. They had maintained some of their former power, enough to be loath to lose what was left. But for the pastors and chiefs saturated with Biblical images, only able to find positions of power in religious office, and with the realities of Nyasaland in 1915 beginning to blur with the plight of the Israelites in Babylon, the World War came as a final crisis easily equated with the end of the world. The fate of the Catholic-connected Njobvualema and that of the Protestant chief, Makwangwala, in the Chilembwe rising of 1915 personifies the behaviour of these two groups in this critical period. More important, it illustrates concisely the historical effects of Catholicism and radical Protestantism in the colonial context.

REFERENCES TO CHAPTER III

[1] Cohn N. *The Pursuit of the Millenium* London 1962, 314–15
[2] 'To go to the mission'
[3] Attorney-General, R. W. Lyall-Grant to Acting-Deputy Governor, H. L. Duff Memorandum of September 1910 S1/1494/19 National Archives, Zomba
[4] Mua Diary 23 April 1908, 27 April 1908
[5] Lands Registry. Document No. 1185 12 October 1905, Blantyre. Montfort Archives, Rome.
[6] Mua Diary October 1946. The incident required the intervention of the District Commissioner.
[7] Personal Communication Rev. R. Saffroy, w.f., Lilongwe. For example, most of the money for Mua church came from the father of Alfred Honoré, w.f.
[8] Interview with R. F. Withers, ex-planter, Blantyre April 1969. Personal Reminiscences. Mua mission was almost fined on two occasions for cutting wood in the Government forest reserve without permission.
[9] There was a large contingent of Montfort missionaries from Limburg. They knew each others' families and went to seminary together, all factors which strengthened their communal life in Nyasaland.
[10] *Rapports annuels* 1906–7 Kachebere
[11] Kachebere Diary 2 December 1909
[12] Pineau *Évêque* 19

[13] Kachebere Diary 2 December 1909

[14] Querel *L'Histoire* Cahier II

[15] Oral Testimony. Petro Johanne Chamoto. Ngoni cowherd in 1904 who drove cattle to Kachebere. Kachebere, August 1969.

[16] Nyasaland Times 7 January 1915

[17] Nzama Diary 8 January 1905. Bourget had to warn the Montfort Fathers that references to their hunting trips in letters to Europe did not convey a sufficiently spiritual impression of the mission work.

[18] *Nsima* is made from pounded maize flour, 'ufa', boiled in water until a thick porridge, capable of being held in the hands, is formed

[19] *Bulletins trimestriels* December 1930, 9. 'After their pious pilgrimage each child received in recompense a lemon or a little salt, and the good-bye included a rendezvous for the next Sunday.'

[20] Bishop Mathurin Guillemé was ordained on 22 September 1883 and had twenty years experience as a White Father behind him

[21] Guillemé to Nyasa missionaries 2 October 1902. A letter found amongst loose papers, Mua Mission.

[22] Accounts of 'Econome' at Mua Mission, 1908. Found amongst loose papers, Mua Mission.

[23] *Rapports annuels* 1907–8. Dupont's report.

[24] The plural of 'Bambo', Father, to indicate respect

[25] *Chroniques* 1904, No. 108 385

[26] Mua Diary 10 April 1934; and on 17 October 1934 'Fr. Champmartin has been made superior of Mua, but alongside this mark of confidence, the Bishops' Conference has added a severe criticism of his running of the mission. (1) for allowing lepers into the house (2) for allowing them to have their household possessions and rags in rooms in the mission, even rooms for visitors (3) for allowing a leper, Moloko, to give Cinyanja lessons to a newly-arrived Father.'

[27] Presents wrapped up in a ball and thrown into the crowd

[28] Mua Diary 18 September 1911

[29] Nzama Diary 17 December 1905. Mother-Superior—Sister Lucie-Marie—and Sisters Eulalie, Thérèsine, Caroline, and Marie-Reine.

[30] And following from notes made by Sister Marie-Thérèse, Providence Training College, which she was kind enough to loan us

[31] ibid.

[32] Nzama Diary 17 December 1904

[33] The care of half-caste children in the Protectorate became entirely the work of the Sisters. For this reason many girls, today women, brought up in their orphanages speak French. The Scots missions, particularly Laws, had a rather penitential attitude towards 'the children of sin'. It is noticeable that in none of the nuns' documents does one find disparaging remarks about the conduct of the children's parents.

[34] Nzama Convent Diary 17 May 1905 Providence Training College, Mulanje, and *Bulletins trimestriels* December 1926, 10

[35] Tambala Mission Diary 11 October 1911, Likuni Mission, Lilongwe and Mua Diary 6 October 1911

[36] Tambala Mission Diary 11 October 1911—27 April 1912

[37] Contained in the 'Nyau file'. White Fathers' Archives, Lilongwe

[38] Interview Father J. Leroux Pirimiti mission, May 1969

[39] Interview Father J. Eyssen Likulesi Catechetical Centre, Phalombe, October 1970

[40] Under 'Mission activities' in a report sent by Auneau to the Propaganda in 1943 were the following: (1) Legion of Mary (2) Brotherhood of Christian Doctrine (3) Brotherhood of Mary Queen of Hearts (4) Pious Association of Brothers and Sisters, 'Oblates of Ste.

Thérèse de l'Enfant Jésus'. (5) The work of enthroning the Sacred-Heart of Jesus Christ in families. (6) Eucharistic crusade.

[41] Oral Testimony, Alexander Hoa-Hoa, Alomwe, Catholic catechist, Neno Mission September 1969. The Matengo were captives of the Ngoni taken around Songea in Tanzania.

[42] Querel ibid.

[43] Utale Mission Diary 30 April 1908. Montfort Archives, Rome.

[44] The Colonial Government's introduction of ridging met with considerable opposition

[45] Short biographies of the White Fathers are available at their archives in Rome. They are contained in an annual publication *Notes nécrologiques*. They tend to be formalized, giving dates of birth, ordination, death, etc. Since they act as official obituaries it is rare to find unflattering remarks about any priest, although later editions are more down-to-earth and give interesting personal details. Priests who died before 1900 can be traced through the archivist.

[46] A Montfort necrology for the Shire Vicariate exists but it gives the barest details. It is used to indicate the anniversary of a priest's death for devotional purposes.

[47] Pineau *Évêque* 199. In 1899 he was obliged to go to hospital for a period in Zanzibar to get some treatment for his rheumatism which had reduced him to crutches. He left finally in September 1911, *Évêque* 261.

[48] Dupont to Nyasa missionaries Chilubula 2 June 1911. His resignation was accepted by the Pope 11 March 1911.

[49] Guillemé had been virtually running the Nyasa Vicariate from Chilubula before being officially appointed

[50] Father Étienne Larue was ordained on 12 June 1891 and was appointed first Vicar Apostolic of Bangwelo on 28 January 1913. Like Guillemé, he was something of an intellectual. He arrived in Nyasaland with Honoré in 1902. He was made Superior of Kachebere in 1906 after four years at Chilubula.

[51] Interview Father X. Uitewaal Likulesi Catachetical Centre November 1969

[52] 'The little barrel'

[53] Government minute S1/1343/23 National Archives, Zomba

[54] Blantyre Mission Diary 20 August 1913. Blantyre Mission. The old spelling was Nankunda.

[55] The British South Africa Charter Co. had narrowly missed absorbing the Lakes Company in 1889–91 under pressure from Rhodes, and was limited to a less privileged position within the Protectorate

[56] 'Mandala', meaning 'glasses' in ChiYao, was the name given to the African Lakes Company head John Moir, who wore glasses, and hence came to refer to the African Lakes Company property in Blantyre

[57] Blantyre Diary. Preamble to foundation.

[58] *Nyasaland Times* 16 April 1914

[59] Charles Domingo was found by the Livingstonia teacher, William Koyi, in Quelimane and later became Laws' house-servant. He was one of the first African assistants at the Overtoun Institute but left Livingstonia under the influence of Joseph Booth between 1907 and 1910 to found his own Seventh-day Baptist Churches. In 1911 he became co-editor with Booth of the 'African Sabbath Recorder'. His history to this date was, in a sense, typical of the time: a Livingstonia discovery who left the institutional Church to found his own. See Shepperson *Independent African*, 159–65.

[60] Eliot Kamwana Achirwa was a Tonga, educated at the Livingstonia mission, Bandawe. After a short period at the Overtoun Institute he met Booth in 1900 and broke with the Institute over their charging fees for education. He spent some time in the South African mines before returning to Nyasaland in September 1908. The Protectorate Government were quick to deport him in 1909 after the success of his Watchtower movement, and he

remained out of the country at Chinde and then Mulanje until the First World War. He was finally deported to Mauritius with his wife in 1916.

[61] Now a national hero of Malawi, John Chilembwe's life is exhaustively dealt with in *Independent African*

[62] Sanderson F. E. *Nyasaland Migrant Labour in British Central Africa 1890–1939* M.A. Dissertation, University of London 1966, 43

[63] Krishnamurty B. S. *Land and Labour in Nyasaland: 1891–1914* Doctoral Dissertation, University of London 1964, 305. Casson's estimate.

[64] A Rhodesian Native Labour Bureau post at Fort Jameson recruited labour from many of the villages around the Catholic missions in Angoniland. Many also went to the Transvaal. Mua Diary, 21 October 1909. 'The men recruited for the Transvaal mines have left Dedza at last, taking with them 5 of our Christians. The villages in our area produced 50 recruits. If all the villages were counted the figure would be hundreds.'

[65] Mua Diary 3 May 1909, and see Krishnamurty *Land and Labour* 263

[66] Also a Tonga who spent some time in the Overtoun Institute, Kadalie left Nyasaland for the mines in 1915. By 1919 he had formed the Industrial and Commercial Workers' Union that was instrumental in bringing South African workers to the verge of a General Strike in 1927.

[67] Report on Emigration from Kasina Mission 1930, White Fathers' Archives, Lilongwe

[68] Shepperson and Price *Independent African* 150–4

[69] ibid. 155–6

[70] See envelope NCN 4/1/1. National Archives, Zomba

[71] Krishnamurty *Land and Labour* 271

[72] Mua Diary 4 January 1910

[73] ibid. 14 February 1910

[74] Gwassa G. C. K. 'Kinjikitile and the Ideology of Maji-Maji' in *The Historical Study* 202–19. Maji-Maji was a mass movement waged by Africans against German colonial rule in southern Tanganyika.

[75] The use of the word 'revivalism' is not strictly accurate in that the people involved were not so much indifferent Christians as pagans wanting baptism

[76] McCracken K. J. 'Religion and Politics in Northern Malawi: 1881–1904' in *The Early History* 229, quoting Free Church Monthly record October 1909, 450

[77] Nzama Baptismal Register, Nzama mission, Ncheu

[78] Mua Diary 2 February 1909

[79] Kamwana differed from the mediaeval leaders in not claiming supernatural powers. His millenarian expectations at the beginning, which included free schooling, were moderate, but his threat to the Colonial Government, which led to his deportation, was some indication that he might, given time, have assumed messianic characteristics. For an excellent discussion of millenarianism in the colonial context see Worsley P. *The Trumpet Shall Sound*, 221–56. London 1957. For a comparative treatment see Thrupp S. L. *Millennial Dreams in Action*. New York 1970.

[80] Nzama Diary 16–23 June 1907 and see also Shepperson and Price *Independent African* 156

[81] ibid. 10 September 1907

[82] Personal Communication Dr. J. M. Schoffeleers

[83] Elmslie W. A. *Among the Wild Ngoni* Edinburgh 1901, 74 mentions similar figures. amongst the Northern Ngoni known as *mfumu ya pansi*. I am indebted to Mr. Leroy Vail, Department of History, University of Malawi, for pointing out this similarity.

[84] I am indebted to Dr. Martin Chanock for first pointing out this important distinction to me in personal discussions. It was a common theme of fund-raising sermons that the Church in Europe should *make up for* the sins of Europeans in Africa by giving to the missions. Personal communication, Rev. Dr. J. M. Schoffeleers.

85 *Rapports annuels* 1910–11 Ntaka-taka

86 Shepperson and Price *Independent African* 183–4

87 Blood *A History* 62

88 *Rapports annuels* 1912–13 Ntaka-taka

89 Moggridge to Turnbull 3 February 1915. A report from Moggridge of a letter he received before the Chilembwe rising from Auneau. S/10/1/6. National Archives, Zomba.

90 Nzama Diary 10 February 1911

91 Mua Diary 27 February 1911

92 Kachebere Diary 25 May 1911

93 A slump at Kachebere was partly the result of an epidemic of sleeping sickness in North-Eastern Rhodesia, which was only arrested by widespread vaccination from the mission in the middle of 1911. The epidemic was at its worst from April to June 1911.

94 Baptism given when the recipient was on the point of dying

95 Mua Diary 19 October 1911, 'Fr. Boucansaud spent an entire evening going round villages between Mua and Ntaka-taka trying to inspire a little practical Christianity in our Christians, but it was little use. In the end, on Fr. Travers' orders, we recruited 19 of the pupil catechists who were able to take them as far as Likuni'.

96 These figures are compiled from the White Fathers' *Rapports annuels* by subtracting the number of neophytes in one year from the number given for the next year. The Montfort statistics are taken directly from baptismal registers, January to January, while the White Fathers' statistics run from June to June. Figures for Bembeke are erratic while those for Likuni and Kachebere show a steady rise. Only Bembeke falls within the geographical area under consideration i.e. close to Ncheu, but since the station was only formed in 1910, its statistics would not be comparable with the others.

97 Retief M. W. *William Murray of Nyasaland* Lovedale Press 1958, 117

98 Shepperson and Price *Independent African* 193–6

99 *Rapports annuels* 1912–13 Mua

100 Mua Diary 3 April 1912. Christians were expected to perform their Easter duties, confession and communion, and to receive instruction on the Faith at this time.

101 Mua Diary 3 April 1912

102 Nzama Diary December 1913, and Mua Diary February 1913. A year later the entry for 1 August 1914 at Nzama was: 'Fervour of Christians getting less and less. Lukewarmness is the order of the day. Few come to mass and there are little communions. Many are at the mines and a lot are on the beer.'

103 The news of war reached most villages by 8 August 1914

104 Witchcraft accusations. These usually consisted of the accusation that a relative had been eating the flesh of disinterred corpses. Such situations could result in the poison ordeal to prove innocence or in the flight of the accused to another village.

105 Utale Convent Diary 7 August 1914. Providence Training College, Mulanje.

106 Siyasiya was a Tonga teacher at Chinyama's school in Nthinda village. He corresponded with Kamwana and his brother, Watchtower groups in Limbe, and with a leading rebel, Anderson Chimutu of the Nyasa Industrial Mission. He spent a period in the Rand in 1913 and on his return became a Watchtower pastor in Chitimba village, Chief Msakambewa's. He was unwilling to participate in the rising because of his pacifist leanings and was only imprisoned for six months. S2/68II/19 and NCN 4/1/1. National Archives, Zomba.

107 Njirajaffa was probably a Yao, known as 'Brother CheJordan', and was appointed by Siyasiya as Watchtower representative in the Ncheu district. He had been in the Negro Industrial Union of 1910 and knew many of the rebels. NCN 4/2/1 and S2/102/23.

108 The leading figure in the Ncheu rising, see Linden J. and Linden I. 'Chiefs and pastors in the Ncheu rising' to be published 1973 in *Dzulo ndi Dzana* edited by MacDonald R. East Africa Publishing House. Chinyama was a Seventh-Day Baptist at the time of the rising and an Ngoni by origin.

[109] Eliot Yohan Achirwa was a firm pacifist and acted as an ambassador at large for Kamwana. In the end of 1914 he was in the Ncheu district trying to rally support for Kamwana, whose stocks were falling owing to the failure of his prophecies to materialize after the promising events of the World War.

[110] Another firm Watchtower pacifist, see Linden J. and Linden I. 'John Chilembwe and the New Jerusalem' in *Journal of African History* 1971 XII No. 4, Appendix 649–51

[111] Wilson Kusita was an Ngoni convert to the Providence Industrial Mission c. 1908. In 1913 he became an itinerant Watchtower preacher in the Ncheu district under the influence of Kamwana and opened schools in Liwonde district. He was executed after the rising, having returned to his Providence Industrial Mission allegiance after October 1914. NCN 4/1/1 and S10/1/6.

[112] The store was run by Njilima's brother Clair and contained, according to the District Commissioner, £300 worth of goods, S1/68/19

[113] BS 1/2/6 National Archives, Zomba.

[114] Peters was writing to America for Watchtower literature at the end of 1914. S10/1/8/3 Trial reports suggest Njilima was firmly convinced that the end of the world was due. S10/1/3.

[115] John Gray Kufa was educated at the Church of Scotland school in Blantyre and ordained a deacon in 1897. He spent some time doing dispensary work around Mulanje in an Alomwe area and was supposed to lead the attack on Mandala stores to obtain guns. His photograph in *Independent African* gives an excellent impression of the standard of dress aspired to by Chilembwe's associates. His small business was confiscated after the rising, and he himself executed.

[116] Eliot Kamwana to Eliot Yohan Achirwa 26 June 1916 S2/68/II19

[117] Yotan Bango, a Yao pupil at the Providence Industrial Mission was sent with a message to the Chief Judge at Tunduru to enlist German support in January 1915. S2/8/19. The reply was non-committal, NSP 1/1/2.

[118] Mitchell to Moggridge 18 August 1914 S10/1/16 mentions the belief that Black Americans were at Karonga. The most militant of Chilembwe's followers was David Kaduya who was being approached in February 1914 about prospects of killing Europeans. Port-Herald security file, NSP 1/2/2.

[119] Kusita to Achirwa. Letter 'E' undated, and Achirwa to Zuze 15 January 1915 NCN 4/1/1

[120] Kamwana, in fact, reported the approaches made to him. Mulanje casebook; testimony of E. Kamwana 11 February 1915 before Mr. Colin Grant, DC Mulanje. BA 1/5/8

[121] Barnekov T. K. 'An enquiry into the development of Native Administration in Nyasaland: 1888–1939'. *Occasional paper No. 48* University of Syracuse 1967, 46–9, and Proc. Leg. Council Nov. 5th–8th 1912 10th Session in Murray S.S. *A Handbook of Nyasaland* Zomba 1932, 129.

[122] *Independent African* Shepperson and Price 194

CHAPTER IV

The Seal of Respectability

It was proved to the satisfaction of the Commission and the general public that Catholic Doctrine is the best safeguard against all types of revolution. The Roman Church gained much in esteem and influence in Nyasaland.

Fr. P. W. Eken 'Een Afrikaansch Oproermaker'[1]

'Ah,' exclaimed a Protestant one day, 'If they were all Catholics we would not have any revolts to worry about.'

Bishop L. Auneau Brouillons[2]

The historical success of Catholicism in Europe had depended to a large extent on the stability of the Institutional Church, its ability to assimilate and control in ecclesiastical forms charismatic and prophetic elements. Although an institutional concept of authority vested in hierarchical office was perennially upheld, Christians undergoing the total *metanoia* demanded by the Gospel were retained as founders of religious orders quite as often as they were lost in schismatic movements. Revolutionary chiliasm[3] was countered in theology by presenting the corporate existence of the Church as a foreshadowing of the parousia.[4]

For nineteenth-century Catholics the Church could not alter; the Christian community with its Pope and Bishops on earth was the shadow of a Heavenly Host above. Although there could be development in the understanding of the *depositum fidei* entrusted to the Magisterium,[5] the Church shared the timeless quality of the Divine Order. Against rapid political change in France and Italy, Catholics pitted a changeless Church and against the uncertainty of secular rationalism, they triumphantly proclaimed an infallible Pope. While the historic, continuity of the Church in its apostolic succession throughout the ages was emphasized, all else was seen as an epiphany of an eternal reality.

The difference from the Protestantism that came to Nyasaland is marked. Far from being a 'religion of the Book' the Catholic missions practised a religion of liturgy. Instead of authority having the immanentist aspect of inspiration and conformity to Biblical texts, it derived from the corporate existence of the Church and the continuity of her office bearers. While the study of the Bible, the basis of Protestant piety, allowed the development of a historical sense, Catholic piety in its adoration of Christ in the consecrated Host, and veneration of the Virgin Mary, dwelt on the timelessness of God in a synchronic dualism of immanence and transcendence. Malawian Protestant pastors who read their Bible from cover to cover were able to associate an experience of the colonial situation with the Jewish nationalism of the Old Testament. Many saw in the history of Israel a reflection of colonial Malawi and the possibilities of a different future. As they were absorbing the Protestant ethic of self-help and personal advancement, Catholics by contrast were hearing the repeated admonition to despise early things, 'kunyoza za pansi pano'. Although Catholics had a promise of a future held out to them it was in heaven rather than in the political kingdom on earth.

The ahistorical Christianity which African catholics learnt was a natural product of missionaries who were in a sense themselves escaping from history in Europe. The priests in Nyasaland were largely the children of Europe's *emigrés de l'interieur*.[6] The Catholicism in which they had grown up prized the virtues of a beleaguered garrison, obedience, refusal to admit mistakes, and an overriding loyalty to the institutional Church. Ida Görres' description of French Catholics in the 1870s can be applied with little reservation to their sons in Nyasaland:

> Their fanaticism was at once chivalric and plebeian, diplomatic and tactless, intimate and indiscreet, wholly spiritual in intent, yet with a child-like and childish obstinacy insisting on the most petty superficialities.[7]

Their position as late immigrants to the mission field in Malawi reinforced the ambivalence of their feelings towards civil authority and Government. With their Mission Societies in France and Algeria dissolved, or in danger of dissolution, the Catholic missionaries needed the security of Government approval and wanted to conform to the administration's wishes. Yet, when the Government approval that they sought was forthcoming they would back off, pleased, but feeling the importance of keeping the State with its 'Holy Liberalism'[8] at arm's length.

The problem of relationships with the colonial administration was compounded by language difficulties. Even had they been psychologically adapted to engage in running battles with the Government of a British colony they were inhibited by a poor command of English. They felt this deficiency most keenly when loyalty to the Church demanded rebuttal of Protestant claims.

> We just do not speak English well enough to enter debates to prove the purity of our teaching and the unselfishness of our work, and so put ourselves on an equal footing with the Dutch Reformed and other missions.[9]

At the same time the failure to speak good English was partly their own choice. Most priests developed an excellent command of ChiChewa in a short time but made no efforts to improve their English until pressed by the two bishops. Their language preference was an indication of their commitment to village life and had in it a subtle defiance of the British authorities.

Bishop Mathurin Guillemé of the White Fathers was the more at home of the two Catholic bishops amongst the ranks of colonial administrators. After Cardinal Lavigerie's speech to French naval officers on 12 November 1890, when at the Pope's behest the head of the White Fathers had put his considerable prestige behind France's Republican Government, the subversive clerical support for a restoration of the Bourbon monarchy in France had received a severe setback. From that date the White Fathers had been consistently willing to work with any government whether liberal or socialist. Their only two sallies into the political arena, in Uganda and Bembaland, had been disasters; the priests had finally to flee the court of the Kabaka and Bishop Dupont soon had to give up his chieftancy over the Bemba. Guillemé had been trained in a tradition that dictated prudence in dealings with both *de facto* and, what the Church considered to be, lawfully constituted authority. In his perennial caution towards the British there was also something of the solidarity of the officer class. He asked the Nyasa missionaries that

> they should always call to mind that the private conduct of European settlers in the colony does not concern them unless it involved behaviour prejudicial to, and likely to harm, mission work.[10]

The best summary of Guillemé's views on the relation between mission and Protectorate Government is contained in detailed instructions issued to missionaries after the First World War. It demonstrates not only the official White Fathers' position but that of the Catholic Church in most colonial territories at this time:

> (missionaries were) to serve loyally the cause of Government in whose country we live; to remind Christians and even pagans under our influence of the legitimacy and necessity of taxation, and to press them to pay their taxes on time. To show by deeds more than by words that the Catholic missionary is primarily a man of God dedicated to the cure of souls, that he is always and everywhere respectful of lawfully constituted authority, and ready to give to all, irrespective of nationality, his dedicated and zealous co-operation.[11]

It was a prescription for mission work that had changed little since the seventeenth century: 'work, labours and thoughts, are but bent on what is heavenly to the exclusion of everything else.'[12]

Guillemé's gentlemanly approach to Government contrasted with Auneau's peasant aggressiveness. There was a tradition of Catholic armed resistance to the Republic amongst the 'chouans' in the Vendée where Auneau had grown up, and many of the Montforts came from anti-republican Brittany.[13] Unlike the White Fathers, the Montforts had been driven out of France by repressive measures against Religious Orders and Auneau had little for which to thank secular authorities. His relations with the Colonial Government were abrasive and characterized by a cruder Ultramontanism than Guillemé's, whose officer mentality was far more attuned to the ethos of the Protectorate administration. Missionaries remember Guillemé as 'a perfect gentleman' and his class approach to Africans and subordinates was entirely in harmony with that of Nyasaland's colonial officers.

The gentleman concept, with its implication that the utilization of power should be suffused with moral purpose and restrained from abuse by inner controls, was, in an African setting, a direct transference of a successful pattern of responsible class behaviour within Britain.[14]

Had the colonial service not shown a disturbing moral relativism towards tribal culture, and impartiality with regard to religious affiliation, Guillemé would have found little to criticize in it.

The Roman Catholic missionaries in Malawi before 1915 were marked by a background as 'emigrés' within their own countries and by their position on the edge of colonial society. In their relations with the Protestants they found themselves in the position of a sect with the Protestants as the Established Church. Their dealings with the Government were often disturbed by a mistaken interpretation of impartiality as hostility. If the Protectorate Government was not for them then it must be secretly against them. If Hetherwick and a number of the colonial officers were Freemasons, it was only a matter of time before a masonic plot to thwart the Catholic missions would be revealed.

Converts around the mission stations absorbed the missionaries' attitudes to the Colonial Government if not by direct instruction at least by precept and observation. The authoritarianism of the mission station matched that of tribal society and colonial rule. Since the epistles and gospels they heard at mass related to a cyclical liturgical year rather than to a historical exposition of salvation history, Catholics were seldom brought in contact with the Jewish idea of linear time. More often than not the priest would preach on a topic unrelated to the Latin gospel and epistle, being more intent on instilling an understanding of the sacraments than of the Biblical texts. The vernacular collections of Bible stories, *Za Mpulumutsi* and *Mulungu yekha*, were all equally devoid of a sense of history and Catholics did not have access to a vernacular translation of the whole Bible. Instruction was aimed at making Catholic Christians more aware of their relationship with a timeless hierarchical Church which brought them into contact with the Divine Order.

By directing the attention of peasants to the Church rather than to any other aspect of life, and by making the Church an all-embracing *corpus christianum* extending its influence into as many parts of daily life as possible, missionary teaching diverted Catholics from any quest for the political kingdom. It put them into a vertical relationship with God at the expense of a horizontal relationship with their fellow man. If traditional religion with its cult of ancestral spirits offered peasants an explanation of life in terms of the past, Catholicism offered one in terms of an other-worldly future. What neither gave was an adequate explanation and analysis of the present. The social malaise which grew up in Nyasaland between 1910 and 1915 resulted in losses from the Catholic mission orbit but it could never give rise to Catholic radicalism. Catholic peasants rejected a future-orientated other-worldliness when they left the Church, usually, for a past-orientated traditionalism. The rejection of monogamy for polygamy, confessional for witchfinding movements, saints for ancestral spirits, implied no fundamental upheaval in world-view. Catholicism had not replaced an African past with an African history of salvation, it had merely opposed that past with a heavenly future.

In these important respects the Catholic missions were at the opposite end of the Christian spectrum to Protestant sects such as the Church of Christ, the Seventh-Day Baptists, and John Chilembwe's Providence Industrial Mission. In these missions a crude historical consciousness was able to come to birth. Since it was formed by comparison rather than analysis it was highly distorted, but it provided a charter for action. In the Chilembwe rising of January 1915 the political consequences of the different theologies taught in Nyasaland became apparent. There was an almost complete absence of Catholics from the ranks of Chilembwe's followers, and Protestants attacked Catholics for the first time since the missions had lived side by side. The virtual discontinuity between the Christianity professed by radical Protestants and by conservative Catholics was demonstrated in an unmistakable way.

The main Montfort station at Nguludi was four miles away from the Providence Industrial Mission at Chiradzulu. The missions had got along well until 1914 with less friction than might have been expected had Chilembwe been a European. Chilembwe and the Montforts were to different degrees, outsiders and the Fathers made an effort to stay on friendly terms with him. They went to tea at Chiradzulu on a number of occasions and the best china would be produced.[15] Although the meetings seem to have been somewhat formal the African pastor had a number of things in common with the priests. Fathers Ryo and Swelsen were great builders and Chilembwe had only recently finished an impressive new church that was the envy of the Protestants in Blantyre. They might well have discussed with Chilembwe how to improve the tone of his new church bell.[16] If such topics failed they were all keen hunters. Chilembwe told Father Guimard that Catholicism was a 'good religion' but he saw it as a continuation of Judaism.[17]

Some contact between Providence Industrial Mission teachers and Catholic catechists at a lower level was inevitable as the two mission fields overlapped. Ngoni from the Ncheu district worked for both missions. Many of the Catholic catechists, like Andrea, Lazaro, and Antonio, came from Njobvualema's area at Nzama, while two, Edward and William, were sons of the chief.[18] Amongst the elders of the Providence Industrial Mission were the Kampingo family[19] and a teacher, Wilson Kusita, from Ncheu. There were a number of Ngoni families in the Shire Highlands who had permanently settled there to work on the plantations. A natural friendship between those with a Maseko background made for a relaxed atmosphere. Any interdenominational marriages were supervised on the Catholic side by the head catechist, Eugenio Matuta, who spoke well of John Chilembwe and was popular at the Providence Industrial Mission.[20] The relationship between the missions was friendly but increasingly competitive towards the time of the Rising.

Since English was not taught in the Catholic schools, and the Fathers frowned on the adoption of European dress and the wearing of shoes, several of the more ambitious Catholics left Nguludi for the Providence Industrial Mission. On the other hand the lure of free education offered by the Sisters meant that the flow was not all one way. One of Chilembwe's important losses was Pio Ntwere who had come with his family to settle in the Shire Highlands from Mozambique in 1903. He soon found work at Chiradzulu and was employed for a while as Chilembwe's gun carrier. Free education, unavailable at the Providence Industrial Mission, took him to Nguludi where he went to school and worked as a *machila* bearer. After his baptism in 1910 he became a Catholic catechist travelling as far afield as Mulanje.[21] In the inter-war period he played a prominent role in the Chiradzulu Native Association and was later made an honorary vernacular grade teacher after over twenty years' service with Nguludi mission.

When the Providence Industrial Mission had been an insignificant Protestant sect there was little conflict with the Montforts. But with Chilembwe's gains, even throughout the anti-mission period, 1912–1915, the Providence Industrial Mission began to expand.[22] In June 1913, two hundred workers on the Bruce Estates approached their manager, William Jervis Livingstone,[23] to plead for permission to build a prayer-house of the Providence Industrial Mission at Nawani's village on plantation land. The request was refused but the prayer-house was built. Although the plantation workers threatened to strike and leave the estates, Livingstone sacked their leader, a man called Lifeyu, and burnt down the prayer-house in front of the congregation.[24] It was widely believed that Livingstone gave permission to the Catholics, but this was not true. The only building for worship allowed on the estate was a mosque.[25] In another incident a prayer-house at Mpotola's village was pulled down with the connivance of Catholics in the area. A third school of the Providence Industrial Mission, at Namchengwa, was reputedly pulled down on orders from the Boma after complaints from the Catholic catechist about its proximity to a Catholic school.[26] Chilembwe spoke to the Catholic catechist at Masanjala's who reported back to the school director, Swelsen, that if these incidents continued there would be 'an exchange of blows'.[27] It was the first intimation that the repeated slights and provocations had begun to tell on Chilembwe and an indication of a serious deterioration in the relations between the two missions.

Even without the aggravation of school disputes there was enough anti-Catholic literature circulating in the Protectorate to inflame passions against the priests amongst the smaller Protestant sects. The Federated Protestant Missions had a vernacular booklet *Mthenga wa ku Nyasa* which contained scurrilous attacks on the Roman Catholic Church. The death of William Tyndale, translator of the New Testament into English, was bracketed with the possible future death of Hetherwick and Dr. Murray for their translation of the Gospels into ChiChewa. It had been written by R. H. Napier of the Blantyre mission and printed at Mvera. Africans who read it might easily have got the impression that the Catholic priests were not only immoral but potential assassins.[28]

Joseph Booth, whose radicalism had been an important formative influence on Chilembwe, supplied his wide circle of *protegés* with Watchtower Bible and Tract Society literature. Tracts came in from the United States as well as from Eliot Kamwana in exile at Chinde. An extract from one of Kamwana's Chi-Tonga translations found in the Ncheu district illustrates the style.

The Kingdom of Great Britain is increasing itself, like the Church of Rome, because Great Britain collects together all the Churches of Babylon that they may pray for their chief, the Pope . . . All such Churches are in agreement with the Church of Rome and whoever refuses to submit to their teachings will be persecuted and perhaps banished.[29]

In the same vein the Watchtower leader in the Ncheu district, Bennet Gospel Siyasiya, wrote to a friend in December 1913 about the 'chirombo popa of the Roman Chalolika'—'the Beast, Pope of the Roman Catholics'.[30] In the language of Watchtower preachers Nyasaland was 'Babylon' and the Roman Catholic missions 'the Beast'. Chilembwe was in contact with Kamwana until the eve of the rising.[31]

The passages of the Book of Revelation that discussed 'The Beast' struck a chord in Nyasaland Africans. The natural association of European whiteness was not with purity and holiness but with fishiness and ghostliness.[32] To be white was to be like the frightening and alien spirits that were thought to emerge from water. The Rev. Harry Kambwiri reported to a Presbytery Meeting at Blantyre Scots Mission on 20 January 1915 that people were saying 'Europeans were *zirombo* (beasts) from the water which we heard of in Revelations'.[33] When Father Guimard was stopped by a group of rebels during the rising a heated debate ensued as to whether he was 'white' or 'red'.[34] The traditional reaction to the European as *mzungu* (not a human being like *munthu*) the African, coming from the water, had found further support in the Jewish Apocalyptic.

The extent to which such teachings were able to influence Africans in the Protectorate can be gauged from the Government estimate of Watchtower strength in 1914.

TABLE II[35]

District	No. of meetings	No. present	Average attendance
Ncheu	58	2,007	35
Limbe	43	1,884	44
Linjisi	31	584	19

This does not, of course, include the many pastors who had access to Watchtower literature but did not attend services. Chilembwe himself and many of his followers were preoccupied with Kamwana's prophecy that the End of the World would come in October 1914. Two of Chilembwe's elders left the Providence Industrial Mission to start Watchtower teaching at schools in the Ncheu district.[36] The outbreak of war stimulated further interest in Russellite literature with its predictions of Armageddon. A widespread fear of impending catastrophe became linked to the idea that the Europeans in the Protectorate were on the point of massacring Africans in a Final Battle. The Anglo-German conflict at Karonga became in the atmosphere of apocalyptic rumours a battle between the British and Black Americans who had arrived to save the Protectorate's Africans from slaughter.[37] J. J. Holmes of the Zambesi Industrial Mission openly admitted later that he thought the end of the world was imminent, and other Europeans in the Seventh Day Adventist mission stressed the importance of the Second Coming in their teaching, even saying that the expulsion of the Turks from Europe would be the sign.[38]

The Roman Catholic missionaries with their close contacts with the villages were not surprisingly the first to register the heightening sense of crisis amongst Malawians. The first rumour came from missionaries in the Muslim Yao area at Nankhunda who reported to Bishop Auneau:

> there was some agitation amongst Mahommedan people; they were all saying that the Arabs will come and we will kill all Europeans and Africans alike who refuse to accept our creed.[39]

The threat of a *jihad* was limited to the Yao districts where the spread of Muslim Brotherhoods[40] and the Islamic renaissance in 1912 had translated the inchoate sense of crisis into an Arab–British battle.

In June 1914 Catholic catechists coming back from their harvesting holiday reported more seditious talk to the missionaries from the Ncheu region.[41] One month later Paulos Mwanye told Bishop Auneau that a Providence Industrial Mission member called Mawson had warned him of an impending massacre. Swelsen made his own enquiries and found rumours that 'John Chilembwe was getting ready to kill all White people, and he was making weapons and spears, and had nocturnal meetings, and that John Chilembwe's Church would rise to Heaven, and the others would fall down and Chilembwe would be the new Noah'.[42] The problem facing Milthorp, the Assistant District Commissioner for Nguludi, when this information was relayed to him by Auneau, was that it sounded like a Catholic attempt to discredit their rivals in the mission field. Milthorp did not like Mwanye, referring to him as 'a very sanctimonious and typically mission youth and a thorough rascal from the look of him',[43] and found no evidence to support the stories. The accusations had been made at the end of a series of school disputes and Auneau was not noted for his delicacy of conscience when the interests of the Church were at stake.

Not trusting the Catholics, but being unwilling to take risks after the outbreak of war, Moggridge, the District Commissioner at Blantyre, turned to Hetherwick who he thought was probably far better informed on subjects of this sort than anyone else in the district.[44] The Church of Scotland dutifully provided a number of teachers who scouted round the Chiradzulu area asking questions and came back with the cryptic information that Chilembwe called his church 'Noah's Ark' and that the belief was widespread that Americans were fighting at Karonga.[45] On 11 December 1914 a confident Moggridge felt able to report back to the Secretariat in Zomba that 'after three weeks hostile and fairly close scrutiny there is little to be feared from this man'.[46]

At the time of writing Moggridge could not have been more wrong. Chilembwe was under pressure from his more militant followers to take active measures to protect his mission congregation from what they took to be an imminent attack by the Europeans. His school inspector, David Kaduya, son of an Mpotola chief from Phalombe, had fought in the Somaliland campaign with the Nyasaland forces against the 'Mad Mullah'. The British-led troops had been badly mauled and Kaduya had seen at first hand the power of religion as an integrative force driving men into a Holy War.[47] He hoped for a crusade against the British. In early 1913, Chilembwe had sent letters to Kamwana at Chinde but had received the reply that: 'It is not the Lord's way to do things by fighting.'[48] Then Kamwana gained considerably in status with the outbreak of war. Under the influence of Watchtower literature many Africans in the Protectorate felt that they were indeed living in the 'Last Times'.[49] Chilembwe's final moderate step, a letter to the newspaper protesting against African involvement in the war, was frustrated by the censor. Kamwana, newly arrived at Mulanje to supervise his congregations at a critical hour, soon saw his influence waning as the weeks passed by without the advent of the parousia that he had predicted.

By December 1914 Chilembwe was suffering from chronic asthma, had lost a daughter and was heavily in debt; his mail was being censored by the Boma and he had been given warning from supporters in Zomba that it was only a matter of time before he was deported. His blindness had reached a point where he was obliged to dictate letters.[50] His idea of history came almost entirely from the Bible. Under the extreme pressure of the newly-proclaimed state of emergency in north Nyasaland, his own predicament, and the urgings of men like Kaduya, it seems that the distinction between Biblical images and political realities became blurred in his mind. Nyasaland was no longer metaphorically Babylon but had become Babylon itself, and Chilembwe was not simply an African pastor in an intolerable situation but the suffering servant who would deliver a saved remnant from oppression. Even if Chilembwe did personally reject a messianic role his long training in the United States and his association with Black Americans cast him as a type of saviour in the eyes of his followers. Wilson Kusita, who had become disillusioned with Kamwana's prophecies, returned to the Providence Industrial Mission in January 1915 and wrote to Eliot Achirwa, Kamwana's representative:

> The people will not be saved by you but here it is possible that we will be saved (because) that John Chilembwe is a real American. Here I am with people that I know and I am not afraid.[51]

It was easy to see Chilembwe as a representative of the invading Black Americans believed to be at Karonga. Salvation was to be rich, educated, and respected, the qualities that supporters of the Providence Industrial Mission imagined were shared by Chilembwe and Black America.

By the beginning of 1915 Chilembwe had been pushed into inaugurating the millennium by the sword. The rising expectations at the end of 1914 had been frustrated. By the end of December there were telltale signs in Chilembwe's letters; he had begun speaking of Africans in the Protectorate as 'my people' and ending with an undisguised eschatological proclamation whose meaning could not be mistaken by readers of the Bible.

> Preach the true Gospel trusting our heavenly Father will help us. Strengthen all weak brethren. Preach the Kingdom of God is at hand.[52]

After dark on Saturday 23 January 1915 the priests at Nguludi were roused by the noise coming from the Providence Industrial Mission. From four miles away came the sound of 'trumpets, yelling, screaming and the sound of an enormous war-drum, fireworks, and gunfire'.[53] It was the beginning of attacks on Europeans in and around Blantyre in which an African policeman was murdered, several Whites killed, and an attempt made to capture ammunition and guns. Although telegraph wires were cut and the Europeans surprised, only the attacks on isolated planters around Blantyre were fully successful. The raids were poorly-timed and bore the marks of hurried planning. As late as 7 a.m. on Sunday morning groups of stragglers were heading towards the township from Chiradzulu. A priest at the new Blantyre mission, Father Guimard, met one such group while on his way to say mass at Limbe. The priest swore on his breviary, taken by the rebels to be a Bible, that he was not a man of war and was allowed to pass.[54]

On the Sunday evening the Assistant Resident sent warning to Nguludi mission to keep a sharp look-out and the next day, 25 January, the Government's attack on the Providence Industrial Mission was clearly audible. Despite a promise made by two planters on their way to join the Midima Volunteers, a European vigilante force, that men would be sent to guard the station, Nguludi was still unprotected on Monday night. A local headman, Sumani, sent word that an attack on the mission by the Providence Industrial Mission rebels was imminent and Auneau wanted no further warning to evacuate the buildings entirely. A very frightened band of two priests and a Brother, together with five nuns and their thirteen coloured orphans plus a number of Catholics who had sought refuge at the mission, set out for the house of a nearby planter, Mr. Fiddes, where they hoped to find help.[55]

Father Swelsen, a tough six-foot Dutch carpenter, bragging that 'he was afraid of no African'[56] refused to obey the orders of his French bishop and stayed on. As the procession wound its way along the bush path saying the Rosary, he prepared to defend the mission. It was an action typical of the more independent-minded missionaries who could be a law unto themselves. He had at his disposal a number of mission servants and employees as well as three guns. Despite the bravado it seems likely that the Montfort priest who had known a well-dressed, gentle African pastor of some learning could not imagine that Chilembwe would give the order to attack Nguludi.

Until this point the mission had remained a well-informed bystander to the Rising. The priests had characteristically warned Catholics in the parish to keep away from the fighting and to refrain from joining in the Government attack on the Providence Industrial Mission. The mission's night watchman had been dispatched to find out if stories about the beheading of Livingstone were true. There was no reason to suppose that Chilembwe would attack the station and Swelsen settled down on his bed to doze.[57]

After Auneau had reached Fiddes' plantation and the nuns had housed their charges in a tobacco barn, it was discovered that one of the girls, Alicia, was missing. Three men with spears and a rifle were immediately sent back along the bush path to try to find her. When they arrived at Nguludi shortly before midnight all was quiet and Swelsen convinced them that there was no reason to return as there would be no assault that night. Swelsen was proved to be wrong.

The attack came around 3.30 in the morning when the moon had gone down. It was led by David Kaduya who had taken control of the military side of the rising. During the Government attempt to capture the Providence Industrial Mission he had defended the mission professionally enough to repulse Boma troops. Alongside him were two violently anti-European members of the Providence Industrial Mission, Thomas and John Lulanga.[58] Swelsen was caught half-asleep on his bed but managed to bludgeon his way through the rebels only to fall, clubbed to the ground and bleeding profusely from six stab wounds, in the mission cemetery. Fortunately for him the crowd's attention was diverted by the wounding of Kaduya who was shot in the leg by Sumani, the Headman, from a hiding place in the bushes. 'Major' Kaduya was taken into the half-built shell of Nguludi Cathedral where a service with hymns and prayers was held.[59] Despite cries that his head should be cut off in usual Yao fashion, Swelsen was left for dead while the rebels set about burning all the mission buildings. The young child, Alicia, who had been hiding behind her bed, perished in the blaze.

The attackers left at dawn and a number of Catholics who had been hiding came out of the bush and placed Swelsen in a *machila*. Supervised by the mission cook, Valentino Mwasika, they managed to carry the priest as far as Mikolongwe station where a special train was waiting to take the rest of the missionaries into a laager in Blantyre. After an emotional scene in which Swelsen begged his Bishop for forgiveness and was given the last sacraments, he was taken to Blantyre hospital where, despite his wounds, he miraculously survived. Kaduya was not so lucky. Transported in Auneau's *machila* by faithful followers of the Providence Industrial Mission he was found by Government troops near Likulesi on his way to Portuguese East Africa: he reputedly asked to be shot outright and there is no record of his ever having been tried.[60]

The Catholic mission at Nzama only escaped the same fate as Nguludi by good fortune. Kaduya and Chilembwe appear to have originally planned a four-pronged attack centring on Zomba, Blantyre, Mulanje, and Ncheu. Nzama fell within the area of the northern focus of the rising. At Ncheu the rising depended for its main support on the Seventh-Day Baptist Church whose most important leader was an Ngoni pastor, Philipo Chinyama. He had his own church and school at Nthinda's village near Dzunje mountain and close to Makwangwala's village of Tyolera. From there he had built up a small network of prayer-houses under the unfriendly eye of the Boma. Government reports on the Seventh-Day Baptists noted an extreme hatred of other missions and creeds especially Roman Catholicism.[61] Part of this hatred stemmed from close contact with Watchtower supporters, contact that proved disastrous for the rebels at the time of the rising.

C. A. Cardew, the District Commissioner at Ncheu, had been a member of the Rhodesian Pioneer Column, guarded the Limpopo drifts against Boer incursions as a member of the British South Africa Company Police, and arrived in Nyasaland with a letter of introduction from Cecil Rhodes to Harry Johnston. The Boma at Ncheu had been founded by him in 1902 and he had spent some time in Tongaland during Eliot Kamwana's rise to fame in 1909, an experience that had taught him to be wary of Watchtower agitators.[62] By 22 January 1915 he had got wind of suspicious activity in his district and, taking the fiery rhetoric of the Watchtower preachers at face value, had Siyasiya, Jordan Njirajaffa,[63] and David Shirt Chikakude,[64] brought in for questioning. As a normal wartime precaution *askari* were sent round the district to confiscate papers and suspicious literature in the hands of African pastors. The Watchtower pacifists had succeeded only in alerting the Boma.

Early on Monday morning 25 January Chilembwe's runner, an Ngoni from the Chiradzulu district called Richard Kuchale, brought news to Chinyama that the rising had broken out in the south.[65] Chinyama was already on the verge of arrest and had warned fellow pastors that *askari* were touring the district. He had been pleading with people he had approached about the rising to keep quiet, but there is every chance that the planning of the rising had reached Cardew's ears. By dawn a considerable body of spearmen had gathered round the Seventh-Day Baptist church at Nthinda, some in full Ngoni war-dress. Despite beatings and abuse from their chief, Makwangwala, they refused to disperse. The Ngoni chief informed the Boma of the illegal assembly and retreated to a beer-drink in a neighbouring village.[66] Cardew barricaded himself into his office and sent off messages to all mission stations warning them of possible attacks and requesting them to come into a laager at Ncheu. Both Makwangwala and Njobvualema were summoned to send spearmen to defend the Boma. The chief of the Catholics received the letter late on Tuesday evening.[67]

Njobvualema's reaction was in many ways similar to that of Makwangwala. He had no love of Europeans and on one occasion the Montfort priests had caught him muttering angrily about the 'Franchesi' while in a drunken stupor.[68] But unlike the African pastors he had a position of moderate political power and a shrewd grasp of political realities within the Protectorate. On a number of occasions before the rising he had come to enquire of the missionaries whether British boats were still reaching the coast of Africa.[69] He knew very well that the British were in a highly vulnerable position after the outbreak of war but rightly calculated that they were not vulnerable enough. He was illiterate and knew nothing of Biblical apocalyptic. Before any decision was made a cow was sacrificed and its entrails read by a diviner. The next morning Njobvualema set out with his warriors to defend the Boma.[70]

Shortly after he had left, the brother of one of his important sub-chiefs, Chikonda, arrived with a letter from Chinyama. A Catholic catechist took the letter to Njobvualema at Ncheu. As the chief's immediate entourage were all unable to read, the task fell to the head catechist who had accompanied the expedition. The message contained orders to kill all the Whites at Nzama.[71] After burning the letter Njobvualema led his forces to Makwangwala's village and sacked it in order to prove his loyalty to the Boma. He was notoriously jealous of Makwangwala's superior education and his habit of riding about in a Government *machila*. As Tyolera was being looted by his rivals' spearmen, Makwangwala lay down on his mat, put his rifle to his throat and committed suicide. He was under suspicion of complicity after a session of interrogation by

Cardew, yet he had failed on all sides.[72] As a final precaution Njobvualema arranged the poisoning of Chikonda once he had learnt that his brother had fled to Portuguese East Africa.[73]

Significantly it had only been the Catholic missionaries who were in any danger. One party of Chinyama's men camped in the coffee plantation of Dombole mission and the daughter of the Protestant missionary at Goa stood watching as two Ngoni in full war-dress passed by.[74] No attempt was made to harm any of the Protestants who staffed isolated stations in the Kirk Hills. Watchtower anti-Catholicism might easily have cost the Montfort missionaries their lives had not Njobvualema already come down on the side of the Boma before Chinyama's messenger reached him. The Ncheu rising was a fiasco of indecision and ill-timing. No attack was made on the Boma and within a few days Chinyama's men were in disarray, fleeing to sanctuary in Portuguese East Africa or south in a futile bid to join up with Chilembwe.

The news of the rebellion produced panic amongst Europeans and Africans alike. An atmosphere of fear and rumour prevailed at Utale where many Catholics came in to protect the mission.[75] There was a frenzied reaction amongst the guards at Ncheu gaol who spat on captured rebels and abused them violently for wanting to kill Europeans.[76] In that unique mixture of frustration and rage that comes from divided loyalties Nyasaland was thrown into a reign of terror that the Government was unwilling, or unable, to stop. On 6 February Father Rivière had to complain to the Resident that mixed bands of Machinga and Ngoni warriors sent by the local chief, KuNgwalo, ostensibly to round up rebels, were pillaging villages around Utale mission.[77] Around Nguludi the Midima Volunteers ran amok burning huts and hauling quite innocent villagers off to gaol.[78] Even when the Government had brought the situation under control the mood of guilt and fear continued to produce savage sentences from the Native Court Assessors at Ncheu. The death sentence was demanded by Njobvualema and Kwataine for all forty-three rebels captured and tried before 5 February 1915. It was through the intervention of Cardew and the Attorney-General that the sentences were reduced to three executions—for men who had threatened *askari*.[79]

Even though, when the Montfort priests came out of their laagers at Zomba and Blantyre, they found their headquarters razed to the ground, their stocks had risen immeasurably in the Protectorate. Amongst Africans in the Chiradzulu District to be Catholic was to be safe from detention; the sale of rosaries doubled.

> Pagans, Protestants and especially rebels wanted to get hold of one so that they would not be arrested. The Rosary had its moment of glory in those weeks.[80]

Auneau's other dubious victory came when the Christians from Nguludi marched in a triumphal procession to take the iron sheets from the roof of Chilembwe's magnificent church which had been dynamited by Government troops. That the roof of the new cathedral at Nguludi should be made from *malata* taken from Chilembwe's 'Noah's Ark' has a poignancy and symbolism that doubtless did not escape Africans in the Chiradzulu district. Several years later old Providence Industrial Mission members refused to talk to nuns who visited their village.

Njobvualema at Ncheu had his share of loot but without the backing of Government permission. Chairs, dresses, English books, and Chichewa Bibles were brought back from Makwangwala's together with a reward of six shillings given to each man by Cardew.[81] The Chief was summoned to Zomba at the end of April to receive the official thanks of the Governor. On his return strange rumours were circulated that the Government wanted all Ngoni to pierce their ears in traditional fashion to distinguish them from the Yao, who were to pierce their noses, and the Alomwe, who wore a hole in their upper lip.[82] Whatever Njobvualema had heard at the Governor's this could only be an expression of his own desire to return to a more simple tribal politics. It seems probable that the Governor had praised the Ngoni's role in the rising and contrasted it with the heavy involvement of the Alomwe and Yao. Njobvualema may have been attempting to reinforce Ngoni power in the Protectorate on the strength of his new-found popularity with the Government. Auneau did report that many of the rebels were carrying Yao amulets and his first impression had been that the rising was an Alomwe rebellion against plantation owners.[83] The Ngoni were relatively unimplicated and it is easy to understand why Njobvualema wanted an obvious distinguishing tribal mark to correspond to the Catholics' rosary.

Auneau gained considerable personal prestige from the rising. Not only had it been his catechists who had warned of trouble coming, but he had been insultingly ignored by the Government, and the Montfort mission at Nguludi left without adequate protection. The promptness with which the Governor sought ways to compensate the mission betrayed a guilty conscience. A public subscription was opened for the rebuilding of the mission, and film and theatre shows put on in Zomba to raise cash.[84] As well as a Government loan there was an outright gift of £800 and the Montforts were given the very valuable concession of being allowed to cut wood in Government forest reserves without payment.[85] The total loss of £1,300–£1,500 was further offset by small sums of money coming from the sale of John Gray Kufa's store and compensation from the relatively wealthy family of Duncan Njilima, two of the leading rebels.[86]

It was in the nature of mission rivalry that what put the Catholics on a pedestal of civic virtue was not to be to the advantage of the Protestants. The meetings of the Commission of Enquiry into the rising that took place between May and August 1915 placed the Protestant missions in Nyasaland under the severest criticism since the 'Discreditable Disclosures' of the 1880s. The only missionary to serve on the Commission was the Anglican Archdeacon, Glossop, who had lost none of the Oxford Movement's respect for Rome. Auneau, Guillemé, and Swelsen, gave evidence in turn and made the most of their hour of glory. The two Catholic Bishops emphasized that no Catholics had been involved in the rising and pointed out the conservative nature of Catholic missionary practice, presenting their Church, as indeed in some respects it was, as a pillar of colonial society and the preserver of law and order. Bishop Guillemé in a scene worthy of the Middle Ages told the assembled gathering that it had always been the experience of the Roman Catholic Church that the widespread distribution of vernacular Bibles led to difficulties.[87]

The Commission's hearings proved to be something of a Roman holiday and the published findings stated the Government's preoccupations and preferences quite openly.

> There is a certain danger that in the absence of adequate supervision religious instruction may possibly be made the vehicle for undesirable propaganda by Native teachers. In the Roman Catholic and Anglican Missions this danger does not exist to the same extent owing to the nature of the religious teaching entrusted to Native teachers.[88]

Despite Laws' and Hetherwick's spirited rebuttals the Commission's contention could scarcely be denied. After four hours close cross-examination Hetherwick was unable to get round the harsh figure of eighty-four baptized members of the Church of Scotland shown to have been involved in the rising.[89]

Bishop Guillemé's disingenuous remarks about the Bible were very much to the point. In an atmosphere of crisis and discussion of the millennium, constantly refuelled by Watchtower tracts, images such as the Babylonian Captivity had inflamed large numbers of Protestant Christians. The desire for independence whether in Church discipline, education, or business, that had characterized the small educated community of Africans in southern Nyasaland had been repeatedly frustrated in the pre-war period. Chilembwe, the 'real American', slighted by Europeans, had provided a Biblical justification for revolt, in the war of the Just and the Unjust. He had personified the plight of the educated African and become a natural figurehead once it was apparent that Kamwana's prophecies could not be realized by passively awaiting the millennium. Africans felt that with Chilembwe 'it is possible we shall be saved' even though it was Kaduya who, in the final analysis, alone took practical measures to do so.

It was ironical that the Montfort priests were better able to understand Chilembwe than his European Protestant colleagues. They had seen it all before, or so they felt, in their seminary Church History classes. Chilembwe was an 'illuminé' who had become crazy with pride and wanted to destroy the Church.[90] They saw him against a backdrop of Hussites and Anabaptists with as much assurance as modern writers place him in the ranks of John Brown and Black slave revolts in America.[91] Overeducation had pushed Chilembwe to the edge of society so that he fitted into neither the European nor the African world.[92] For them the rising was a religious matter, the product of a misplaced emphasis on personal inspiration at the expense of apostolic authority, and overhasty Africanization of the Church. They felt proud not to have made such mistakes and were pleased that the Protectorate Government shared their views on the self-evident rationality of their mission policy. The Catholic missions were in the enviable position of being able to say 'I told you so' and rarely refrained from doing so in the subsequent years. At the first signs of Watchtower activity and at the reopening in the 1920s of the Providence Industrial Mission by Dr. Daniel Malekebu flurries of letters were sent in to the Government.[93]

The Chilembwe rising, by differentiating the Christian Missions quite clearly in front of horrified Government officials and planters, was a turning point for the Catholic Missions in the Protectorate. Despite their foreignness, close association with Africans and absence from colonial social life, the priests had proved themselves as upholders of law and order. Their willing participation in the war effort together with the nursing service of the nuns was to confirm a growing consensus of opinion arising from the Commission's findings. In times of trouble the Roman Catholic missionaries were reliable. They not only knew the 'native mind' but also knew the meaning of authority and discipline. They were the sort of missionaries a young colony needed. For a while the Church was both Mater and Magister.

REFERENCES TO CHAPTER IV

[1] Eken P. W. *Een Afrikaansch Oproermaker* Meerssen c. 1922, 39. Trans. from Dutch.
[2] Auneau L. *Brouillons* MSS. Pencilled notes for short articles. Montfort Archives, Rome.
[3] The term is used by Cohn N. in *The Pursuit of the Millenium* London 1962, 422
[4] Adam K. *The Spirit of Catholicism* London 1929, 79—'Her liturgy seeks to adumbrate and anticipate by means of visible and transitory signs the glories of eternity'
[5] This was the thesis of John Henry Newman's *Essay on the Development of Christian Doctrine* first published in 1845
[6] The name given to French Catholics in the nineteenth century because of their attitude to secular society and change
[7] Görres I. *The Hidden Face* New York 1959, 26
[8] Eken *Een Afrikaansch* 43—'hoogheilig liberalisme'
[9] Mua Mission Diary 12 July 1909
[10] *Règlements et instructions* Guillemé to Nyasa missionaries 10 February 1919
[11] ibid.
[12] Quoted by Muller K. in *Concilium* March 1966 from a Propaganda Fidei document of 1659 'Ad exteros', 9
[13] The Vendée had given rise to an anti-republican peasant movement in 1793 inspired by conservative Catholicism, see Dansette *Religious History* Vol. 1. 77, 121
[14] Cairns H. A. C. *Prelude to Imperialism* London 1965, 93
[15] Oral testimony of George Njoloma, Nankhule village, October 1969. Njoloma lived at Chilembwe's house at this time and remembers playing with his children.
[16] Oral traditions collected in the Chiradzulu district ascribe the cracking of Chilembwe's bell to a number of Europeans. Most popular is William Jervis Livingstone, though the mission cook at Nguludi, Valentino Mwasika, was adamant that it had been Father Ryo who had told Chilembwe to heat the famous bell. Father Ryo worked in Nyasaland from 1906–39 and had the reputation of being a near saint. He was a great walker but practised the penance of wearing outsize shoes to hurt his feet. Although he had a child-like personality he was an adept linguist speaking ChiYao, ChiLomwe, and ChiChewa. He came from a farming family in Brittany and is remembered by his parishioners as being very talkative and friendly. Father William Swelsen came from a prosperous farming family in Schimmert, Holland, and arrived in Nyasaland in 1908. He survived not only the rising but an attack of blackwater fever in 1918 to be joined on the mission by his brother, Jean Swelsen. Oral testimonies from Father Leroux, Pirimiti and Father Eyssen, Likulesi, August 1969.

[17] C.O. 525 166. p. 593, Public Records Office, London

[18] It was the Montfort policy to transfer catechists from station to station and Nzama became something of a catechists' training school, since it was the first Montfort mission. By 1915 Nguludi was the administrative headquarters though this changed shortly after the War to Limbe mission.

[19] Wallace Kampingo escaped across the border into Portuguese East Africa in a group of Chilembwe's close associates and relatives including his cousin, Stephen Mkulichi. He crossed back over the border to look for Chilembwe and was captured. During his trial he turned King's evidence. Trial records of 20 October 1915. S10/1/3. National Archives, Zomba.

[20] Oral testimony of Pio Ntwere in a series of interviews at Nguludi, May–August 1969, Alomwe Catholic catechist, and of Chief Michael Gordon of Gordon village, Chiradzulu, Providence Industrial Mission member in 1914, interviewed by Lee Higdin, a Peace Corps teacher at Chiradzulu Secondary School August 1969, to whom we are indebted for this information.

[21] Pio Ntwere ibid.

[22] New schools were opened including the Ncheu school staffed by Wilson Kusita who attempted to open another at Chief Jalasi's. Ncheu District Book quoted in Kusita's trial BS 1/2/6. The Bruce Estates were sufficiently extensive to oblige Chilembwe to build on European plantation land.

[23] Shepperson and Price *Independent African*, 80–1, for details of Livingstone

[24] Evidence given by A. L. Bruce in Case 77. S10/1/3

[25] Mwalimu, Yao headman on Magomero Estates C.O. 525/66 p. 435. P.R.O. London.

[26] Oral testimonies, Ben Mononga, Namuthakoni village, Chiradzulu, a worker in Chilembwe's garden in 1914 and Augusto Liboti, house servant at Nguludi in 1914, George Village, Chiradzulu. February and May 1969.

[27] Pio Ntwere tells the story that Swelsen misheard this as 'change of blows' and spent some time looking in his dictionary to discover Chilembwe's meaning

[28] C.O. 525/66. pp. 311, 477, P.R.O. London

[29] In an affidavit of H. Silberrand, DC Ncheu 29 June 1915. Government translation from ChiTonga S2/68/19

[30] B. G. Siyasiya to D. S. Chikakude 27 December 1913. The letter was significantly sent from the North Rand.

[31] C.O. 525/66. p. 565

[32] Personal Communication Dr. J. M. Schoffeleers

[33] C.O. 525/66. p. 455

[34] C.O. 525/66. p. 593

[35] Comparable figures are to be found for the West Nyasa District i.e. Kamwana's home territory of Tongaland, where there were fifty-one 'churches' with some 1,000 adherents in 1914. Governor of Nyasaland to Secretary of State for the Colonies. 6 March 1916. S1/49/19.

[36] Turnbull to Moggridge 15 February 1915 and 23 February 1915. S10/1/6

[37] Shepperson G. 'Myth and Reality in Malawi' *Fourth Herskovits Memorial Lecture* Northwestern 1966 deals with the theme of Black American saviours in some depth.

[38] C.O. 525/66. pp. 407, 661

[39] Montfort Archives Rome

[40] Personal communication from Mr. R. Greenstein at present researching on Islam amongst the lakeshore Yao

[41] Oral testimony. Father Auguste Baslé, Pirimiti mission, October 1970.

[42] C.O. 525/66. p. 254 Father Basle arrived in Nyasaland in 1908 and was at Nankhunda in 1914.

[43] Mitchell to Moggridge 18 August 1914. S10/1/6

44 Moggridge to Hetherwick 14 November 1914. S10/1/6
45 Moggridge to Secretariat 11 December 1914. S10/1/6. 'Noah's Ark' is another symbol of the saved remnant and fits in well with Chilembwe's final vision of himself and his mission.
46 Moggridge to Secretariat 11 December 1914. S10/1/6
47 Oral testimonies. Pio Ntwere and Ben Mononga confirmed by Kosamu Mpotola from Mptola's village, Chiradzulu, in an interview at the Providence Industrial mission, August 1969.
48 C.O. 525/66. p. 565.
49 Shepperson and Price *Independent African*, 230, quote a letter from a Nyasaland Watchtower adherent and in Linden *John Chilembwe*, 635–44 the importance of millennial expectations is discussed.
50 For details see Linden *John Chilembwe* and C.O. 525/66. p. 466
51 Kusita to Achirwa 16 December 1914 NCN 4/1/1
52 Chilembwe to Kusita 22 December 1914. NCN 4/2/1
53 Auneau L. *Brouillons:* Notes on the burning of Nguludi
54 Blantyre Mission Diary 25 January 1915 and Utale Convent Diary 8 March 1915 and C.O. 525/66. p. 593
55 Auneau L. Letter of 5 February 1915 in *Le Règne de Jésus par Marie* February 1915, 111–15. Montfort Archives, Rome.
56 Oral testimony, Valentino Mwasika, cook at Nguludi, Ntonya village, August 1969
57 Oral testimonies, Mwasika, Ntwere, and Liboti
58 Oral testimony, Mononga, Ntwere
59 Further indication that even at this late stage the rebels believed themselves to be fighting a Holy War
60 Auneau *Brouillons*
61 S2/68/19
62 Claud Ambrose Cardew was born at Sandhurst in 1870, the third son of Sir Frederick Cardew, a former Governor of Sierra Leone, and uncle to General Montgomery. After retiring at 51 from the colonial service he lived as a recluse until his murder by the son of his cook in September 1959—see Hickman A. S. *Men who made Rhodesia* B.S.A. Company. S. Rhodesia 1960, 40 and *Nyasaland Times* 25 September 1959, 6 October 1959, 17 November 1959.
63 'Brother CheJordan' had been appointed by Siyasiya as Watchtower representative in the Ncheu district while the latter was in the Rand. He was still in gaol in 1923 when most of the other rebels were released on ticket of leave so was probably implicated in the rising. S2/102/23 NCN 4/2/1.
64 David Shirt Chikakude remained in gaol until 1921 when he was released on ticket of leave. He was a faithful Watchtower preacher and was being investigated again in 1923 for questionable preaching. S2/102/23. For full details of Watchtower supporters see Appendix of Linden *John Chilembwe*, 648–51.
65 Case 42. 4 February 1915, and Cardew to Moggridge 6 February 1915. S10/1/6
66 Oral testimony, Griven Chinkasi, a pupil teacher at Chinyama's school at the time and Thomas Kabanga-Ndau *nduna*, Chief Makwangwala's Dzunje, Ncheu September 1969
67 For full details of the rising see Linden *Chiefs and Pastors*
68 Eken *Een Afrikaansch* 32
69 ibid.
70 Nzama Mission Diary 27 February 1915
71 Oral Testimony. Maurillo Karvalo, Ngoni catechist, Nzama Mission, September 1969, and Nzama Diary 21 June 1915 and 23 June 1915. The priests were probably assembling evidence for the Commission at this time.
72 Oral testimony, Chinkasi and Kabanga-Ndau

[73] Nzama Diary 30 January 1915

[74] Personal Communication, Miss E. Smith. On asking some African children about the war-dress she was told as if it were an everyday occurrence that they were going to *nkhondo*, to the war.

[75] Utale Mission Diary 6 February 1915

[76] Nzama Diary 3 February 1915 'Ah, inu mufuna kupa azungu'—'Oh, so you want to kill Europeans.'

[77] Utale Diary 6 February 1915

[78] Oral Testimony, Benito and Vito Ntwana, Yao catechists from Nguludi Mission interviewed September 1969. The Government were unable to convict a number of the rebels as the Volunteers had destroyed the evidence by burning down their huts. Turnbull to Moggridge 4 February 1915 S10/1/5.

[79] Chinyama, Kusita, and Kuchale, were later executed: see Linden *Chiefs and Pastors*

[80] Auneau *Brouillons*

[81] Nzama Diary 8 February 1915

[82] ibid. 6 June 1915

[83] ibid. 31 January 1915. A letter from Auneau with news of the burning of Nguludi attributes the rebellion to a certain Mr. Dickie, a nearby planter who Auneau thought had enraged the Alomwe—'fanaticisé les Angourous'.

[84] Blantyre Diary 7 August 1915. One performance raised £60.

[85] Auneau *Brouillons*

[86] Nzama Diary 25 August 1915, and Blantyre Diary 2 January 1915. £80 from the Njilimas. For details about John Gray Kufa see Shepperson and Price *Independent African* and for Njilima see Linden *John Chilembwe*, 651.

[87] Details of Guillemé's performance at the Commission are contained in *Monsignor Mathurin Guillemé, July 3rd 1859 to April 7th 1942* published on his death at the White Fathers' press, Bembeke, and in C.O. 525/66 p. 298. The lack of the Bible was considered to be a distinguishing mark of Catholic Christians. When asked what was the difference between the Providence Industrial Mission and Nguludi, the Providence Industrial Mission members invariably said that the Catholics were not allowed to have the Bible. The *Zambesi Industrial Mission* of December 1929, 9, carries an interesting article by Rev. Holmes on Catholic efforts in the Chiradzulu area showing how the Bible was still equally important. 'In all these villages there is the continued menace of the Roman Catholics who adopt such mean methods to entice the people. We do not fear our own Christians going over to them as they know very well that the Roman Catholics would deny them their Bibles and intelligent Natives think a lot of their Bible and believe it is the Word of God. In a heathen village the Roman Catholics go in, put some beads round the necks of a few children and maintain that this is now their village.' Guillemé was also of the opinion that the Old Testament was sufficiently salacious for it to be imprudent for an unmarried woman to read it.

[88] *Report of the Commission of Enquiry into the Nyasaland Native Rising* Paragraph 44. Supplement to the *Nyasaland Government Gazette* 31 January 1916, Zomba 1916.

[89] Auneau *Brouillons* and Eken *Een Afrikaansch* 38

[90] Father Brung in a letter to *Messager de Marie-Reine des Coeurs* February 1915, the Montfort magazine for their Canadian province: 'Ce fameux John Cilembur [*sic*] fier, orgueilleux et quelque peu illuminé.' Auneau L. in *Onze Missionarissen* May 1915 wrote an article 'Christenvervolging in Shire' translated into Dutch: 'Under the pretext of driving out the Europeans his main aim seems to be to attack the Catholic Religion and deal it a mortal blow.' Trans. Dutch. Each of the Montfort Provinces had its own magazine.

[91] For example Rotberg in *Strike a Blow and Die*, Introduction

[92] Eken *Een Afrikaansch* 14, 15 talks of 'gedeclasseerden'—'marginal men'. Although this book and the magazine articles are aimed at the pockets of Catholic readers and

are therefore often grossly distorted they provide some interesting insights into the rising.

[93] The hostility did not extend to the ranks of the catechists, as both Pio Ntwere and Eugenio Matuta worked with Dr. Malekebu in the Chiradzulu Native Association. Dr. Malekebu shared with John Chilembwe experience of the United States and with Dr. Banda a medical degree.

CHAPTER V

The Crisis of the First World War

War in Europe, war here against the Germans, a religious war, persecution
almost. You might almost think that we were close to the end of the world.

Nzama Mission Diary 30 January 1915[1]

As the Chilembwe rising had destroyed the illusions of the European population
in Nyasaland about its superior race relations, so the scales finally dropped from
the eyes of Africans during the First World War. Much of the success of
colonial rule depended on bluff. The European, *mzungu*, had been considered a
different species from *munthu*, the African.[2] Like the Ngoni before him he was
widely held to be invincible and all-powerful. British rule in Nyasaland had
been unpleasant but far less oppressive than former Ngoni raids and the contemporary administration of Southern and Northern Rhodesia. After the campaigns against the Germans there were no longer grounds for believing in the
essential superiority of Western civilization.

Within a year of the declaration of war and the initial battle around Karonga
large numbers of Malawians were winding their way north, each man with his
load for the front. In a six-month period in 1918 two Catholic priests baptized
more than one hundred and fifty men dying on the supply routes from disease
and exhaustion.[3] Porters would often have to travel for a whole day before they
were able to find food; many were treated little better than pack-ponies.[4] For
these hundreds of *tenga-tenga*, who had no way of knowing that equally appalling mortality was occurring in Europe, the supply columns seemed like
European-organized death marches.

Since many of the Catholic missionaries were French nationals, it was not
long before the French Consul was demanding their repatriation for service in
the trenches.[5] Bishop Auneau put up a spirited resistance arguing that French
priests would be of more service to their Government if they stayed in Nyasaland and spared their country the cost of repatriation.[6] On 27 July 1916
exemption of missionaries from active service was revoked.[7] Although the
priests were not obliged to return to Europe several had to serve in the East
Africa campaign. One Montfort, Father Ryo, volunteered to return and fought
at Salonika.[8]

Since the Catholics were not allowed to take posts as chaplains in an official
capacity, Auneau held out for medical service. Fathers Régent, Martin, and
Grolleau, were drafted into the Ambulance Corps in 1916 followed by Fathers

Rivière and Guimard a year later. Two other Montforts, Habets and Ten Dyck, volunteered, and the Sisters provided four nurses for the front.[9] It was a big loss to the mission and in April 1918 Auneau let the Government know that lack of missionaries was having a deleterious effect on Catholic schools;[10] he astutely pointed out that their absence from stations meant that catechists were teaching without adequate supervision. In the light of the Commission of Enquiry's reflections on mission schools, the Government could hardly ignore the Bishop's plea. A month later Grolleau and Martin were released from their duties at the front.[11]

On the whole Monsignor Auneau had a 'good war'. Despite lack of personnel, money, and supplies, Nguludi cathedral was completed thanks to the Government's guilty conscience. Built largely by Father Régent, it was officially blessed on 7 December 1916. Catholic schools spread out triumphantly into the old area of the Providence Industrial Mission at Masanjala's, Tembeta's, and Maleta's.[12] To his intense annoyance, the disgraced Hetherwick was banned from competing in the same region and the Catholics were given an official monopoly for several years.[13]

The Bishop lost his pectoral cross in the burning of Nguludi but none of his episcopal vigour; undaunted he had his Goanese and African parishioners collect £16.3s.5d. for a new one. But the 'effroyable guerre' eventually came even to Auneau; owing to the shortage of shipping reaching the African coast the cross never arrived from Europe.[14] In June 1918, with instincts unimpaired, he bought thirty-five acres of good ground on the right bank of the Lower Shire to found St. Michel de Chikwawa on land originally owned by the British South Africa Company.[15] The district had already been evangelized from the distant Neno mission so there were thirty catechumens to greet the priests when they arrived in the village of Mikolongo.[16] For the first few months, until bricks had been baked and a small house built, the missionaries lived in a cotton barn donated by a local planter.[17] The foundation on 23 July 1918 by Fathers Baslé and Leroux of Chikwawa Mission brought the Catholics for the first time amongst the Mang'anja, where they were to have very little success for decades.

Thanks to pressure from the South African Catholic Bishops who met to-gether at the Council of Johannesburg to discuss the impact of the war on the Church in South-Central Africa, the White Fathers, who did not qualify as a Religious Order, also escaped repatriation.[18] In all, fourteen White Fathers and two Sisters served in the East Africa Campaign, many in active service in the Transport Corps. From the Central Region Fathers Mazé, Paradis, Boucansaud, and Sarrazin went into transport while Father Roy acted as a chaplain and stretcher bearer after 1918.[19] The work of the priests and nuns during the war was often heroic. Sister Jacques du Sauveur left Utale mission for Karonga in 1916 and worked without respite until her sudden death from smallpox in September 1918. In the same year Father Habets succumbed to the epidemic though the other Sisters survived. Three priests were awarded the Italian Bronze Medal for their war service.[20]

The most technically distinguished military record was that of a Canadian priest, Father Ernest Paradis. He volunteered in 1916 along with Father Mazé and joined the Nyasaland Volunteer Reserve in Karonga. By April he had been moved to the South African Rifles to supervise convoys going to Fife in Northern Rhodesia. Three months later, having survived the assaults on Luwiwa and New Langenburg, he went to Lupemba where Bemba troops were being used against the German forces. With the help of Father Sarrazin over one hundred of the Bemba were baptized during the fighting. He was first cited in dispatches while at General Northey's headquarters in Njombe and by the end of the war had become senior transport officer for all troops east of Nyasaland and north of the Zambesi.[21]

The military service of priests like Paradis was important for the Catholic missions in a number of ways. Not least was the fact that an officer's pay was a welcome contribution to mission funds.[22] More important it finally set the seal of respectability on Catholic priests in the eyes of planters and Government officials. The priests had proved themselves as officers and gentlemen and had loyally served the British Empire. After the war Paradis acted as education director for the White Fathers and was able to use his prestige in the complicated negotiations that went on with the colonial administration. He thoroughly offset cantankerous personalities like Auneau. At the same time the priests were able to act as unofficial chaplains at the front. Paradis arranged for mass a room belonging to a Catholic A.D.C. of General Northey and was able to hear the confessions of troops fighting with the Nyasaland Field Force.

On the other hand the war brought evangelization within Nyasaland almost to a halt. Missionaries were made to run errands for the Government even when they were not on active service. In July 1917, Fathers Rivière and Toublant had to leave to buy maize in German East Africa, while Father Julien[23] was sent to buy beans around the Dedza district.[24] All food supplies were funnelled to Fort Johnston, and Ntaka-taka Mission was turned into a huge depot for maize awaiting shipment down the lake. In 1916 there were 180,000 kilos of maize and 50,000 kilos of beans collected from around the Dedza region piled up at the mission.[25] In the south at Blantyre and Nankhunda the Montforts were hosts to German nuns and priests from Tanganyika. It was the second time that the missionaries had sustained an invasion from German clerics; during the republican revolution in Portugal German Jesuits had been expelled from Mozambique and turned up at the White Fathers' stations at the end of 1910.[26]

The conduct of the war widened the gulf between missionary teaching and the actual behaviour of European 'Christians'. As in England, recruiting officers passed through the villages with drums banging and trumpets blaring.[27] If interest in 'joining the band'[28] failed to bring unsuspecting Africans from their huts, promises of huge financial rewards were made. Chiefs welcomed the opportunity to get rid of awkward villagers and would direct army officers to their huts. Africans were tricked and press-ganged into joining a war in which they had no stake or interest.

At Ntaka-taka the Ngoni chief Kachindamoto, who wanted to please the British, subjected his sub-chiefs to the most humiliating intimidation. When the first South African troops arrived in Nyasaland in August 1915 and officers went round recruiting porters, Kachindamoto summoned his Chewa sub-chiefs and ordered them to provide six hundred men. When each headman in turn refused to volunteer members of his village the Ngoni chief refused to allow them to leave the *bwalo*[29] until a ransom was paid for every man. The Chewa held out for twenty hours in the hot sun with women bringing food from their villages until resistance began to crack. Eventually 'volunteers' were produced and the headmen were able to go home to bed.[30] But when porters began to return from Karonga in a pitiful physical condition it required more than trickery or force to flush out villagers. Men fled into the bush or emigrated to the mines to avoid capture as harrowing tales from the front were brought back to villages all over the Protectorate.

The priests in transport did everything in their power to alleviate the sufferings of Africans in their charge but were obliged to obey orders. Discipline was invariably excellent in their columns, as they could hold the threat of transfer to a South African officer over any recalcitrant men.[31] At Old Langenburg, Father Régent was able to build a small hospital for African soldiers and carriers but it was totally inadequate for the volume of sick and wounded. By early 1917 conditions at the front were perhaps as bad as in Europe. Government censors did not think to read nuns' correspondence too thoroughly and Sister Jacques' letters give some idea of the appalling conditions in which African troops and carriers fought.

> If this campaign goes on much longer I am afraid of becoming a pagan. What an existence! Our hospital is so crammed that patients sleep on top of one another. We have a dysentery epidemic and most patients have fever. And to crown it all plague has broken out at Karonga.[32]

Both Fathers Paradis and Mazé came back with tales of women ordered from their villages for raping and of the brutality of officers towards even the most emaciated porters.[33]

The impact of the war was compounded in Nyasaland by a very poor harvest in 1916. As tons of food were shipped out to Tanganyika and Ntaka-taka was piled high with maize, ordinary villagers were on the verge of starvation. The cost of goods soared as small Indian stores, profiteering from the shortages, sprang up around Dedza.[34] The last year of the war was the worst. Weakened by lack of food Africans in the Protectorate were overtaken by two devastating epidemics, smallpox and Spanish influenza. With most of the remaining maize being turned into beer a combination of famine and disease accounted for the deaths of hundreds of Malawians.

As more and more Catholic catechists were called up for work as porters on the over-extended supply lines, mission work ground to a standstill. A total lack of medical supplies at the mission stations meant that at the height of the epidemics the numbers of patients treated by the nuns and priests dropped from the usual thousands to hundreds. At every station schools were shut. No supplies got through from the Mother-Houses in France and Algeria. The priests who remained were reduced to abject poverty on a monthly income that rarely exceeded £2 for each missionary. By the end of 1917 the Mua diary was carrying entries like the following.

One of the Fathers is a little anxious about the Adoration of the Cross this Easter. It looks as if he is going to have to perform in a pair of completely holed socks. His shoes are just a collection of holes bordered with leather. Father Champmartin wants to help him but only has one pair of red socks which he had saved for the occasion.[35]

Even if the priests had the money they would have been lucky to get hold of new shoes. The only people with money and goods were European officers and Indian traders.

At the beginning of the war when some of the Fathers were volunteering there was an optimistic feeling that the war was in some sense a good thing. It was widely felt that a little military discipline would 'stiffen the moral fibre' of Africans. The White Fathers practised a martial discipline in their own daily lives and thought it would do their parishioners no harm.

A letter from one of our Christians conscripted into the army tells us that his rifle is too heavy and his food inadequate. In short it's a tough job, not a bit what he expected. But all that is for the good, especially for those who are far from being solid christians.[36]

But this muscular Christianity did not survive the reality of war when it was brought to the mission's doorstep. The same priest was later to write:

We have several boys on *tangata* [37] work staying here, too sick with dysentery and enteritis to continue home. These unfortunate people are just skin and bone so weak as hardly to be able to walk. It is to be feared that several will never leave Mua.[38]

As the war progressed and more of the missionaries were involved, it was realized by even the sternest of priests that the war was an unmitigated disaster for the missions.

It is clear that the ruthless exploitation of Nyasaland Africans in a European war did begin to tell on the White Fathers. But trained as they were in obedience to lawfully constituted authority they never once protested openly. From Guillemé's worried directives to his clergy issued after the war it is apparent that considerable friction had grown up between missionaries and Government but had stopped short of official complaints.

I must ask you, yet again, never to interfere in Government affairs. Limit yourself to pointing out to the relevant authorities those abuses of which you are absolutely certain. By acting in this way you will stay in the role of missionary which cannot be that of a policeman.[39]

The silence of the Catholic clergy was accepted, if not understood, by their African laity. It was assumed that the priests were as much a victim of circumstance as the countless *tenga-tenga* they attempted to help on an individual basis. Compared with the racism of many other officers, some of whom treated their porters like animals, the priests appeared saints. Government nurses were reported to have refused to care for sick Africans [40] but the nuns worked for them devotedly throughout the war.

It is difficult to exaggerate the shock to Africans forced to participate in the war. If they were Christians they had been told repeatedly that baptism committed them to living under the Ten Commandments of God, including 'thou shalt not kill'. When they asked their priests how could they fight in a war which involved breaking the fifth commandment, they were told that there was a right to self-defence.[41] When the Father-Superior was questioned by his catechists about what he thought of the war, he was likely to give the evasive answer that war was bad but this war a necessity. It was being fought on French soil and many of the priests wanted to see the Germans defeated. British propaganda magnified by rumour had most Africans convinced that Germans bombed villages and tortured Africans.[42] As in Europe it was generally believed that there was no alternative to war. But however much the carnage was justified and accepted by the missions, nothing could lessen its psychological impact on Africans.

As the soldiers and porters drifted back to their villages at the end of 1918 the disillusionment with the *Pax Britannica*, which had its origin around 1909, had overtaken most of the Christian community. The shock of the war and the Chilembwe Rising did not inaugurate the total rejection of European institutions, but it did accelerate a return to traditional ways of life that had begun earlier. Younger Africans could not remember a time when the British were not in control, and were confirmed in their resentments. Older men who had lived through so many changes felt a sense of disintegration heightened by the events of the war years. There seemed to be no security. The impact of the war even on isolated missions such as Mua was summed up by the Father Superior in an entry in the station diary in July 1917: 'there has been a pagan renaissance which has quite frightened us'.[43]

The feeling of panic and crisis which had produced the Chilembwe rising was in no way dissipated by its violent suppression. Before an eclipse of the moon on 4 July 1917 the Montforts at Nguludi thought it wise to preach a sermon to quieten the fears of their parishioners. It was the same mood as had prevailed at the outbreak of the war.

> Some of them think that the Europeans are going to kill all the blacks; others are spreading the rumour that it will be the end of the world. Several have been sacrificing goats and chickens.[44]

The European image of bringers of peace and stability had died on the long supply columns to Karonga. It had been mortally wounded when its main African imitators were shot after the Rising, and was finally buried at the front in Tanganyika. And it was several years before it could be resurrected in the minds of Protectorate Africans.

The Catholic Church had not differentiated itself sufficiently from the colonial administration, in the eyes of villagers, for missionary endeavour to remain unaffected. The nuns at the front were upset to find that the men to whom they had ministered so lovingly refused baptism as they lay dying. The soldiers and carriers told the Sisters that 'they did not want to go with the Whites when they died'.[45] Sister Jacques du Sauveur was distressed and unable to understand their attitude but the reason for their refusal to enter a 'white' heaven is obvious from her letters.

> They find it very odd that we wash them, tend their wounds, and if need arises feed them like babies, because for the most part they have only received blows and ill-treatment from the *azungu*.[46]

However much they wished it to be otherwise, the Christianity they professed and practised seemed part of the colonial process that was sacrificing Africans in a cruel war. Against their dedicated medical work had to be set the tacit approval of the Church for a war that had made it necessary.

The alternative to the religion of the Europeans was a return to well-tried solutions to the problem of evil and suffering. Unlike traditional religion which explained personal misfortune in terms of the malign activity of witches, or returning spirits, Christianity of the institutional type had provided no coherent account of the crisis that had overtaken Nyasaland. The best Western Christianity had produced was a promise of an imminent end to the present distress, in chiliastic Protestant sects, or for Catholicism its end in Heaven after the individual's death. The eschatological explanation never lost its appeal but at the same time the immediate post-war period saw a resurgence of witch-finding.

At Njobvualema's *mwabvi* ordeals began again after a break of several years and the chief began forcing girls into polygamous marriages in defiance of the Montfort mission.[47] The poison ordeal had claimed so many victims that by 1920 the Ncheu Resident, Cardew, sent complaints to the Portuguese Resident at Vila Coutinho that *mapondera*, professional administrators of the ordeal, were crossing the border unimpeded and touring villages. At Mtengo-Mbalame on the other side of the border opposite Nzama mission two *mapondera*, Nchizang-wangwa and Tumbankombe, had established themselves and were receiving visits from villagers as far away as Mua Mission. Cardew had discovered twenty deaths in the Ncheu district and there must have been many more undetected.[48] Christians and pagans alike would flock to the *mapondera* to prove their innocence of witchcraft.

All the missions in the Central Region registered a change in atmosphere in the villages they evangelized.[49] At Kachebere, Mpezeni II, who had lived monogamously in keeping with the demands of the mission, began to take additional wives.[50] It took a decade before the widespread rejection of mission teaching was reversed and rate of recruitment into the Institutional Churches improved. The following table shows the rate of recruitment into the White Fathers' missions for four year periods from the beginning of the war to the 1930s.

Statistics for the Montforts in the same period are affected by their un-relenting proliferation of mission stations and their lowering of the length of time spent in the catechumenate. Some of their new stations such as Mulanje had phenomenal success owing to the immigration of Alomwe labourers. From 1918 to 1923 the number of Christians in the Shire Vicariate rose from five to ten thousand. But between 1923 and 1929 the figure shot up to thirty-nine

TABLE III[51]

Mission station	Total no. of new neophytes in 4-year period		
	1914–18	1922–26	1929–33
Kachebere	1,328	1,980	3,819
Ntaka-taka	311	568	885
Bembeke	300	541	834
Mua	258	267	441
Likuni	344	235	469
TOTAL	2,541	3,591 ($\times$ 1·4)	6,448 ($\times$ 1·8)

thousand.[52] The slowing in rate of recruitment shown by the White Fathers' figures is therefore masked.

Table III is deliberately arranged in a descending order which corresponds to the level of 'Ngonization'. Kachebere mission at the top recruited from a district in which the Ngoni way of life predominated, while Likuni, at the bottom, served an almost entirely Chewa population. Mua and Bembeke were mixed congregations with most Chewa around Mua mission. The impact of the war is most marked in Chewa districts; for them the Europeans had initially come as liberators from the Ngoni colonists of the nineteenth century. But neither missionaries nor colonial administrators had returned to them their lost Phiri chieftancies.[53] Wherever Principal Headmen were Ngoni the missions tended to side with them while they found it difficult to work with the diffuse authority of Banda chiefs in the Central Region. After the war the Chewa fully understood that they would not be able to manipulate European institutions as the Ngoni had done to find ways of gaining power. They looked for other methods of advancement and means of assertion and found in the nyau societies a potent weapon against both European and Ngoni alike. The key to the missions' failure in Chewa areas lay in the transformation of the nyau societies into militantly anti-Christian sects, a phenomenon that was to dominate the life of the missions in the Central Region throughout the colonial period.

REFERENCES TO CHAPTER V

[1] Nzama Diary 30 January 1915, Montfort Archives, Rome

[2] It was popularly believed that like mzimu, a spirit, the Europeans had come out of the water

[3] Rapports annuels 1917–18 Ntaka-taka diary entry for 15 July 1918. In the epidemics after the war there were reports of 7–8 per cent mortality in supply columns between Fife and Karonga. Report of Lt. MacPherson 4 February 1919 S2/5/19. National Archives, Zomba.

[4] Oral testimony, Jakobi Mbalule

[5] Blantyre Diary 12 November 1914

[6] Nguludi Diary 24 November 1914 and Blantyre Diary 9 January 1915

[7] Nguludi Diary 27 July 1916

[8] Oral testimony, Rev. J. Leroux s.m.m.

[9] Gelfand M. *Lakeside Pioneers* Oxford 1964, 83, mentions a total of six nuns. Blantyre Diary 15 December 1916

[10] The lack of missionaries was, in fact, trivial beside the lack of funds to pay catechists. Many worked on reduced pay and some for nothing before they were conscripted.

[11] Swelsen J. 'Historical survey of the Montfort Fathers' Mission' MS BC/534 Catholic Secretariat, Limbe

[12] Nguludi Diary 7 December 1916

[13] Hetherwick to Laws 20 May 1916. Hetherwick Correspondence. Quoted in Ross *Origins* 335.

[14] Nguludi Diary 7 October 1917

[15] Chikwawa Mission Diary 23 July 1918

[16] ibid. 27 July 1918

[17] ibid. 31 July 1918

[18] The White Fathers were not a Religious Order with vows of poverty and therefore not legally entitled to the privileges of monks and nuns in wartime

[19] *Rapports annuels* 1917–18 and Paradis *Notes*

[20] Querel *L'Histoire* Cahier III

[21] Details taken from an envelope marked 'Ernest Paradis' containing biography and personal diary presented to Bishop Julien after Paradis' death. White Fathers' Archives, Lilongwe.

[22] Most of Paradis' pay went not to the missionaries but to the building of Bembeke Church

[23] Fr. Oscar Julien, a Canadian, was consecrated Bishop on 24 March 1935 after Bishop Guillemé resigned as Vicar-Apostolic in 1934

[24] Blantyre Diary 28 July 1917

[25] *Rapports annuels* 1916–17 Ntaka-taka

[26] Mua Diary 1 November 1910 and Blantyre Diary 15 December 1916.

[27] Oral Testimony. Mattias Kalibotona. Ngoni. He was aged about 15 at the time and later became a Jeanes teacher. Jeanes teachers or 'Jeaners', as they were sometimes called, were an important part of British attempts to improve education in Nyasaland. They were supposed to be both a type of school inspector and community development worker. They were to supervise 15–20 schools and attempt to update teaching methods and ensure the Government curriculum was being taught, as well as setting a personal example themselves of hygiene and good agriculture at home. The Jeanes teachers were named after a rich Quaker from Philadelphia, U.S.A., Miss Anna T. Jeanes, who started a fund to train Negro demonstrators to assist teachers in the South. The American Phelps–Stokes Committee suggested the idea for Africa and centres were set up in Kenya, Zambia, as well as Nyasaland. Kachebere, August 1969 and Louis François Villy W.F. Kasina Mission, September 1969. Also in *Rapports annuels* 1916–17 Ntaka-taka diary entry for 11 July 1916 'Drums and trumpets, a real circus'.

[28] Oral testimony, Kalibotona

[29] The open space in villages equivalent to the English village green

[30] Paradis E. 'The 1st levy of Tenga-tenga in Nyasaland' MS White Fathers' Archives, Lilongwe

[31] Oral testimony, Louis François Villy W.F.

[32] Sister Jacques du Sauveur to Mother-Provincial 18 February 1917 in *Bulletins Trimestriels* December 1920, 13

[33] Oral Testimony, Louis François Villy W.F.

[34] Mua Diary August 1917

[35] ibid. March 1917

[36] ibid. September 1917

[37] The Government claimed the right to levy labourers to do an amount of work 'equivalent' to their tax

[38] Mua Diary January 1918

[39] *Règlements et Instructions* Guillemé to Nyasa missionaries 25 December 1919

[40] Sister Jacques ibid.

[41] Oral Testimony, Pio Ntwere. In the Catholic catechism of the day the relevant passage read as follows: 'Hence by this commandment it is forbidden to procure abortion. But to repel force by force against an unjust aggressor, while careful to preserve due moderation in a blameless self-defence is permitted by every law and right.' *The Catholic Catechism* New York 1932. Article 222, 65.

[42] Oral testimony, Vito Ntwana

[43] Mua Diary July 1917. It is estimated that in the period 1917–18 there were 123,000 Nyasalanders involved in the war in some capacity, mainly as soldiers and carriers. S1/946/19.

[44] Nguludi Diary 1 July 1917

[45] Sister Jacques du Sauveur to Mother Provincial 16 September 1916 in *Bulletins Trimestriels* December 1920, 12

[46] ibid. 'azungu' is the plural of *mzungu* i.e. Europeans

[47] Even at Njobvualema's the process had begun before the outbreak of war, see note 102 Chapter III.

[48] Cardew to Resident at Vila Coutinho 22 July 1920. S2/30/22.

[49] For the Dutch Reformed see Retief *William Murray* 117–28

[50] Kachebere Diary 25 July 1917

[51] These statistics are drawn from the annual reports of the White Fathers for the period 1914–34. They include babies, dying people etc.

[52] From statistics prepared by Auneau for benefactors in the United States so possibly on, the high side.

[53] See Chapter IX

Above: *The 1889 Mponda Mission: top left, Br. Chrétien, top right, Fr. Heurtebise, bottom left, Br. Antoine, bottom right, Fr. Mercui, centre, Fr. Lechaptois*

Below: *A Montfort catechism class in the 1920s*

Bishop Adolphe Lechaptois

CHAPTER VI

Nyau Societies and Holy Liberalism

We are christians. We used to dance the nyau but we stopped as immoral things went on. The bad thing in this dance is that you dance naked in the presence of many people. Things are sung which are shameful, which in English are called 'obscene'.

Likuni mission teachers to Governor 1928[1]

I would especially like to impress on you that 'decency' is a relative term. To insist on the standards adopted by some of the over-civilized inhabitants of Europe, who having confused decency with prudery, are ashamed of their bodies, would not only be unreasonable but definitely harmful to the development of your race.

R. H. Murray, Provincial Commissioner, Lilongwe 1929[2]

The nyau societies which came to play such an important role in opposing mission influence at the village level in the Central Region were extremely ancient Chewa institutions.[3] Like the Catholic Church itself the nyau was not simply a system of religious beliefs but a society with extensive claims on its membership. Its cult was shared by all the Chewa-speaking peoples of Malawi from Undi's kingdom on the Zambia/Mozambique border to the Mang'anja of the Lower Shire Valley. Unlike the centralized territorial rain-cults the societies operated at the level of the village-cluster, and oral traditions suggest that in pre-colonial times there was some tension between the royal rain-shrines and the nyau societies of the commoners.[4]

The 'centrifugal' nyau, and a constant threat of poisoning, may have been the two most important factors in curbing the power of the centralized chieftancy in Chewa society. The opposition of the nyau to the centralized authority of the mission station and its hierarchy of priests and catechists would, then, represent no new role for the societies. Power changed hands in the nineteenth century from the declining Phiri royal house to the powerful Ngoni paramounts with their *nduna* and finally to the missionaries. The Ngoni colonists had not made any serious attempt to eliminate the nyau cult until the arrival of the missionaries, so that it had continued unchanged until the First World War. After this, in the 1920s, the growing influence of the missions at the village level produced open conflict.

Nyau dances were performed during the communal female initiation rites at puberty, *Chinamwali*, and at funerals. On these occasions dancers dressed in structures representing animals, or wearing masks caricaturing a particular human being, would perform on a specially consecrated piece of ground known as the *mzinda*.[5] Behind the masks were considered to be spirits of men and animals so that when the nyau moved into the village from the bush there occurred a re-enactment of the Bantu primal myth in which men, animals, and spirits lived in harmony. Yet at the same time the dancers abused onlookers and the songs accompanying the dances were obscene. Only men were initiated and able to drum or dance so that the nyau performance was characterized by a pronounced sexual antagonism. Within a social functional context this vituperative behaviour from male performers provided some resolution of conflict within the Chewa matrilineage; the societies offered husbands living in their wives' village some relief from the social pressures on them, and the obscenity bound together men of different status and from different villages.[6]

Initiation into the societies was reserved to boys over the age of puberty who were presented by a sponsor. During the ceremony in the bush the neophyte underwent a symbolic death and was taught the secret vocabulary and songs. In the past all men were initiated although many became only nominal members who simply watched the performances. While the hierarchy of the societies was not as complex as some of the Luba secret societies, each region was controlled by an 'elder of the forest' called in the Central Region *mfumu dziko*, the chief of the land, and each village with a *mzinda* had its own nyau elder. These offices were by no means sinecures, as court cases concerning nyau dancers were outside the jurisdiction of chiefs and headmen and tried by the nyau elders in special courts.[7] Since the nyau traditionally behaved in a violent way, molesting women and stealing chickens, jurisdiction over nyau cases was important in village life. The nyau formed a society in which normal Chewa values and behaviour patterns were reversed and over which traditional authorities could not exert direct influence. With its theological, social, and legal dimensions the nyau was integral to Chewa culture.

The survival of the nyau into the twentieth century depended on the Chewa ability to accept political domination by centralized chieftancies while maintaining village life intact. Where there were massive military invasions, as for example along the southern limits of the lake by the Yao, the local Nyanja were swamped and the societies died out, but where a handful of invaders grabbed power, as in the Lower Shire Valley where Livingstone's Kololo porters conquered the Mang'anja, the nyau survived. The main promoters of the nyau today in the Chikwawa area are the descendants of the Kololo, Katunga, Kasisi, Makwira, and Masseah.[8] The situation in the Ngoni colonized areas was more complex and depended on the numerical strength of the Ngoni aristocracy and their ability to assimilate Chewa captives successfully into their states. As a general rule Chewa incorporated into the Ngoni regiments were obliged to give up the dances but the nyau still thrived within, and on the edge of, the Ngoni State where there were Chewa headmen who paid tribute but kept a degree of autonomy.[9]

The problems facing the European administration of Nyasaland resembled those of the Ngoni inasmuch as they had to maintain political control over a large population with few personnel while assimilating people into alien institutions. At the turn of the century there were only 314 Europeans in the colony, most of them missionaries.[10] The missions and plantations were the main contact points in this process and by the First World War they had not been entirely successful. It was clear from Chilembwe's following that neither the mission élites nor the rank-and-file of plantation labour in the Shire Highlands had come to terms with British rule. The proliferation of the Independent Churches led by anti-European pastors was further proof of this failure.

Where it was accepted, the mission-station hierarchy of the Institutional Churches offered a new channel for the attainment of social status, and this alone might have provoked the opposition of the nyau societies. But before the nyau had time to feel bypassed at the village level, the priests were branding the dances as immoral and actively opposing them. This was not the product of a blanket condemnation of village life. The proposition that black people were morally and intellectually degraded had been condemned in a papal encyclical of 1839, 'In supremo apostolatus', and the first Vatican Council had opposed the notion that Reason without Faith was incapable of formulating valid moral principles.[11] The missionaries would not have questioned that village culture did contain its own morality had the proposition been put in an abstract way. However, the superficiality and dogmatism of much of their training did not give them the intellectual flexibility to place specific moral issues in a social context. They were no moral relativists. That many priests transcended the limitations and narrowness of their training to develop a human warmth and sensitivity to the life and problems of Africans around them, did not stop their attempting to impose a rigid moral code on Malawian societies.[12]

The nyau was immoral in the priests' minds because of the sexual content of the songs, the appearance of naked dancers in the presence of women, and because they had reason to believe that there were instances of adultery taking place after the performances.[13] They were aware of the fact that throughout the performance the dancers were obliged to observe complete sexual abstinence, a period of five nights. As early as 1909 the White Fathers had gathered details on the nature of the dances and songs and had forbidden catechumens and Christians to participate. The Mua diary has the entry that year:

> This morning the Father-Superior had to go to Makombe to 'excommunicate'[14] two catechumens who have just joined the famous Zinyau society. He discovered that they had left for Blantyre.[15]

This was not the result of an indiscriminate attack on dancing. Whenever possible missionaries went to view the dances themselves or obtained detailed information from their catechists about what went on at certain ceremonies. New converts, eager to reject the past, often gave them highly coloured testimonies, but slowly a solid body of fairly accurate knowledge grew up and was available to new missionaries. Dances that took place during the day, without any mixing of the sexes, were viewed favourably. The initial reaction of the priests to the nyau should be seen, therefore, more in the context of a mild

Jansenist prudery than in the sense of premeditated cultural imperialism. It was an attitude as typical of country priests in Ireland and Italy as of Catholic missionaries in Nyasaland. When gramophones and modern dancing in western style began appearing in villages for the first time in the 1930s the Fathers were even more disapproving.

> Really, the old native dances that had to be banned in the name of morality seem like a vicarage tea-party to these imitations of western civilization.[16]

The nyau societies were already geared to becoming an important force in opposing missionary influence in the villages by the middle of the war. The combination of labour migration, the breakdown of large villages, the return of soldiers from the front who were greeted as heroes because they had a little money,[17] and the increased powers of District Commissioners after the 1912 ordinance, had eroded the authority of traditional chiefs and headmen. Although the price of *mzinda* might amount to twenty goats, headmen were coming back from the war with the equivalent in cash, or were able to earn it in a two-year period at the mines. The number of *mzinda* increased and Chewa chiefs like Dzoole, Matanda, and Mkanda, lost control of them.[18] The hierarchical structure of village life began to disintegrate as personal wealth became no longer the prerogative of the chiefs.[19]

The older style of village life in which seniority was all important was lamented by older people. It was widely felt that young people no longer respected their elders.[20] From the reports of District Commissioners there was more to this than the habitual complaints of the old about the young.

> (Youths) have of recent years evinced an inclination to emancipate themselves from the disciplinary responsibilities of village life and obedience to authority, and to adopt habits prejudicial to native family life.[21]

But being illiterate,[22] the connection between their subjective feelings that things were falling apart, and the overall political context of the European presence in Southern and Central Africa, could never be made by traditionalists. Instead their resentment was directed at the one tangible and constant feature of European rule, the missions and their network of schools. The trouble lay, for hundreds of villagers, with the priests and their bush prayer-houses. Not unreasonably the nyau set about combating them.

The initial response of the nyau to Catholicism was the absorption into the cult of the key religious figures of St. Peter, St. Joseph, and the Virgin Mary. Masks were invented which held these important Catholic figures up to ridicule and began to appear with increasing frequency at performances. 'Maliya' portrayed a white woman with prominent breasts made of *magwebe*, the fruit of a palm, a very ruddy complexion, and an animal's tail for hair; the dancer would appear with an imitation baby. As the mask 'Josephe' was being danced the accompanying song made allusion to the doctrine of the Virgin Birth. It was a common nyau song that normally referred to the test of manhood undergone by a girl's fiancé after her first initiation rites. 'Wagona, wagona, wagona ndi gojo—

She slept, slept, slept with an impotent man.'[23] 'Christian' masks were kept as request items that required extra payment to the dancers.

This assimilation of alien elements into the nyau is not without precedent. The Mang'anja wear masks with long flowing garments attached which may have resulted from contact with Arabs on the Zambesi.[24] One of their animal structures can be little other than an imitation of a Portuguese cavalry horse.[25] In the 1920s there were reports from the Central Region of masks depicting the Governor of Nyasaland and the King of England.[26] District Commissioners were very often portrayed. At Mua the mask for the District Commissioner was known as *kanioni*, a corruption of the name of the wartime Resident, Mr. Kenyon-Slaney, whose devotion to duty was not appreciated by the Chewa.[27]

The more radical change in the nyau after the war was the mounting of a campaign to enrol school-age children into the societies. The pre-war and certainly very ancient regulation was that the boys had to be adult, or at least well past puberty, before they were eligible for initiation.[28] The waiving of this regulation was a deliberate attack on the mission schools. Unlike the passive return to *mwabvi* taking, the nyau societies took positive action against the influence of missionaries and catechists.

Missions in the Central Region began to feel the pressure by the early 1920s and complaints began to pile up on the desk of the Provincial Commissioner in Lilongwe. Even though he could not share the missionaries' alarm he was ready to admit that the nyau was changing its regulations.

There is no doubt that the 'Vinyau' has of late years entirely altered its character. Originally no women[29] or children were allowed to belong to the society . . . now, however, women and children are encouraged if not forced to join and it has turned into a kind of secret society.[30]

Likuni was naturally the first mission to register a serious decline in school attendances; eighty out of one hundred and forty-six of the schools were affected and Father Louis Villy was complaining that in all but three of the schools the nyau were a nuisance. Table IV shows the decline that had set in at the four worst schools.

TABLE IV[31]

Village	Average no. of attendances each year		
	1917	*1921*	*1922*
Mbingwa	76	87	25
Buluzi	78	9	Closed
Msewa	44	—	0
Santi	56	14	0

The drop from 254 pupils to 25 in the space of five years was entirely the result of nyau pressure. The rapid decline in 1922 was the response to an official denial by Bishop Guillemé of rumours that he was about to allow nyau members to be baptized. By 1930 as a result of changes in education policy in the Protectorate[32] the number of schools around Likuni had been reduced to eighteen serving a total of forty-eight villages. From 30 per cent of the villages not a single child went to school. The average number of pupils registered in these schools was thirty-seven but these children only gave an average attendance of seven.[33] At Bembeke where there were Ngoni and Chewa under chiefs Masasa and Kasumbu respectively, there was a 70 per cent attendance in the villages without nyau and an average of forty-nine students registered in the schools. In the schools serving the twenty-nine villages which danced nyau there was only 35 per cent attendance and an average of only twenty-nine students registered per school.[34] The nyau villages were, of course, in the Chewa area under Kasumbu.

The reaction of the missionaries to the nyau's aggressive tactics was a mixture of frustration and repression. In May 1918, Father Chateauvert was trying to play the harmonium during Benediction but was unable to make the music heard for the sound of nyau drums outside Mua Church. He rushed out on to the *mzinda* and pushing aside some women slashed the drums with his knife. The next day the Ngoni regentess, Nyathei, wrote to the Boma demanding compensation for the drums. The resident, Aplin, fined the priest thirty shillings and ordered him to pay their owner ten shillings compensation.[35] It was a humiliating defeat for the Mua missionaries and the nyau started up in force all over the district.[36]

Although the initial response was invariably to lash out, it was soon tempered by the realization that the nyau societies were far more than immoral dancers to be condemned from the pulpit. The White Fathers set about studying the societies with varying degrees of acumen and objectivity. Fathers Braire, Roy, and Denis all put their observations on paper and their notes are an eloquent testimony to their intimacy with village life.[37] The nyau's attempt to de-activate the mission schools could not be countered by violence since intimidation was one of the main weapons of the societies themselves. In any case the British Residents were unwilling to countenance brawls between catechists and dancers in their district.

Aplin's attitude in the Mua dispute was typical of that taken by the Government when the clash with the missions became sufficiently serious to reach a national level in the 1920s. While the Government's desire to maintain 'native culture' and avoid detribalization was mindful of the political advantage of a compliant peasantry, it was backed also by the sincere liberal conviction that every man had the right to order his own life. The Protectorate administration had in the past suffered the justifiable protests of missionaries about tax collection and labour migration. The nyau issue gave them the opportunity to turn the tables and to act as the protectors of African interests from missionary encroachment.

The Catholic missionaries found it very hard to take competition in the field of moralism. If there is an 'infantile disease' of liberalism it is self-righteousness; the priests found the smugness of some of the District Commissioners infuriating.

The discussion was soon off the ground. In short we had just come here to bother the blacks and we ought to just leave them in peace. A negro who goes around dancing naked in front of men and women is no danger to them morally because they are accustomed to it. Polygamy is a good thing because human nature demands it. The conversation went on until 11 p.m.; it was very icy and interspersed with long silences. Fr. Villy brought it to a close by saying to the Father in French: 'Go on, tell him to stop talking such twaddle. What on earth is the point of arguing with a fellow like that. Let's go to bed.' Mr. Foster understood every word so that was the end of that little session.[38]

Their aggravation was compounded by the knowledge that the District Commissioners lacked their detailed information about events in the villages. In the wave of poison ordeals after the war more than twenty villagers had died in the Mua region and the missionaries had interpreted the District Commissioner's refusal to intervene as sheer laziness.[39] In one instance two people had died of *mwabvi* in the village where the District Commissioner was camping without his knowing.[40] Usually, though, the Residents discovered a percentage of the deaths but were unable to prosecute for lack of evidence.

Part of the reluctance of the District Commissioners to involve themselves in nyau cases was simple expediency. The average length of time spent by a District Commissioner in one Boma after the war was eighteen months to two years.[41] They had to administer large and densely populated areas with a continual to and fro resulting from the need to find paid work. Tax collection, encouraging cash cropping, judging cases, consumed most of their time. If missionaries living in the closest possible contact with the villages had to listen to nyau drums under their window, it was improbable that the constantly changing Government officers would be able to combat a cult that operated in villages that they perhaps only visited once a year.[42] Even had they agreed to ban the societies as the priests wanted, it would have been almost impossible to enforce the ruling against widespread opposition.

Since it was rare for District Commissioners to be able to build up any detailed knowledge of their districts beyond the annual maize production, when enquiries into the nyau began to be carried out by Government officers after 1922 an extraordinary mass of undigested information began pouring into the Zomba Secretariat. The difficulty facing the District Commissioners was that they were studying an institution that was changing virtually while they watched. Dr. Sanderson, the medical officer at Dedza, and the very influential R. H. Murray, Provincial Commissioner in Lilongwe from 1927 to 1930, held that the nyau was an extension of *chinamwali* and a form of initiation rite for boys. Hodgson at Dowa, who had some anthropological training, guessed that it was a degenerate religious institution.[43]

Another problem in assessing the Residents' reports on the dances is that they had probably been treated to expurgated versions. As Villy remarked, anyone who imagined that the real nyau would be put on as a public performance for Europeans must be 'rather simple indeed'.[44] The assurance with which several of the colonial officers pontificated about an institution of which they knew very little earned them the disdain of many missionaries.

Between you and me, the DC's are the most frightful nitwits. As long as they get their *msonko*[45] and you don't get yourself killed, all they ask is to be left alone. They have no way of finding out what is going on. How can you expect them to know anything when they are changed so often.[46]

The only systematic study of the nyau to reach the Government came from a Dutch Reformed missionary, Rev. J. Jackson, in February 1924. He also connected the dances with *chinamwali* and presented them as a form of carnival association that had grown into a secret society. As a result of the different reports the official understanding of the nyau was that the cult was a type of initiation rite that had been originally for girls and was now extended to include boys.

R. H. Murray, who was the main protagonist of this view, disliked missionaries in general and the Dutch Reformed in particular. Presiding over the many inter-mission skirmishes in the Central Region his feelings were understandable.[47] Although the Catholics assumed that the fact he was a Freemason automatically made him anti-clerical, his most biting comments were reserved for Protestant ministers.[48]

> The Low Church missions . . . wish not only to induce Government to attempt the impossible task of making the Native moral by legislation, but claim the right to define morality.[49]

More than any other Government officer Murray cast himself in the role of spokesman for—what he took to be—inarticulate Africans assailed on all sides by the legions of Puritanism.[50] It was his views and recommendations that were accepted by Zomba, and Government policy towards the nyau-mission dispute can be largely attributed to him.

By 1924, the missions' attempts to get nyau banned piecemeal, district by district, had given way to a more concerted effort at the national level. The approaches were initially made through Green, the Provincial Commissioner at Lilongwe. The priests at Likuni pleaded their case with him for a complete suppression of the nyau throughout the Protectorate. They had before them the example of Northern Rhodesia where the administrators of the British South Africa Company had at the beginning of the century, unsolicited by missionaries, banned the nyau for repeated breaches of the peace.[51] Missionaries at Kachebere had been complaining ever since that whole Chewa villages had been moving across the border into Nyasaland where they could dance legally. Bishop Guillemé, thoroughly exasperated by being ignored by the Phelps–Stokes Commission,[52] wrote to Lilongwe in May 1924, describing the nyau in unusually immoderate language as 'a secret society the first purpose of which is lubricity and robbery by performing a dance ceremony for the dead'.[53] The Government reply was to request more information about the societies in lieu of concrete action.

The weakness of the Catholic campaign in the 1920s was that the complaints never settled on one issue to pursue it to the bitter end. They ranged over such points as the violence that occurred during and before the performances, their obscenity, the nyau interdict on children attending school, and the potential security risk of secret societies to colonial rule. The administration were able to counter the points one by one; they wanted detailed evidence of violence, ignored a threat of sedition which they well knew to be unfounded, and philosophized about the concept of obscenity.[54] The alleged interference with Africans who did not want to participate in the dances, and the possible effects of night dancing on education, were taken more seriously. A directive was sent to District Commissioners telling them to inform villagers that the convenience and freedom of natives who did not participate in the nyau was the responsibility of the headmen.[55] In reply to the accusations that schoolchildren were being stopped from going to school District Commissioners were asked to make sure that it was the children who refused to attend school and not the teacher who refused the children.[56]

The 1924 District Administrative Ordinance, which fully recognized village and sectional courts, allowed the Government to transfer the responsibility for nyau back to the villages. Since the headmen who were supposed to decide on the nuisance issue were usually prominent nyau members themselves the Government directives were either naïve or a deliberate refusal to listen to the missionaries. The latter were reduced to bringing charges of assault or breach of the peace, but always found it difficult to get villagers to come forward and testify in court. The nyau was increasingly able to intimidate Christians and the priests could give them no protection. The missionaries' policy of bringing every possible infringement of the law to litigation was skilfully manipulated by Ngoni chiefs like Kachindamoto[57] and frayed the nerves of District Officers.

By the end of 1927 incidents between Christians and nyau members had increased alarmingly in number and gravity. Zealous catechists were contesting the admission of children to the dances and spending time during their lessons in denouncing the cult as superstition. The growing numbers of uninitiated villagers were a constant reminder to the nyau of their losses to the mission. Dissension broke out in houses where only one member of the family was initiated and Christian husbands were forced to stay in their huts while their wives were bullied into attending the dances.[58] Pressures had built up sufficiently in Matanda's area around Likuni mission for Christian families to be moving out of nyau villages. On the other hand there were two cases reported of the killing of nyau members by Christians, in one instance, when they had insisted at dancing during the funeral of a Christian's mother.[59]

Likuni mission with its fiery Canadian Father-Superior, Father David Roy, was at the centre of the conflict. In May 1928 some catechists captured the sacred nyau masks after a performance and the Provincial Commissioner at Lilongwe, R. H. Murray, threatened to prosecute the mission if they were not returned. The nyau took the law into their own hands and burnt down two prayer-houses and set a trap to topple one of the Likuni missionaries from his bicycle as he went on his rounds.[60] Despite his Quebec English, Roy was more than a match for R. H. Murray.

If it becomes a question of morality and civilization we wonder to see such a sudden love of native customs by people whom we thought did not care so much for these things. For example the Government has taken the property of the land [*sic*] from the natives—their most cherished possession; they have forbidden slave trading, *mwabvi* drinking, made game laws, reserved many trees, put [*sic*] the hut tax and given the country other Principal Headmen.[61]

It was because of forthright letters of this type that Father Roy became the first casualty of the nyau war of attrition. Within a month the Governor was pressing Monsignor Hinsley, the Apostolic Delegate, for Roy's removal. Whatever Guillemé's private feelings on the matter—and Roy's only offence that distinguished him from other White Fathers was to wield the pen to as much effect as his opponent[62]—Hinsley's directive, 'correct the imprudence but do not quench the zeal', resulted in the Canadian's departure to the quieter waters of Lake Bangwelo.[63]

Since it was apparent that frontal assaults on the administration by missionaries had negligible results, the Dutch Reformed and Roman Catholic Missions changed their tactics and began sending deputations of African teachers and chiefs to Lilongwe. The Dutch Reformed gathered together an impressive group to visit Lilongwe in October 1927 consisting of the Yao chief, Ndindi, and the Ngoni paramount, Gomani, along with two other Ngoni chiefs, Jere and Chiwere, together with mission teachers and some token pagans. They made the case to the Government officers that the degree of intimidation and coercion had reached unacceptable levels. They pointed out that the nyau was being danced at the funeral of any villager who could pay for it while in the past only the most important chiefs were given the honour.[64] This alleged chiefly monopoly was probably never true but it was a genuine expression of the chiefs' anxiety at the proliferation of the societies beyond their control.

R. H. Murray succeeded in keeping the anti-nyau lobby at bay for a few more months. The Christian complaint about obscenity in the nyau had annoyed him since he saw the issue in terms of an educational technique in an initiation rite. The mission teachers knew from experience that it was not educational but were unable, quite naturally, to talk in sophisticated terms about the resolution of social conflict in a Chewa matrilineage. Murray had reached the conclusion that the basis of the nyau hostility to the missions was the fear that the bush schools taught children to despise their elders. He saw the way round the difficulties to be the invention of a Christian initiation rite and an increased appreciation on the Christian side of the non-formal education of village culture. Since the problem was not the clash between old and new pedagogy, or Christian and pagan initiation rites, but a more profound opposition of two religious systems, the Provincial Commissioner's solutions were not surprisingly widely misinterpreted. Most people came away from a Council Meeting of chiefs at Lilongwe in the beginning of 1928 firmly convinced that Murray had advocated the initiation of all children irrespective of religion.[65] The Likuni mission teachers wrote a shocked letter to the Governor and it was clear that the nyau issue would eventually have to be resolved in Zomba.

After complaints had been made by the Dedza Planters' Association, who were frightened that excessive night dancing might reduce the availability and efficiency of their labour, the issue reached the press. An article on the societies appearing in a November issue of the *Nyasaland Times* was an amalgam of the Dutch Reformed and Government positions; it dwelt on the impossibility of banning the societies and was characterized by the kind of bland urbanity that was calculated to enrage the Catholic missionaries:

Chinyawo, as now practised seems to bear an extraordinary resemblance to something well-known in many lands . . . as 'carnival'.[66]

Father Ernest Paradis' reply to this was an emotive article in the May 1929 edition of the periodical *East Africa* entitled 'Devil Dancers of Terror' in which he gave details of the abuses that went on during the dances.[67] He had written a more moderate plea for prohibition of the societies in a January edition of the *Nyasaland Times*[68] in which he had hinted at the possibly seditious nature of such secret societies. There was also talk of an appeal direct to Rome and London, but Hinsley quickly quashed the idea; he did not relish a head-on collision with the Colonial Office after all his careful building up of good-will.

The climax to the nyau debate came in a speech from the Governor to the Legislative Council at Zomba on 29 April 1929. It was a strong repudiation of the missionaries' accusations and reiterated the Government's position for the benefit of the Colonial Office in London.

Government has not itself been able to obtain any evidence which would justify the suppression of Vinyau or the prosecution of any members of that society . . . They (the Chewa chiefs at Lilongwe) said that they could see no reason why because they were not Christians they should be accused of doing things that no decent native would think of.[69]

When the Governor took the floor in the Legislative Council he could not plead ignorance of the societies' nature. He had at his disposal considerably more anthropological data than at the beginning of the disputes. Hodgson at Dowa believed that the evidence for 'totemism and re-incarnation' in the cult was overwhelming and accurately assessed that the masks represented 'the re-incarnated spirits of the dead'.[70] Another Resident, O'Brien at Liwonde, suggested that *mpingu*, the demand for sexual abstinence throughout performances, was breaking down because people travelled from villages distant from a *mzinda* to watch the dances and thereby gained a certain anonymity.

O'Brien suffered from the initiation/education fallacy but his suggestions for reforming the nyau were sensible and later adopted in the Central Region.

We should seek out the tribal authorities and give them back the power of supervision over these ceremonies, concentrating initiations and using our influence upon these chiefs to elevate the standards of instruction given.[71]

As a result of a meeting of chiefs in Lilongwe under Murray's chairmanship a set of regulations was drawn up for the owners of *mzinda*. It was an important document in that the Banda chiefs were attempting to exercise some central control over the societies and bring back their pre-war discipline. Women and pre-pubertal boys were forbidden to participate, and the dancers forbidden to demand presents. Mission and Government interests were safeguarded in the injunction that effigies were to be of animals and not of men, paths and roads were to be kept clear, and all accidents or fights reported to the Boma.[72] Since the latter instruction would have undermined the juridical autonomy of the societies it was unlikely to be heeded.[73] The chiefs finally insisted on the taboo on sexual intercourse being properly observed; in this directive, at least, the chiefs were taking the role of religious reformers.

It was difficult, however, for the Government to issue a simple directive that Principal Headmen should be the final arbiters of whether nyau dances were being conducted properly and should be allowed to continue. Murray would have liked to return the nyau to the few Chewa Principal Headmen but since most chiefs were Yao or Ngoni this would have led to a ban on nyau in all but the most staunch Chewa districts.[74] The final Government circular to be sent out gave power over the nyau to village rather than Principal Headmen thereby negating their main aim of centralizing control of the societies and boosting the power of the few Chewa chiefs. Not even Murray's ultra-British concern for the underdog could reverse the consequences of Yao and Ngoni colonization in the nineteenth century. The nyau remained where it had always been, in the hands of minor sub-chiefs.

From the point of view of effective legislation the final Government position was ludicrous. It suffered from the perennial defect of Protectorate executive action, taking away with one hand what it gave with the other. The Government had tackled a problem that grew out of the control of the nyau by minor headmen and had responded to it by placing the responsibility firmly in the same men's hands.

> Whenever such spontaneous complaints based upon a real desire for specific action are received, administrative officers should inform headmen that the remedy lies in their own hands.[75]

After eight years of investigations, reports, invective, and memoranda, the nyau dispute was back where it started from.

Once the Government had been through the motions required of Indirect Rulers, R. H. Murray made a last bid to salvage some sort of a truce in the Central Region. On 25 September 1929 a conference of Dutch Reformed teachers and missionaries met with nyau leaders at his house in Lilongwe. The nyau leaders reiterated their old complaints that the Christian catechists divulged the nyau secrets to school children and encouraged disrespect.[76]

> We Achewa cannot allow our customs to disappear. They are the precious legacy of our ancestors. We hold to them as sacred things. If they hold their tongues and do not divulge our secrets they will be left in peace.[77]

The one result of the conference was that the Dutch Reformed teachers promised to respect the secret vocabulary and songs of the nyau. Murray, donning the mantle of *pedagogus universalis* ended the meeting by delivering homilies to all present.

You Christians, I would ask you to remember that the price you will pay for failure to reach an understanding is the de-tribalisation of yourselves and your children. How great a price this is you will probably hardly realise.[78]

Guillemé was visited by the Governor later in the year to patch up the quarrel and the two big missions in the Central Region called off their campaign. Both Dutch Reformed and Catholics had been defeated by 'Holy Liberalism'.

The Catholic priests were neither willing, nor able in conscience, to come to terms with the nyau and the confrontation continued at village level, resulting in countless *milandu*.[79] The clash came between the transition rites of the two religious systems. After a life-time of mission influence it was rare to find even the hardiest of nyau members courageous enough to turn away the catechist who appeared at his bedside. Once baptized the mission was able to claim the body for a Christian burial while the nyau was equally determined to bury the corpse according to custom with dances. Since the mortuary rites were the principal occasion for dancing nyau the societies were seriously threatened by the Catholic practice of baptizing *in articulo mortis*.

The macabre squabbles over corpses that took place were in earnest as both parties believed that the fate of the man's spirit hung in the balance. The nyau came to take active precautions of hiding their dying members in the bush in case a catechist or priest found them and succeeded in inducing a death-bed conversion.[80] It was the firm belief of priests and catechists alike that a man's eternal destiny lay in their hands in the last moments before his death. The Father would often speak of the Merciful God whom the nyau were said to have offended but there were also more Joycean methods of inducing contrition if this failed.

With the development of the Legion of Mary[81] in the 1940s the mission had a powerful group of lay Catholics to protect funerals and oppose the nyau in the villages. Women in the Legion were occasionally assaulted by nyau members and the legionaries often had to resort to violence to keep the dancers at bay. The following description of a Christian funeral gives some idea of the intensity of feelings involved.

> Catechists and Agurupa spent all day in the hut singing canticles and reciting the Rosary. The night was spent in prayer with everyone on the watch. The next day the men of Catholic Action were filled with resolution and the cortège set off. As the procession crossed the *bwalo* where they held their bacchanalia an attempt was made to force the cortège on to the *mzinda*. 'We'll not let that happen,' said Peter Kalilombe[82] who was in the lead. Juvenale made a grab at the mat[83] but a good punch knocked him for six; he rolled around on the ground howling all the while. The canticles for the dead redoubled in volume and the cortège went on, followed by all the fanatics in a fine rage, gritting their teeth with anger.[84]

Since the nyau did not attempt to initiate Christian girls forcibly during this period, the female initiation rites remained a pagan ceremony without too much friction with the mission over the dances. The occasions for dancing nyau in the

Mua area were increased by a one-night performance called the *gule wa mizimu*, the dance of the spirits, in which a dancer would perform at the grave of a deceased relative who had recurrently appeared in dreams. This seems to have acted as a substitute for possession cults which were absent in the district, and enabled the nyau to make up for their losses to Christian burials.

The timing of the beginning of the struggle between Catholic missions and nyau societies bore some relation to the length of time the missionaries had been active in a district. For example, in the Central Region the clash came about eighteen years after the foundation of the Catholic missions, in the 1920s when systematic punishment of tax defaulters got under way. In the Lower Shire Valley where Chikwawa, the first Catholic station, was only founded in 1918 there was an almost identical time-lag. It was correlated in both districts with the growth to maturity of a generation of young men who could not remember a time when the mission was not influential in the affairs of the neighbourhood. It was the fate of these men that was being contested in each area.

It was on the Feast of the Immaculate Conception, in December 1935, one of the hottest months of the year, that two Montforts, Kerrec and Heraud, threw caution to the winds and belaboured a group of nyau dancers with clubs and sticks. The nyau had been deliberately provocative and were dancing to rival the Catholic festival.[85] The following week the mission suffered a near-revolt from its catechists who refused to continue teaching. The leader of the protest was William Chafulumira, the head catechist and an articulate traditionalist who was later to become an author. After persistent pressure on the Boma from the priests the nyau was finally banned in the district in May 1936. The strength of the nyau in the area could be judged from the reaction.

> General fury even amongst the Christians. A visit from Father Kerrec to Karvalo, an Ngoni from Ndalanda,[86] has made him realize how bitter the banning has made people.[87]

Three days later the nyau at the village of the Kololo chief, Kasisi, retaliated by snatching the body of a young Christian before burial and performed dances around it. The ban was simply ignored and dances started up again around the mission. Unlike the situation in the Central Region the *corpus christianum* was not sufficiently strong to pit Christian against traditionalist.

> All, both Christians and pagans have put up a solid front to save the nyau and its leader Kasisi. Out of sixty Christians only three put up any resistance whatsoever.[88]

In those areas of the Lower Shire Valley unaffected by Sena migration conditions were ideal for the nyau. In contrast with the Central Region, the missionaries could not enlist the support of powerful Ngoni chiefs to combat the dances. Statistics for nyau membership collected in 1966 gave 105 active societies in the Lower Shire Valley with a total membership of 5,000. Many of these were in the Kololo chieftancies; the average membership at Masseah's was 400, at Makwira's 721, at Katunga's 809, with Kasisi as the leading promoter with 1,241. The two Mang'anja chieftancies of Lundu and Chapananga averaged 1,072 and 927 members respectively, while at Chief Ngabu's the patri-lineal Sena had wiped out the societies.[89] The intense heat from November to March, and mosquitoes from the swamps along the river, reduced European settlement to a minimum. Both Kololo and Mang'anja chiefs at Chikwawa had the same stake in traditional life so the missionaries faced implacable opposition from all sections of society. Within a few years of their first confrontation the missionaries resigned themselves to the fact that the nyau societies in the Lower Shire were there to stay. They continued to complain about the effect on their schools but, lacking the support of their own Christian congregations and any great local interest in Catholic education, were unable to compete in the way that the White Fathers further north could do.

Throughout the Chewa-speaking areas of colonial Malawi the nyau resisted the missions until Independence, when a performance on the steps of Mua Church symbolized their victory over the Catholics. In one sense their triumph was warranted; they had withstood the pressures of both Ngoni and European missionaries for over sixty years. None the less the Independence movement owed nothing to the nyau. Nyau members could neither read nor write and were interested only in village politics.[90] As societies, rather than individuals, they played no part in early nationalist movements like the Nyasaland African Congress.[91] This was not for want of contact; letters from the Congress were reaching Ntaka-taka as early as 1947 and the Ngoni chief Samson Kachindamoto was a supporter.[92] The societies were the refuge for traditionalists who were unwilling or unable to rise in the mission élites and lower-paid posts in the colonial administration.

As a result of accommodation to the European presence much of the religious significance of the nyau had been lost even before the First World War. By the 1920s financial interest had become an important factor for dancers, alienating many non-active members.[93] The charge for a performance today can range from ten shillings to £3 plus a goat. Since the quality of the performances and of the masks produced is a subjective judgement, haggling can arise over the price and dances can even be stopped through disputes over money.[94] The societies had to compete with men returning from the mines with money and as the cash economy became daily more of a reality for isolated villages,[95] the dancers began to raise their prices from the traditional chicken. Ex-soldiers who came back from the war disillusioned with what Western civilization had to offer, but unwilling to return to being underdog in their wives' village, joined the societies in droves, so increasing the level of violence associated with the performances.

The degeneration in the life of the societies in the colonial period represented a partial acceptance of the Western definition of value and status, coupled with a paradoxical refusal to enter fully into Western institutions. It could only be placed at the door of the missions inasmuch as elementary education stimulated in villagers ambitions and goals which could not be fully realized within traditional society. Where these ambitions were less intense, as in the Lower Shire Valley, a 'purer' form of nyau survived. The Catholic missions affected the nyau directly by decreasing the number of chinamwali ceremonies and increasing the number of Christian burials. The response was to diversify the occasions on which nyau might be performed and to recruit members from lower age groups.

The nyau opposition to bush schools was misguided in that it failed to see the schools as trivial when placed in the context of labour migration, tax collection, and the economic demands of colonialism beyond the borders of Nyasaland. The schools were only minor agents of disruption against this background of an already disrupted traditional society. The Protectorate administration had reason to be grateful that the nyau's attack was directed at missionaries and their employees rather than Government officers and Boma police. The societies were given the most sympathetic treatment of any indigenous institution in Nyasaland, even being called upon by the Government to dance at the Queen's Birthday.[96] However much they might seek to reduce its local impact and moderate its worst effects the Government officers were part of a system that in the final analysis exploited Malawian villagers for the profits of colonialism in Southern-Central Africa. The bush schools were the portal, not to the Church as Cardinal Hinsley would have it,[97] but to the consumer society; they produced in a small measure the expectations that fed villagers into a capitalist economy[98] and drove men into the mine compounds in search of radios and gramophones. In this sense the nyau attack centred on the mission schools was on target.

Intelligent men like O'Brien were convinced that the insertion of Africa into a world economy would destroy institutions like the nyau.

> The Dzinyao must go with the march of progress, but its elimination must be gradual through gaining the native's confidence and his faith in our better institutions, which he will not fail to adopt of his own accord in substitution for his own primitive methods the moment that confidence is established.[99]

The gap between the self-image of the colonial administrators and the view of the *Pax Britannica* held by most Africans in the Protectorate never closed in the subsequent half-century. The nyau cult did, of course, change as villagers responded to European rule but from being the greatest storehouse of religious symbols and most elaborate ceremony of the Chewa people to being a secret organization bent on intimidating those trying to reject the past. The growth of secondary education and the rise of the Protestant Mission élite left the nyau behind in the villages. But it did not destroy its appeal to the mass of peasants in Chewa areas who saw in it an assertion of their identity against the Ngoni and European colonists. For the Catholic missions who concentrated on the evangelization of these peasants it remained an insuperable obstacle to their attempts at building a *corpus christianum*.[100]

REFERENCES TO CHAPTER VI

[1] Likuni teachers to Governor 4 September 1928. Trans. ChiChewa. White Fathers' Archives, Lilongwe.

[2] R. H. Murray. This was contained in a paper prepared for the Nyau-Mission Conference of 25 September 1929. The paragraph was deleted on objections from Rev. W. H. Murray—see a letter of 3 September 1929. NC 1/21/2 National Archives, Zomba.

[3] Rev. Dr. J. M. Schoffeleers who has studied the societies in the Lower Shire Valley suggests that they were taken by the Bantu from hunting rituals of the bushman-type culture in Malawi or the Congo. Similar figures of men wearing animal structures occur in bushmen cave paintings in South Africa.

[4] Oral Testimony, Kambambe, shrine official at the Msinja shrine, interviewed with Makewana in the Lilongwe Land Development Scheme, May 1971. Both Ntara and Rangeley record the tradition that the prophetess Makewana's attendants, *matsano*, were drowned during their initiation rites in the sacred pool of 'Malawi' and that henceforth nyau dancers were banned from the region of the shrine and the chieftancy of Chadza, the Phiri chief in charge of the shrine. In Kambambe's testimony it was stated that the drowning was caused by the nyau.

[5] *Mzinda* originally meant 'town'—see Gamitto *King Kazembe* 68, 77

[6] The fullest account of the nyau with bibliography is contained in Schoffeleers J. M. *Symbolic and Social Aspects of Spirit Worship among the Mang'anja* Doctoral Dissertation, University of Oxford 1968. His analysis of the social functional aspects of the societies leans heavily on Evans-Pritchard's treatment of obscenity.

[7] Schoffeleers *Symbolic and Social Aspects* 341. Oral testimony of a Mang'anja headman. 'You cannot arrest and punish an animal which has hurt you because what it did was pure accident. There is no case because there is no accused.' This was the justification for the special nyau court.

[8] ibid. 320

[9] Interviews undertaken in collaboration with Mr. Bill Rau of U.C.L.A. (University of California, Los Angeles) around Chipata in the area of the Fort Jameson Ngoni, and at Kandeu, Chief Gania's, on the end edge of the old Maseko paramountcy.

[10] Murray *Handbook of Nyasaland* 25

[11] Kieran J. A. 'Some Roman Catholic Missionary Attitudes to Africans in the 19th century' *Race* X 3, 1969, 341–59. The Vatican Council's statement was directed against the fideist position and from it followed the conclusion that the principles on which African societies worked *could* enshrine basic moral tenets.

[12] The theology of the seminary manuals came from a low-water mark of Catholic thinking. Fr. Louis Bouyer describes the Catholic intellectual climate in the 1840s. 'The faith of the man in the street, based on the most fantastic apologetics, the most extravagant philosophising, was practically all there was to be discovered under this name . . . The Jesuit Perrone—he and his like—who had retained, or renewed, contact with the sorely decaying scholastic tradition, would have furnished the only example of a catholic thinker who was not an amateur.' Bouyer L. *Newman. His Life and Spirituality* London 1958, 247. The only solid philosophy learnt would have been scholasticism with its view of a relative Natural Law informed by Revelation.

[13] Paradis E. 'Accusations against the Vinyau' April 1929 NC 1/21/1 and Personal communication. Bishop J. Fady W.F.

[14] 'Excommunicate' would have meant the imposition of a public penance—a common punishment was exclusion from the sacraments for two months

[15] Mua Diary 19 April 1909

[16] *Rapports annuels* 1933–4 Bembeke 473–4

[17] There was also the genuine relief that someone came back alive. A touching entry in the Mua Diary in December 1917 describes the return of Father Paradis on leave. 'That evening and for the rest of the week there was a procession from all the villages to see the Bwana who had come back from the war. He received at least fifty chickens.'

[18] Dzoole belongs to the Mwale clan, Matanda is Banda, both from the Lilongwe district, while Mkanda has one of the few Mbewe clan chieftancies in Malawi and lives at Mchinji on the Zambian border.

[19] The changing importance of the cash economy can be judged from the different observa-

tions made in 1903 and in 1927. Father Alfred Honoré w.f. wrote in 1903: 'We made these purchases by means of exchange articles worth £2 since money has no currency amongst the natives ... The people will only accept money to pay their tax ... When you do see money it is shillings. Any other coins will be refused by the natives. For them the hut tax is three shilling pieces and not two shilling pieces and two sixpences.' Personal Diary Alfred Honoré w.f., February and May 1903. R. H. Murray in his labour report for 1927 wrote that nothing has impressed on him more the demand for money that existed among the natives than their readiness to work in a half-nourished condition if thereby they could obtain a few extra coppers. Such a state of affairs was quite a modern development S1/428/27.

[20] Even as early as 1904 Alfred Sharpe was writing that the authority of the chiefs had diminished: 'At the present day when chiefs are not allowed to use any of their old methods, the people formerly subject to them often refuse to obey or take any notice of their direction'. Colonial Reports. B.C.A. Protectorate 1904–5 Cmd. 2684 London H.M.S.O. quoted in Barnekov *An enquiry* 45–6.

[21] Annual Report B.C.A. Protectorate 1912–13 Cmd. 7050 London H.M.S.O.

[22] See Chapter VII for details of literacy amongst nyau members

[23] Jackson J. 'Description of the Chinyao Dance, Central Province, Nyasaland 1929. MS Afr. 556 Rhodes House Library, Oxford, and Braire to Paradis 26 March 1929. White Fathers Archives, Lilongwe, and Schoffeleers *Symbolic and Social Aspects* 362.

[24] This compares strikingly with the almost naked Chewa dancers who appear with their bodies daubed with clay and a few feathers. *Akapoli* which imitate the ostrich and herald the dancers are naked in the Central Region.

[25] From a collection of colour slides of nyau figures in the possession of Rev. Dr. J. M. Schoffeleers.

[26] NC 1/21/2

[27] Mua Diary September 1945

[28] Stannus H. S. 'Notes on some tribes of British Central Africa' *J. Royal Anthropological Institute* Vol. XL 1910 'Children are carefully excluded' 334.

[29] Only a few old women known as *namkhungwi* were allowed to associate with the dancers, bringing them food to the *dambwe* where the masks were made.

[30] Acting Provincial Commissioner at Lilongwe to Zomba secretariat, 23 June 1922 NC 1/21/2

[31] Report from Villy to PC Lilongwe, August 1922. White Fathers' Archives, Lilongwe.

[32] A severe cut-back in the number of bush schools/prayer-houses was demanded by the Government in 1927. See Chapter VII.

[33] From reports on schools sent to Bishop Guillemé in 1930. White Fathers' Archives, Lilongwe.

[34] ibid. Kasumbu is a good example of an independent Chewa chief. He survived the Ngoni raids by siting his village on top of Dedza mountain and was very reluctant to accept a Catholic school when first approached in 1907. Personal Diary of Alfred Honoré w.f. 18 September 1907.

[35] Mua Diary May 1918.

[36] ibid.

[37] One such piece of work by Father P. Braire 'Association des danses déguisées' MS 1927 is in the possession of Rev. F. X. Lapointe w.f. while there are also scattered notes in the nyau file at Lilongwe. Most of this material on the nyau has been incorporated into a manuscript book on Malawi by Father Hovington *Angoni, Ayao et Achewa aux bords du lac Nyassa* in several volumes in his possession at Ludzi mission, Malawi.

[38] Mua Diary August 1919

[39] ibid.

[40] Mua Diary July 1921

[41] Provincial Commissioners moved as fast. At Lilongwe there were Green, 1924–6, Murray 1926, Anderson 1927, Murray 1928–9, and Vassal 1930.

[42] Hodgson wrote for example in 1924 that in the absence of an Assistant Resident he was unable to perform even the ordinary work of two men properly. Further it was difficult to suppress secret societies and the tendency was to drive them underground where they might become dangerous NC 1/21/2.

[43] Hodgson to Zomba Secretariat 14 April 1927. S2/23/22.

[44] Villy to Provincial Commissioner 23 June 1922. NC 1/21/2.

[45] Tax

[46] Paradis to Eken 28 December 1928. White Fathers' Archives, Lilongwe.

[47] For details see Chapter VII

[48] The Nyasaland Lodge was connected with the Grand Lodge of Scotland and most of the Nyasaland masons were Colonial Officers. British 'fair-play' usually seems to have got the better of any anti-Catholicism despite the priests' fears of French-style anti-clericalism. S1/2690/22, S1/672/23, S1/275/19.

[49] R. H. Murray to Zomba secretariat May 1927. S2/23/22.

[50] For example R. H. Murray to W. H. Murray 16 June 1929 said that speaking for the pagans, he could state quite definitely that they were only too anxious that their children should be educated S2/23/22.

[51] The District Book for East Luangwa c. 1905 carries details of nyau songs and makes it plain that the reason for banning was the immunity of the nyau from prosecution: 'no-one would ever dare bring a case against the nyau . . . because the nyao are supposed to be spirits'. National Archives Lusaka. I am indebted to Dr. Martin Chanock for finding this information.

[52] The Commission had been in Nyasaland studying education in the previous month but had ignored the White Fathers' and Montfort Missions. See Chapter VII.

[53] Guilleme to Provincial Commissioner, Lilongwe 15 May 1924. White Fathers' Archives, Lilongwe.

[54] NC 1/21/2

[55] Zomba Secretariat to Acting Provincial Commissioner, Lilongwe October 1927. NC 1/21/2

[56] ibid.

[57] See Chapter IX

[58] Braire to Guillemé 10 May 1924, White Fathers' Archives, Lilongwe, for example of this type of intimidation

[59] Anderson to Zomba Secretariat in a covering letter for details of the Dutch Reformed deputation. 13 October 1927. NC 1/21/2.

[60] It is difficult to make out from correspondence what exactly the 'trap' was, possibly a rope across a bush path, or a pit covered with leaves

[61] Roy to Provincial Commissioner Lilongwe 29 June 1928. White Fathers' Archives, Lilongwe.

[62] Roy's letters are scribbled all over in Murray's handwriting and the Provincial Commissioner appears to have been very nettled by them

[63] This was in the same diocese at the time. Roy's parting shot was a most unapologetic apology to Murray in which, referring to the ambush of Father Louis Denis at Likuni, he wrote: 'In such circumstances I thought it was time to speak aloud while yet alive.' Roy to Provincial Commissioner Lilongwe 6 July 1928. White Fathers' Archives, Lilongwe.

[64] The Government treated all such deputations as put-up jobs by the missionaries. Any complaints from the deputation were effectively nullified by a parallel catalogue of Christian misdeeds carefully appended by the Acting Provincial Commissioner. 13 October 1927. NC 1/21/2.

[65] Likuni Mission teachers to Governor 4 September 1928 'At the last meeting . . . the

PC said that . . . anyone who does not follow the customs of forefathers had got no wisdom. Even christians shall be done chinamwali.' A translation probably made by a priest. White Fathers' Archives, Lilongwe.

[66] *Nyasaland Times* 27 November 1928

[67] *East Africa* 14 March 1929, quoted in *Nyasaland Times* 16 April 1929

[68] *Nyasaland Times* 29 January 1929. Paradis wrote another strong article in ChiChewa in the African-language newspaper *Zoona* 28 February 1929.

[69] Reported fully in the *Nyasaland Times* 3 May 1929

[70] Hodgson to Zomba Secretariat 15 April 1927. S2/23/22.

[71] O'Brien to Zomba Secretariat 9 May 1929. NC 1/21/2.

[72] 'Regulations with regard to Vinyao Dance' attached to Government Circular of 27 April 1929. White Fathers' Archives, Lilongwe.

[73] The leading Chewa chiefs who signed the document 'We, the Chiefs of the Achewa tribe', of course, would have been pleased to see a curtailment of the power of minor headmen. They had been pushed into the position of centralized authorities over the Chewa and were behaving accordingly.

[74] By this time R. H. Murray freely admitted that most educated members of the community were opposed to the societies but he had become entrenched in his position and did not want to lose everything in careless wording of the Government's directive.

[75] Acting-Governor W. B. Davidson-Houston to Administrative Officers 27 April 1929. White Fathers' Archives, Lilongwe. Davidson-Houston was an Irish Protestant gentleman from Cork who would have felt at home handling 'reactionary' priests.

[76] R. H. Murray to Zomba Secretariat 27 September 1929. NC 1/21/2.

[77] Report on the conference sent by Roy to Paradis 27 September 1929

[78] Report on conference sent to Zomba Secretariat 25 September 1929. NC 1/21/2.

[79] Plural of *mlandu*, a court case

[80] The Mua Diary gives one instance of a hunt for a dying man, Isofou from Madziansatsi village. 'After dinner and breviary, I went off to Isofou's village, saying the Rosary for him as I went. The head of Catholic Action was right—he had gone . . . I started chatting with people when Herman came up with the news that scarcely had Fidelis Muyeye left when Isofou's brothers ran off to his relatives. The nyau came shortly afterwards to get him . . . They had made a hammock from blankets and taken him over the Namukokwe to his village.' August 1940.

[81] The concept of Catholic Action was promulgated by Pope Pius X in an encyclical in 1905, 'Il fermo proposito'. It gained further support from Pius XI in the period 1922 to 1939 and was strongly championed by Pius XII as a weapon against communism. The more militant 'Action Française' groups immediately aroused opposition in Europe and the idea became transformed into a non-political group of pious associations like the Legion of Mary. In the African context even groups like the Legion of Mary could be quite militant—see Chapter IX.

[82] The father of Bishop Patrick Kalilombe w.f., formerly Rector of Kachebere Major Seminary

[83] In traditional burials the corpse was wrapped in a sleeping mat rather than put in a coffin

[84] Mua Diary June 1941

[85] Certain para-liturgical celebrations such as a procession of the Blessed Sacrament had a glamour that could, up to a point, rival the nyau in attracting villagers' interest. An example from the Mua Diary May 1921. 'The procession was led by one of our sawyers, Mangani, with the cross . . . Then came the little girls resplendent in white dresses made for them by the nuns. Each was carrying an oriflamme and the biggest girl held a banner of Our Lady. The boys dressed as best they could followed each with his oriflamme. One was carrying the St. Joseph banner; behind them came the women of the Blessed Sacrament Guild

followed by the men, each with their own banner. The seminarians were in front of the dais. Then followed four little girls all dressed up with a crown of flowers and each with a basket of petals. On a signal they turned round, gave a deep curtsy, and threw a handful of petals. Finally there was a dais borne by the carpenters. The decorations that the Sisters had made were splendid, cut silk with lace and beads; all in the best possible taste. Then behind the dais came the jostling crowds, the "populo" which, as in former years, were led by Father Champmartin, baton in hand to keep everyone at a respectful distance.'

There are instances in which the nyau put on performances to rival the Catholic liturgy which had a moderate pull on villagers for whom any colourful event broke the monotony of daily life.

[86] This was Maurillo Karvalo, an Ngoni catechist from Nzama. It is a good example of the way the mission used Ngoni Christians as intermediaries between the mission and the Chewa-speaking people of the country.

[87] Chikwawa Diary 12 May 1936 and Heraud to Auneau 14 August 1937. Montfort Archives, Blantyre.

[88] Chikwawa Diary 28 May 1936

[89] Schoffeleers *Symbolic and Social Aspects* 324

[90] For a discussion of the political role of the nyau see Linden I. 'Initiation rites and nyau societies; a study in local politics at Mua' *Chilema Conference on the Interaction of Christianity and African Societies* August 1971.

[91] The Congress was led entirely by products of the Protestant missions: Rev. C. Chinula, C. J. Matinga, C. W. Mlonga and J. D. Phiri.

[92] Mua Diary February and March 1947

[93] Details of the impact of the cash economy are given in footnote 19

[94] Schoffeleers *Symbolic and Social Aspects* 332

[95] See footnote 19.

[96] Personal Communication, Mr. Gomo Michongwe, Dept. of Education, University of Tanzania, Dar-es-Salaam

[97] Recommendations of the Apostolic-Visitor 10 August 1928—see Chapter VII

[98] Illich I. 'Schooling: The Ritual of Progress' *New York Review of Books* 3 December 1970 Vol. XV No. 10, 20–6. While not accepting Illich's extreme position it is certainly true that in colonial Malawi schooling was one of the most important formative influences structuring society. Where Illich overstates his case is in presenting schools in isolation as the sole generator of consumer expectations.

[99] O'Brien to Zomba Secretariat 9 May 1929. NC 1/21/1.

[100] The first signs of waning of the power of the nyau have recently come from the Mua area; the funeral of Rita Kafulama, an important Banda chief, was not accompanied by dancing. Government approval of the societies may therefore turn out to be more damaging in the long run than mission opposition which stimulated resistance.

CHAPTER VII

From Prayers to Pedagogy

> The secular instruction given in these schools has only a secondary import-
> ance in our eyes, but it is unfortunately necessary, for without it we would
> have only very few come to learn the catechism.
>
> Father Guillemé to Nyasa missionaries[1]
>
> The fact that the Government is unable at present to supply the kind of
> education which would benefit the African does not seem necessarily to imply
> that it must permit a type of education which would be harmful to the
> Natives under its protection.
>
> Rev. E. D. Bowman to Gaunt[2]
>
> The Government are to call the tune, but the missions are to pay the piper.
>
> Bishop Cathrew Universities' Mission to Central Africa[3]

There was nothing fortuitous in the main target for attack by the nyau societies
being the educational institutions of the Catholic missions. From the moment
missionaries arrived they made their first task the training of catechists, who
would have a double role as teachers and auxiliary evangelists. Implicit in this
sharing of the work of evangelization was the belief that all missionary endeavour was directed towards the creation of a self-supporting indigenous
Church. Until the first Malawian priests were ordained in the late 1930s, the
catechists were the leaders of the African Church, priests in all but name and
sacramental duties.

The speed with which the first Fathers got catechists into the field is some
measure of the importance they attached to them. They were chosen from the
best married students at the mission school and given special training. By 1905,
barely two years after the foundation of the White Fathers' stations, catechists
were sent out from Mua and Kachebere to work in Central Ngoniland.[4] They
had to staff twelve schools with almost 1,000 pupils. As they were barely more
than a few months ahead of their pupils, each catechist was obliged to return to
the mission for refresher courses, after three weeks' teaching in the bush.

The Montforts opened their first school at the mission within six months of
arriving at Nzama. Pupils were divided into those 'who knew their letters a
little', and the rest; women, girls, and young children, were taught in a separate
class.[5] The White Fathers held classes of one hour each, morning and afternoon,

for four days a week. Reading, writing, addition, and subtraction, were taught in an 'upper' class, while two-thirds of the pupils had to be content with a little reading in the lower class. Afternoon lessons ended for everyone by chanting parts of the catechism in unison. Additional catechism lessons were given on Sundays at 8 a.m. after mass, and workers at the mission were given instruction three times a week.[6]

The conditions in which these first schools operated were primitive in the extreme. It was some time before a shipment of slates arrived at Nzama, and school equipment was a luxury. Away from the station, catechists gave catechism lessons weekly in the shade of a tree on the *bwalo*. Children had to write in the dust with their fingers and, instead of blackboards, the catechist used a crude cloth-board. But this was an improvement in many ways on the hot crowded conditions in wattle and daub huts, or at the mission school, where all age-groups would squeeze in to hear the 'Mau a Mulungu'.[7]

Nor were educational methods sophisticated. As in France, the lesson was largely a matter of chanting after the teacher. The method was sacrosanct for the catechism.

> Word for word teaching, learnt by heart, must be considered as the norm for instruction in the vicariate. A word for word recitation will count for $\frac{3}{4}$ the examination for admission to the catechumenate, and explanation $\frac{1}{4}$. For admission to baptism it will be $\frac{1}{2}$ and $\frac{1}{2}$. Failure to recite the catechism word for word will be considered sufficient grounds for exclusion from baptism.[8]

In practice, there was leniency shown towards older people in the examinations, more attention being paid to conduct during the catechumenate, than to their intellectual abilities. At Kachebere, where there was an unfailing supply of catechumens, a stipulation was made that children should at least know the alphabet before they were permitted to end their period of postulancy and enter the catechumenate.[9] But beyond this rudimentary demand educational attainment was never linked to Church membership.[10]

The Fathers were equally quick to produce books in the vernacular. By the beginning of 1903 Winnen had an ABC and a complete set of New Testament stories on the way to Europe for printing. They came back in 1906 from the St. Peter Claver missionary printing office in Salzburg. An edifying preface had been added in Austria which provides a fascinating glimpse of Europe's genteel and philanthropic Catholics.

> I trust your nice book will be an apostolate of light, and piety, in extending the knowledge and love of Our Saviour amongst the civilized White Man and the savage Blacks.[11]

'Za Mpulumutsi'[12] and a collection of Old Testament stories, 'Mulungu yekha'[13] were the Catholic substitute for the Bible.[14] Together with the catechism, they presented basic Catholic Christianity to their African readership without omissions or embellishments. The 'Katekismu wa Akatolika'[15] translated the 'false Gods' of the first commandment liberally into a prohibition of sacrifice to the 'mizimu',[16] ancestral spirits; it made up for such modifications with an equally liberal sprinkling of angels, one of whom, in mortal combat with Lucifer, looked remarkably like Joan of Arc.

Preparation for baptism at the White Fathers' missions was the most rigorous period of religious instruction undergone by any prospective Roman Catholic. Candidates were given special catechism lessons at the station, that lasted six weeks.[17] Lessons were limited during the last week to an explanation of the sacraments the catechumens were about to receive; they were allowed to stay throughout the mass for the first time, and details of the priest's actions at the altar were explained. If all religious instruction before this time had demanded rote learning, the emphasis for this week was on explanation. The central Catholic doctrines concerning the Eucharist, baptism, and penance, had to be understood. Formal instruction ended in the last three days before baptism; the Fathers led the catechumens in prayers and exhorted them to persevere in a blameless life.[18]

In theory and in practice, baptism was the Catholic initiation rite. The Fathers made no bones about the fact that the day of the catechumen's baptism was the most important in his life. Great stress was laid on the change that was to take place in the state of the person. This was not a piece of hypocrisy. The Fathers genuinely believed that at baptism the catechumen was being saved from eternal damnation. In the dictum, 'Extra Ecclesiam nulla salus',[19] so archly proclaimed by the Church to the anti-Catholic and secular Europe of the late nineteenth century, lay the key to Catholic aggression, whether against the 'Protestant Sects' or the nyau societies.

The gradual unveiling of the central part of the mass, at the end of the catechumenate, added to the neophytes' sense of having entered into the Christian mysteries. Furthermore the catechumenate was very selective; the Montfort nuns invited to instruction at the mission only widows and the first wives of men in the villages they visited.[20] The neophyte tended to become separated from other villagers. He had entered the *corpus christianum*, with its own set of rules, hierarchy, and ways of reaching positions of importance in village life. There is no doubt that baptism was for many the genuine Biblical 'metanoia';[21] they were converted and their way of life altered. Many of the first neophytes became catechists and gave a lifetime of service to the evangelization of their districts. They did so on a pittance; the 1908 budget for thirty-eight catechists at Mua was £63 for the entire year,[22] less than 3s. per month. There was nothing unusual about such low pay at the time, only it has to be remembered that the level of education of the catechists, however low, qualified them for jobs in the towns and mines at a much higher rate. Catechists gained in status within their villages but this was no less true of well-paid workers returning from the mines, and of clerks at the local Boma.

To describe Catholic education before the First World War is, then, to talk about religious instruction in preparation for baptism. There was never any pretence that the small amount of secular instruction provided by the missions had any other purpose than to attract villagers into the catechumenate. Father Bourget wrote almost by way of apology in 1903: 'the writing and reading that we are teaching are only a means for us'.[23] At Mua it was decided to move the catechism part of the lesson to the beginning, so that 'the people will understand that you can attend the catechism instruction without being obliged to sit through the rest'.[24] Only fourteen out of 171 catechumens at Mua in 1907 were not attending the mission schools.

The missionaries saw their first task as preaching the Gospel. They realized that the secular side of the instruction they provided lured people into the orbit of the mission stations, but they did not consider it as an integral part of their vocation and ministry. None the less they did make a significant contribution to the education of the people around the mission in small ways, unconnected with formal schooling. The District Commissioner wrote of Mua before the war:

No special Industrial School is attached to this mission, but many Natives in the neighbourhood will be found to be good sawyers, carpenters, bricklayers and brickmakers, local labour having been employed by the Fathers for all mission work; also good gardeners can be got who have learnt their work in the mission gardens.[25]

By walking enormous distances the priests were able to visit distant schools once a week, and their tight control over catechists meant that a certain minimum standard was maintained in formal teaching at the beginning. After the first wave of baptisms in 1907–8 the number of Catholic catechists mounted, the bush schools began to multiply, and the Fathers took an increasingly smaller share in the teaching. From 1908 to 1911 rambling networks of bush schools of a lower standard began to spread out from the White Fathers' stations, and were visited less frequently.

TABLE V[26]

Year	No. of W.F. schools	No. of teachers	No. of pupils
1908	26	25	3,000
1909	41	50	4,000
1910	96	119	5,500
1911	133	152	7,500
1912	190	239	10,500

Owing to continued pressure on the Governor, Sir Alfred Sharpe, from Church of Scotland missionaries, grants-in-aid for education were begun in 1907. Livingstonia and Blantyre shared half the available £1,000 between them. The Dutch Reformed and White Fathers were given £125 each. The Montforts, who had been slower to train catechists, concentrating on a Central Mission School where the teaching was done by the Fathers, were only able to sport three schools, so declined to put in a bid.[27]

The Catholics, unlike the Scots, insisted on keeping their education free. Auneau only gave way in 1938 to Government demands to introduce a fee of

1d.–4d. for classes 1–2, and 6d.–4/- from substandard to standard 4 classes.[28] He had not taken kindly to being threatened with a loss of his grant-in-aid.

> We Catholics consider it our duty to give Catholic children, first of all, and even sometimes non-catholic children, an elementary education, without exacting fees, if it is in our power. It seems to me strange to say the least, that the exercise of this duty should be censured by a suspension of the Grant-in-aid.[29]

Even so, it was several years before the fees were collected properly from Catholic pupils. Since both bishops held that 'we must always maintain the religious basis of all education given by us',[30] the fear was that religious instruction and contact with the Church might be denied villagers who could not raise sufficient money. While the exactions of tax collectors continued unabated and Catholic standards remained low, children might stay away from Catholic schools if fees were demanded.

As early as 1883, the Livingstonia mission was charging 6d. for English classes,[31] and, by 1910, £400 per annum was being collected in school fees. The Northern Ngoni were accustomed to the idea that education came with a price tag. But Samuel Smiles had still to reach the Maseko and Chewa villages around Mua. On reading how the four Church of Scotland stations had collected £144 from their congregations in 1908, the Fathers were moved to write:

> This is of great interest to us. People who are living around our mission are very far from seeing their way to supporting our work. To take all the time, that's fine, but the idea that they should contribute something themselves, that has yet to dawn. It is extremely hard to ask for money, though, when they have barely enough for their own needs.[32]

Part of the trouble was that the French missionaries were not used to demanding money from the laity; after the Concordat with Napoleon the French Church had been State aided. The French catechism lacked the sixth commandment of the Church, that of financially supporting its priests.[33] A Church Tax, *mtulo*, applied half-heartedly by the Fathers was widely ignored. But when an attitude of dependence on the mission came to include education it became positively damaging. African Catholics, in most cases, accepted the priests' indifference to education, and undervalued it in relation to other goals. While Nyasaland Protestants sometimes absorbed the Scots virtues of self-help and thrift, its Catholics often took literally 'having no thought for the morrow'. And when the morrow came it was not surprisingly a colonial Nyasaland stratified into a Protestant élite and a Catholic peasantry.

While it is true that Catholic education was rudimentary before the 1920s, it would not be correct to conclude that withholding advanced education from Africans was an express policy of the Catholic missions. One group of Africans, the seminarians destined to become priests, were given intensive training with the aim of achieving high standards. In the Shire Vicariate during the 1920s there was a European-staff-to-student ratio in the Minor Seminary of 1:20, while at the Teachers' Training College it was 1:125.[34] There was one priest to fourteen pupils at the White Fathers' Seminary, which must have been one of the lowest pupil/teacher ratios in the country at the time.[35]

The first formal catechists' school was begun by the White Fathers at Mua in 1911. Pupils from Ntaka-taka who had been taking English lessons the previous year with Father Boucansaud,[36] made up the majority of the students. The syllabus consisted of reading, writing, geography, history, and grammar, taught by a rather eccentric Breton, Father Joseph Mazé, while Boucansaud took charge of religious instruction. Although Mazé had a doctorate in canon law, he was in many ways an unfortunate choice to direct the Catholics' first attempt at higher education. Much of his time at Mua was spent working on a ChiChewa 'Life of Christ' with the co-operation of his pupils; he wrote far into the night and often did not turn up for classes the next morning.[37]

The Catholic immunity to ambitions in the field of secular education was by no means universal. The catechists' school netted many young men who appreciated the value of a good education and command of English in the colonial setting, much to the distress of the priests.

Amongst our pupils there are far too many who have no real desire to become catechists. Some have openly admitted that they don't want to and others would just be incapable of doing the job. It's easy to spot the ones who are not interested in becoming catechists, they are far too eager to learn English, and indifferent to everything else.[38]

The mission's response to this overeagerness for the forbidden fruits was to close several schools around Mua and replace them by catechists giving nothing but religious instruction on the *bwalo*.[39] The teaching of English remained an exception in the Catholic schools before the war. Father Brinkhorst alone taught English for a while at Kachebere, before being moved into the North East Rhodesian side of the Vicariate.[40] The missionaries found English a strain and they were loath to provide the villagers with the, albeit meagre, intellectual equipment for emigration to towns and mines.

In March 1912, Guillemé decided to change the catechists' school into a Minor Seminary. A nucleus of the six best pupils was chosen, and an ability to read and write made obligatory for subsequent entry to the seminary. The seminary was directed by Fathers Villy[41] and Roy with the help of two African teachers. During the war many pupils left to look for paid employment and the seminary was closed before the beginning of 1919. The Montforts made some attempts at starting a Minor Seminary at Nzama in 1914, and a Canadian priest began giving English lessons at the local store, but the experiment was discontinued.

The effect of the war on Catholic educational efforts was similar in Nyasaland to that in other African countries. As in Uganda, catechists went on working for reduced and sometimes no pay, but the exigencies of war did not result in any increased delegation of responsibility to local Church leaders.[42] Because of the shortage of money and supplies, only 200 of the White Fathers' catechists were kept on with pay, teaching sometimes in up to four different schools in a day.[43] The most they could hope for was one shilling a week, and if they lived more than seven miles from their schools a little salt in addition. They were allowed three months' holiday to prepare their gardens between November and January, a month after Easter for harvesting, and a couple of weeks in winter. They were expected to come back to the mission each month for a refresher course lasting one week, attend a three-week retreat in February before the re-opening of schools, and bring their Christians to mass every Sunday.[44] However well disciplined and devoted to their work, they could hardly provide an adequate education for the 20,000 pupils who attended their schools.

By the end of the war even these catechists had been drafted as porters and all educational work had been brought to a halt. Schools fell into disrepair. When mission work began again in earnest at the beginning of 1919 Guillemé was disturbed by the abysmally low standards that prevailed in the newly opened schools.

If like you I only attach secondary importance to secular education in schools away from the mission, I see the work of the mission school in a different light. And here I must regretfully say that the school is being treated far too simply as a way of getting children into the catechism.[45]

This was a new note. However his main concern was the low level of intake into the Minor Seminary, which was reopened that year. Good unmarried catechists were still looked on as potential recruits for the priesthood. The only concession to higher educational standards outside the seminaries was the opening of a Normal School at Nguludi. There was some reduction in the numbers of catechists in the White Fathers' Vicariate; those remaining were paid better. The annual budget for each catechist was £2 in 1921; those with over ten years' service to the mission had their Hut Tax paid in addition, and any with over fifteen years' service were given a bonus of £6. Where there was a poor response to the mission, catechists were withdrawn from a village in order to concentrate their efforts more.[46]

Catholic education policy continued to rest on a widespread network of bush schools giving an elementary education to as many villagers as possible; an élitist education was reserved for a few seminarians. Auneau, who had received reinforcements of Montforts from Holland, established schools in Protestant areas as a preliminary to opening full mission stations. Despite the fact that he was £2,000 in debt, and forced to shut down several schools in the Blantyre area,[47] he wanted to expand at all costs. In July 1921, preceded by four of their best catechists, the Montforts moved into a store at Port-Herald.[48] Fortunately for the missionaries it rained early that year and the early rains were attributed to the powers of the newly arrived *Aroma*. Disputes began immediately with the South Africa General Mission at Chindidi, which had been established in the hills since 1900. Unperturbed, the Montforts extended their schools as far north as Lundu's.[49] On 12 September 1921, Sisters Marie de St. Florent, Maurille, and Alice, the last being one of the first English Daughters of Wisdom in the country, opened a girls' boarding school on some land bought by Auneau in Limbe.[50] This was later to become Limbe mission.

At the same time, Auneau, who saw the whole territory from Port Herald to

Port Amelia as his ecclesiastical plantation, began correspondence with Antonio Centeno, Director of the Portuguese Nyasa Charter Company that ran Northern Mozambique, with a view to starting Montfort missions there. Centeno seems to have been worried about the subversive potential of Islam in the area. His request for missionaries had a familiar ring.

> We wish to establish Catholic missions in our area, especially those which have no other aim than civilising the Natives, teaching them religious principles and particularly willing to combat Islam which is spreading everywhere.[51]

In the highly-charged nationalist atmosphere after the war, the Portuguese were still unwilling to see non-Portuguese priests in their colonies.[52] The Montforts went all the same. In May 1922, two Montforts, Baslé and Lebreton, set out on an enormous 600 mile trek, mostly on foot, into the Malokotera district, Concelho da Montepuez, north of the Lulio river.[53] Unable to continue further, and with their shoes worn to shreds, they founded the first Montfort station in Portuguese East Africa, Santa Maria da Namuno, followed by another mission later in the year on the coast at Porto Amelia.[54] In a repeat performance of the White Fathers' difficulties in the previous century, letters passed between Rome, St. Laurent-sur-Sèvre, Nguludi, and Mozambique, to resolve the problem of ecclesiastical jurisdiction.[55] Eventually the ruffled plumage of Monsignor Raphael, the Archbishop of Mozambique, was smoothed over by the Prefect of the Propaganda, Cardinal Van Rossum, and the Montforts were allowed to stay.[56] Father Martin was sent to the coast as liaison officer between Auneau and Raphael.[57]

Within two years Auneau decided to move closer to Zomba, too, but the Governor was resisting, declaring that no mission should be set up within ten miles of the town centre. The Daughters of Wisdom had been promised the chance to staff the hospital at Zomba at an earlier date, but the idea seems to have been squashed by the Scots;[58] the nuns had already taken control of education for European and coloured girls in the Protectorate. But the broken promises gave Auneau a little leverage and he was able to insert a mission on the outskirts of town in exchange for the Sisters. The priests vacated Nankhunda, making it available for use as a Minor Seminary. On 2 February 1925, the first fifty pupils arrived at 'Le petit séminaire de L'Enfant-Jésus' to begin their schoolwork. They had been largely taken from the better students at the Nguludi Normal School.[59]

As the White Fathers were opening their first new station since the war at Kasina in 1925, almost next door to the Dutch Reformed centre at Nkhoma, the Montforts were opening their fifth[60] at Mulanje, next to an old Church of Scotland mission. The arrival of the Catholics coincided with the peak of the Alomwe emigration from Portuguese East Africa to Nyasaland. The Alomwe settled piecemeal under Mang'anja chiefs who employed them to test out the new Catholic schools.[61] One of the Mang'anja chiefs, Mabuka, invited them to settle on his land and they seem to have been generally welcomed.[62] Many of the new immigrants settled around the Catholic mission at Chisitu. Huge open air masses were held and the baptismal records indicate an unparalleled rush into the Catholic Church: 1926—164, 1927—530, 1928—2,050, 1929—1,500, 1930—1,500, baptisms per annum.[63] The Alomwe found in the Catholic mission free, readily accessible, though rudimentary, education, and a way to attain the limited number of headmanships available to them under the Mang'anja. The proliferation of Catholic schools produced by the new mission sparked off a Protestant–Catholic confrontation of epic proportions.

Since the Protestant Missionary Federation of 1904 in which the Catholics did not participate, friction between missions had invariably been the result of Catholic clashes with 'the rest'. The first major confrontation was between White Fathers and Dutch Reformed in the Central Region. Between 1908 and 1914 there was a race to start new schools and occupy all available areas. On average the Dutch Reformed were opening up 111 new schools a year.[64] They were easily outstripped by the Catholics.

TABLE VI[65]

Mission Society	Increase in schools 1910–15	Staff increase Europeans	Staff/Student ratio
Dutch Reformed Church	150%	Nil	1:2,249
White Fathers	154%	21%	1:416
Montfort Fathers	393%	83%	1:449

In December 1910, Rev. W. H. Murray from Mvera, attempted to get the Catholics to accept some sort of pact.[66] Father Travers, who was Dupont's link with the Nyasaland side of his Vicariate, and Vicar-General, was very reluctant to agree to any spheres of influence.[67] His reticence, though, was somewhat equivocal. At Kachebere the Catholics had been pressing for spheres of influence to keep the Dutch from their most profitable mission field.[68] Missionary attitudes towards spheres of influence were entirely pragmatic. When one side wanted to break into an area, its Christian autochtones put up the cry of separate spheres. The tactics of the religious scramble for Nyasaland were often clothed in high-sounding phrases such as 'liberty of worship'; the reality was that occupation was nine-tenths of the law.

Dates for meetings between representatives of the two Churches were postponed three times, so it was Guillemé who supervised the final arrangements. He made a rather touching appeal to the Dutch Reformed:

> As none of us is sufficiently acquainted with the English language I should ask permission to appoint as our representatives two of our missionaries who speak Dutch.[69]

But when the meeting finally took place on 27 April 1911 between Hoffmeyr, Murray, Freiburg, and the White Fathers Onstenk[70] and Ter Maat, an almost common language singularly failed to create any atmosphere of bonhomie. The meeting, around a big table at Mr. Cruise's house[71] in Lilongwe, lasted for four hours and was presided over by the District Commissioner, Mr. Ockenden. With icy politeness the Catholics elaborated on their sixteenth-century claims while the Protestants spoke of their orders from the Transvaal. After a little bargaining in which the Catholics were offered an area west of Malingundi mission, extending across the border of Portuguese East Africa, almost entirely Chewa so relatively refractory to missionary penetration, the meeting ended with a mutual agreement on a two-mile limit between schools. And 'Mr. Ockenden seemed a little uncomfortable'.[72]

The opening of the Catholic mission at Tambala's put paid to any hope of a continued détente. The relations between the missions deteriorated further and Guillemé had to meet Murray personally in March 1912. They agreed that catechists should not in future be permitted to discuss the tenets of each other's creeds with villagers. There had been a number of instances of 'Daki'[73] catechists telling horrific tales about Roman Catholics.

The Aroma are 'zimfiti'[74] who will eat your body after you have died; they gave you that little cross in order to recognise their prey when you are in the grave.[75]

Much of the trouble then and later was caused by zealous catechists trying to better their opponents. The authority of each catechist stemmed from his particular mission; each identified with his own creed as a personal authorization to challenge chiefs, and keep his Christians in order. Teachers from other missions, with different doctrines, threatened the position of the Catholic catechist in 'his' villages. The differences between denominations inevitably became accentuated.

Alongside a knowledge of Christian Doctrine each catechist of distinction equipped himself with a grounding in 'Church History'. In practice, it was little more than a list of ways in which other denominations were heretics, and the excesses their heresies had led them to. Dutch Reformed catechists from Nkhoma would be likely to know that the Jesuits were a 'Society of Satan', and most Protestants, even if they barely knew who the Virgin Mary was, were well aware that Catholics worshipped her instead of Christ. However, not all theological discussion between denominations was on the level of insults. While no mediaeval disputation, the following dialogue between a Dutch Reformed catechist, Rubeni, and his Catholic counterpart, Mikael Finyeza, is a good example of the type of polemics and apologetics of which several of the bush catechists were capable.

So the Malingundi Boer said, 'Leave the bad things behind, the things that make you drunk'. And I replied, 'The things that make you drunk are not forbidden, but it is true that God forbids you to get drunk. You go on about beer, but at Cana the Lord Jesus made six calabashes of wine out of water.' Then they all began shouting, 'Did you not know that the Lord made that wine in one day so that it did not have time to ferment.' So I answered, 'The people at the wedding boasted about the wine, saying that it was better than the previous one'. I asked them, 'What made it better?' So they replied that they would leave that topic for the moment.

During the argument Calvin, Henry VIII, and the Boer War were all discussed.[76]

There was far more to the debate than differing opinions of the strength of the wine at Cana. Beer drinking was often taken to be one of the marks of the Roman Catholic Church. The theological justification of the Protestant ban on alcohol was shaky, and many villagers resented it on more mundane grounds. During the 1930s a song about how the Protestants had tricked the people about beer was quite common in the Kasungu district.

> Kale, kale, Aprotestanti anatiyenga
> Musamwa moa
> Lero talowa Ecclesia, Lero talowa Ecclesia
> Akatholika.[77]

(In the past the Protestants tricked us. You must not drink beer. Today we joined the Church. Today we joined the Catholic Church.)

Since beer drinking was an important element in traditional life, in libations and other ritual activities, the Catholic position had much in its favour. However this liberality was not motivated by thoughts of adaptation. Attempts were made to stop Catholics joining in libations[78] while simple secular drunkenness was tolerated. To what extent the Protestant ethic, and abstemiousness with regard to alcohol, contributed to the attitude of many Protestants towards education, is difficult to demonstrate without firm sociological data from each region. Suffice to say, the heavy consumption of beer that took place, and still takes place, in Catholic villages was no spur to Catholic advancement.

The Government's view of the repeated mission disputes was inspired by liberal ideals. Whenever possible most District Commissioners behaved as trustees for the Africans in their district. They tried to be sure that chiefs and headmen really wanted the school of a particular denomination, and attempted to make missionaries come to agreements amongst themselves, without imposing solutions from above.

> The matter is thus entirely in their own hands. The Government is only too ready to countenance and assist all reputable missions . . . but it is no proper part of Government to undertake the division of missionary spheres of influence nor can any such division be satisfactory which does not rest on a mutual and friendly understanding between the missions themselves.[79]

None the less such high Lockian thoughts were salted with pragmatism. The choice of schools was just the sort of decision the Government wanted left in the hands of the chiefs. It gave them the illusory sense of being masters of their own villages.

> The Native is not in a position to contract freely as an individual with whitemen and the Government as his guardian supplements his incomplete individuality. It is part of government policy to allow a *certain amount of influence*[80] to Native Chiefs and if missions are to be allowed to establish Churches and Schools in direct defiance of their wishes, nothing could be more calculated to undermine their influence.[81]

Bishop Joseph Dupont

Above: *The first Malawian Sisters of the Congregation of the Servants of the Blessed Virgin Mary, Nguludi Cathedral 1928*

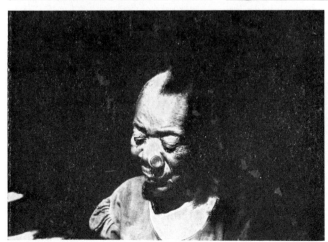

Above Left: *Malawian Sister with orphans c. 1930*

Above Right: *Father Andrea Makoyo: ordained 1938*

Left: *Rita Kafulama: the last Mwali*

Catholic missionaries were neither liberals nor pragmatists. Friendly and mutual understanding between Protestant Churches and the Catholics was a rarity. The two-mile limit agreed on between the Dutch Reformed and the White Fathers lasted but a short while. If Ockenden had imagined squabbling could be stopped by such a simple expedient he was sadly mistaken. The letters soon began passing between the missions again.

> I don't know whether you took the trouble to measure the distance from our school building at Mzingo to Chirundu. Allow me to tell you that I measured the distance, and found Chirundu's villages less than two miles from our school building at Mzingo's.[82]

After 1912, the tape-measure became an indispensable piece of the evangelists' equipment and the sight of priests intrepidly pacing their way through thick bush not uncommon.

As the Montforts began their expansion after the war the number of meetings at the Boma, presided over by harassed District Commissioners, increased. The honest-broker policy of the administration produced long and acrimonious discussions between missionaries in an atmosphere of *odium theologicum*. Following one such bitter session at Chikwawa after the founding of the Montfort mission, the Resident was reduced to the not unduly perceptive comment, 'it would appear to be the wish of each to exclude the other'.[83] Even the most idealistic of colonial officials might have lapsed into repressive measures, had it not been for the legal stiffening provided by a Royal Instruction of 9 August 1907, and the more general provisions of the Berlin Act of 1885. The former requested Governors in Nyasaland to 'promote religion and education among the native inhabitants of the Protectorate', while the latter guaranteed freedom of conscience to Africans and made missionaries a special object of colonial Government protection in international law.[84]

The Government came very near to intervening in mission affairs with a heavy hand after the Chilembwe rising. Andrew Bonar Law,[85] leader of the British Conservative party and himself a son of a Presbyterian minister, wanted to see ten full miles between each main mission station and properly delimited spheres of influence, but was constrained by international law.[86] In English law the executive could only intervene in religious meetings 'as of lawful purpose' when they caused an open breach of the peace. The Protectorate Government was legally bound to approach the missionary problem with some delicacy. Strict rules regarding distance from rival institutions might be applied to formal schools, but not to prayer-houses, religious meetings, and church classes. Since what went on in wattle and daub huts in the bush was difficult to control, and the distinction between 'prayer-house' and 'school' semantic rather than real, even this degree of Government supervision could not easily be enforced. The dispute over the Mulanje mission and its schools provided something of a test case for the Government.

Auneau had chosen for Mulanje a veteran of the Blantyre campaign, Father P. Régent. On 1 November 1925 Régent fired his first warning salvo at an unsuspecting District Commissioner.

We have already been nearly all round the Mlanje district. There is plenty room [sic] for our mission and certainly a big work to be done amongst the natives. Then would you kindly let the Provincial Commissioner know that we are ready to start work, and give us the permission to open a school on the Likabula plot where we will be staying for the rainy season.[87]

An anxious correspondence ensued between R. H. Murray, then Acting Provincial Commissioner in Blantyre, Anderson, the Resident, and Rev. Reid, the local Scots missionary. The District Commissioner accurately forecast 'endless trouble for the Resident if the Marist Fathers are allowed to come here'.[88] Reid summoned all the chiefs and headmen for a feast on Christmas Day and unseasonably denounced the Montforts.[89] Rumour was rife that the Fathers had cleft feet under their cassocks.[90] By February 1927, things had begun to get serious; a Chief Nzenje, a Catholic adherent, kidnapped one of his headmen, Nkhota, who had permitted a Scots school to be built in his village. The issue worked its way up to the Governor who ruled that the Catholics might open prayer-houses, but not schools. Régent nonchalantly informed the Government in his 1927 school returns: 'In all our prayer-houses agriculture, hygiene instruction and games have been started only in January 1927.'[91] Gaunt, the new Director of Education, despairingly commented: 'He has turned his 116 prayer-houses into schools.'[92] It was far more simple than that; the Montforts stubbornly refused to recognize any difference between prayer-houses and schools.

While Régent was fighting on the eastern front the even more formidable Father F. Nicolas, operating from the Nzama mission, was trying to break into an area controlled by the Zambesi Industrial Mission in the north. Viewed by an impartial observer the tug-of-war between Nicolas and all the Protestant missions at the education board meetings at Ncheu, had the elements of comic opera. One incident was remembered clearly by a local planter.

This proselytism aroused all the long established Protestants. I remember Ferguson of Dombole mission making an impassioned speech condemning the R.C.'s and asking that immediate action be taken to stop their activities. This was greeted with enthusiasm by all the Protestants although they agreed in practically no other matter, and was listened to very quietly by the French R.C. priest. Ferguson finished his peroration by pointing to the Union Jack flying outside the Boma office and saying, 'Whose flag is that', 'Whose flag is that?'. And I remember the RC priest saying quietly, looking carefully at the flag, 'Zee flag of Lib-ar-ty'.[93]

However, the Government were not amused. Nicolas almost provoked the first intervention in mission affairs on grounds of a breach of the peace since the Chilembwe rising. The Provincial Commissioner considered him 'a menace to public order'. The Montforts' efforts at Mulanje and Ncheu ended in a worried letter from the Governor to the Secretary of State for the Colonies, Amery,[94] on the policy to adopt in such situations when the missionaries were causing an open breach of the peace through rivalry.[95] Only a timely warning from Auneau seems to have kept Nicolas from being removed from the Ncheu district altogether. Nsipe mission opened in 1928 on the strength of Nicolas' efforts, and

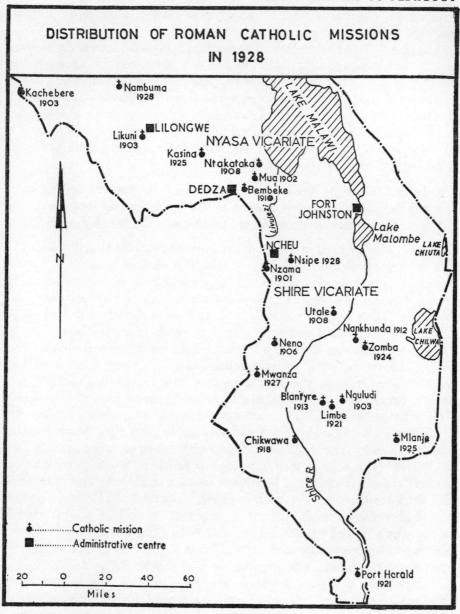

DISTRIBUTION OF ROMAN CATHOLIC MISSIONS IN 1928

Kachebere
1903

Nambuma
1928

Likuni
1903

LILONGWE

NYASA VICARIATE

Kasina
1925

Ntakataka
1908

Mua 1902

DEDZA

Bembeke
1910

LAKE MALAWI

FORT
JOHNSTON

Lake
Malombe

LAKE
CHIUTA

N

Livulezi

NCHEU

Nsipe 1928

Nzama
1901

SHIRE VICARIATE

Utale
1908

Nankhunda 1912

LAKE
CHILWA

Neno
1906

Zomba
1924

Mwanza
1927

Blantyre
1913

Nguludi
1903

Limbe
1921

Chikwawa
1918

Mlanje
1925

Shire R.

Catholic mission
Administrative centre

20   0   20   40   60
Miles

Port Herald
1921

a year later, Mwanza mission to the south of Nzama. Undeterred, Auneau managed to continue to expand.

The arrival of the Phelps–Stokes Commission in Nyasaland, on 22 April 1924, caught the Catholic missions in the middle of a phase of rapid expansion, for which they had neither the funds nor the personnel. The Commission's three-week tour of the country to survey educational institutions was stage-managed by Hetherwick, even to the point of having all the Commission's mail sent to his own address.[96] He was a personal friend of the Governor, Sir Charles C. Bowring, past Grand-Master of the Nyasaland Lodge, and nurtured a profound dislike of Catholics. In 1915 he had been very piqued by

> a decided favour for Anglican and Roman Catholic missions and methods which the Scottish Churches consider to be not only without adequate reason but entirely opposed to the spirit and traditions of the British Empire.[97]

This favour had resulted in the Montfort expansion into the Chiradzulu area.

The Phelps–Stokes Commission met their first Catholic missionary, Father Rivière, as their train steamed out of Blantyre station on the way to Beira. He managed to thrust a letter of complaint through the train window.[98] The *Nyasaland Times* had optimistically told its readers that the balanced composition of the Commission was 'bound to result in an unbiased view'.[99] Hetherwick made sure that not a single Catholic institution was visited. The Catholic educational work, 375 bush schools catering for over 20,000 pupils in the Shire Vicariate alone, was given seven lines in the Commission's final report. Its final remark was to be echoed in all later studies of missions in Nyasaland: 'It is unfortunate that this important work cannot be adequately described.'[100]

Hetherwick was right to be jealous of the Catholic glory after the war and the Chilembwe rising. The Montfort Fathers were given an education grant of £65 in 1919 although none of their 247 teachers had been formally trained in a teachers' training institution. The White Fathers, who did have legitimate technical school teachers, such as Brothers Omer, Willibrord, and Placide, together with Father Champmartin, sent in a return of 175 village schools visited regularly by a 'trained educator'. They were given £100. None of the Montfort schools could properly be graded and the White Fathers' claim to have 'trained educators' was a definite exaggeration. On the other hand, the Z.I.M.[101] with 90 Grade I and 80 Grade II schools only got £100 also. The Seventh-Day Baptists with 39 Grade I schools were given a paltry £20.[102] If the distribution of Government money was any indication where its heart lay, then it was certainly not with the more fundamentalist Protestant denominations.

Of the three main interest groups in the Protectorate after the First World War, the planters, the missionaries, and the Africans, the Government had only to contend seriously with the first. With the exception of a few activists like Levi Mumba,[103] Africans could be effectively stifled in the web of colonial bureaucracy. The Protestant missionaries at Blantyre who had been so vociferous in the past were discredited in the 1915 rising from which they had yet to recover. The Government's official policy on African education tended to lean towards the views of the majority of planters. Planters were notoriously suspicious of 'highbrow learning' that gave the labourer 'an exaggerated idea of his position'.[104] The Governor did not put it in that way but seems to have been of the same opinion. He felt that education should 'establish discipline, form habits of truthfulness, manliness, and readiness for social service'[105]—generally make Africans more governable. The emphasis of the Phelps–Stokes Commission was different but amounted to the same thing; the African should be educated for life in the village. Dr. Jesse Jones, the head of the Commission, with truly American concern for the antiseptic values, wanted hygiene as top educational priority.[106]

The Catholic lack of interest in material transformation, and stress on education as a means to spiritual formation, meant that many planters were happy to accept Catholic schools on their estates whereas they were often chary of the Protestant Industrial Missions.[107] After the 1915 Rising Catholics earned the planters' respect even more by being 'in touch to a special degree with Native opinion'.[108] The only highbrow education dispensed by the Catholics was to seminarians who would disappear to Kipalapala Major Seminary for ten years. When Father Travers, the Vicar-General of the White Fathers, returned from greeting the new Governor, Manning, in March 1911, he put part of their conversation on paper. It is a good illustration of the way Catholic missionaries, planters, and Government, favoured, albeit for different reasons, the same type of education for Africans.

His Excellency, Governor Manning, told him of the complete satisfaction with our missionaries felt by both government and the European settlers. He laid great stress on one point which far from disturbing us, encouraged us to continue with our well-tried methods; it is that on being converted and getting an education in our missions the native does not lose his African 'character';[109] he keeps his station without any feelings of discontent or humiliation, and is not obsessed by a passion to become in all things as much like the *Azungu* as possible.[110]

Manning apparently then went on to compare Nyasaland Catholics with 'Natives from other missions who with very little learning become very self-important'.[111]

When the debate on education opened after the departure of the Phelps–Stokes Commission, many Catholic laymen began to look critically at the education open to them in Catholic schools. Several found it wanting. Their most revealing complaint was that it was virtually impossible to learn English in Catholic institutions. Guillemé and Auneau not only positively believed in vernacular teaching, they lacked teachers qualified to teach English;[112] the first English Daughters of Wisdom were lost to Africans at a European girls' boarding school in Limbe.[113]

Nyasaland Catholics knew very well that fluency in English was a passport to 'middle-class' clerical jobs. Edward Michongwe, whose son was the first Malawian delegate to the United Nations, left for Rhodesia in 1921 after he heard that Catholic schools, under English Jesuits, taught English there.[114] Another ambitious Yao Catholic, Vito Ntwana, one of the first African teachers at Zomba Catholic Secondary School, left for South Africa in 1925 to learn book-keeping. He had spent from 1920 to 1922 trying to improve his English at Nguludi Normal School but had become increasingly dissatisfied with Catholic educational standards.[115]

The period of Montfort expansion undoubtedly resulted in some further decline in already low standards. The Protestant schools in the bush were not much better, though. The Scots showplace institutions at Blantyre and Livingstonia diverted attention from the rather poor grassroots education provided over large areas of the country. The Director of Education's assessment of all Nyasaland's teachers in 1927 was that eight-tenths of them were underqualified;[116] he estimated that Catholic teachers were nine-tenths underqualified. An African Protestant writer, George Simeon Mwase, gives perhaps the most accurate picture of Catholic education in the 1930s.

> We all know that Roman Catholic Schools are the last weak schools ever been in our country. I do not mean that they are bad Schools, but I say that they are weak, in teaching high standards.[117]

It was an opinion shared by even the most devout of Nyasaland Catholics.

Gaunt, the first Director of Education, was one of the first fruits of the recommendations of the Phelps–Stokes Commission; he was a conscientious and able educationalist and began a six months' tour of schools in May 1926. He met the minor seminarists from Mua at Bembeke, heard their band, and gave them a short examination, the results of which seem to have pleased him.[118] But when the Director of Education sat down in December that year to draw up some draft proposals for an Education Ordinance, the Montforts were opening up prayer-houses at the rate of one a week in the Mulanje district. Auneau had foreseen stricter standards and was accelerating the expansion of his network of schools, hoping that it would prove impossible to close them at a later date.[119]

The Catholic campaign at Mulanje resulted in two revisions of Gaunt's draft proposals as the harassed Director of Education discovered loopholes through which the Catholics could, and did, continue to expand their network of 'schools' against the Government's wishes. It was apparent from the final draft that, while discussions about curricula and teacher training programmes were deferred until an education conference convened in Zomba for May 1927, the Government was going to insist immediately on properly trained teachers.

> It may be assumed that village schools with unqualified teachers in charge and with inadequate means of supervision may be actually harmful to the community. The influence of a native teacher in the neighbourhood of his school is very great and it appears unwise to grant such powers to an ignorant and unqualified native.[120]

This was taken by Auneau to be an attack directed at the Catholic teachers. He insisted during an interview with the Governor on 31 March 1927 that unqualified teachers might be intellectually quite able to provide good elementary instruction. With typical flair for touching the administration's chief phobia he concluded the conversation:

> I may add that a supereducated native may not be reliable, as has been proved

in the case of John Chilembwe and the many supereducated natives who followed him in 1915.[121]

It was a very nice touch and Auneau's mixture of tenacity, shrewdness, and sheer cheek won him an important concession. In April, the Governor agreed to the teaching of reading and writing in Catholic prayer-houses.[122]

Notwithstanding, when the Education Conference opened in Zomba on 17 May 1927, the Catholics lost at the conference table some of their gains from the Governor. A general outcry against the Government's assumption of control over an education system almost completely financed by the missions, was tempered on the Protestant side by the *arrière-pensée* that given enough rope the administration might hang the Catholics. The Church of Scotland minister, Rev. E. D. Bowman, was adamant in holding out for an absolute minimum of secular instruction in prayer-houses. Since the Catholics used secular education as a 'bait', to use Gaunt's expression,[123] this was, whether intentionally or otherwise, a blow at Auneau and Guillemé. While it is true that many villagers made no distinction between schools and prayer-houses[124] which taught the Three Rs, so that pupils would be drained from genuine schools, it must have been obvious to Bowman that prayer-houses were the main vehicle used by the Catholics to expand their influence.

The two Catholic Bishops seem to have survived the rigours of the conference by feigning Gallic incomprehension and a measure of rustic simplicity. Given Auneau's campaigns outside the conference room to increase his prayer-houses and turn them into crude schools, his inability to distinguish between the two, at this late date, must have angered all present.

> The Rt. Rev. Bishop Auneau said that he would like to see both reading and writing taught in schools. He thought that it was good for natives to be able to write letters to one another. Also letter writing increased revenue through the Post Office. It was pointed out to Bishop Auneau that the resolution did not refer to schools but only to church classes or prayer houses.[125]

As a result of the 1927 Education Ordinance the Government took control of education in Nyasaland. A Department of Education with teams of school inspectors was formed, curricula were drawn up, and standards for teachers were defined. Recognized mission schools with properly qualified teachers were eligible for Government subsidies. An Advisory Board on Education, comprised of the education secretaries of the different Mission Societies, was set up, but the Government attempted to reserve the right to impose penalties on missions that did not comply with regulations, particularly the stipulation that a return for schools under the supervision of each missionary body had to be made each year.

After the conference the Scots had qualms that the rein they had given the Government might have been a little too free. They were just as worried as the Catholics that their resources would not be adequate to raise the education given in their schools to the level demanded by the Government. Hetherwick began extolling the virtues of his unqualified teachers in terms very reminiscent of

Auneau before the conference. The Scots were also up in arms about the proposed composition of the Advisory Board on Education, two Roman Catholics, two or three members of the Federated Missions,[126] and one delegate from the Universities' Mission to Central Africa. Compromises were made all round. Teachers with long experience in mission schools were given honorary vernacular grade certificates, and the membership of the Advisory Board was boosted to include four Protestant missionaries. Bowman was rewarded with the post of head of the Jeanes training school at Domasi, the leading Government institution for Jeaners who were to be school inspectors and community development workers.[127] These compromises were made law in the 1930 Education Ordinance.

Auneau, while assuming the pose of blank opposition to the Government's new educational measures, had begun to prepare for the evil day when the Education Ordinance became law. During his visit to Nsanje in January 1927, he insisted that catechists be sent to Nguludi Normal School for training rather than being taught at the mission by an unqualified priest.[128] But at Nguludi tiles were loose, teaching went on in acute poverty, and all the pupils had to be financed by the station that sent them.[129] For young men used to the hot climate in the Lower Shire the school was not very enticing.

> Monsignor wants the teachers sent to Nguludi, but they all come back hungry and ill; they don't like the Normal School.[130]

Conditions were not much better in the White Fathers' training school at Kasina, where there was the added inconvenience of inadequate water supplies.[131] The school was moved to Likuni in 1928 and Father Chateauvert put in charge of the all-important English classes.[132] Two Montfort Fathers, Swelsen and Eyssen,[133] were sent away for training in educational methods at Strawberry Hill College in London. Fathers Bossard and Arnaud, the former with a French diploma in agriculture, were given teaching certificates by the Government without further training. However, such certificates were given on condition that the priest spoke competent English and, more important, worked full-time in education in recognized schools.[134] For the White Fathers, who withdrew nine priests for full-time teaching, this represented a considerable commitment to education at the expense of their normal mission work.[135]

While these preliminary attempts at upgrading were being made, the Catholic delegates to the Executive Committee of the Board of Education[136] kept up Auneau's rearguard action. Father Paradis tried to get the question of reading and writing in prayer-houses reopened at the very first meeting. A vote was taken and the two Catholics were the only members voting for the motion.[137] Had it not been for the intervention of Mgr. A. Hinsley, these obstructionist tactics might have continued into the 1930s.

On 7 December 1927, the Rector of the English College in Rome had a private audience with the Pope and later talked with officials of the Propaganda where

> I was instructed to dwell everywhere on the importance of the school. It is the atrium or portal of the Church . . . If anywhere, I was told, it is a question of

building a church or building a school, the school should have first preference, even if the building has also to be used as a church.[138]

By January 1928, Hinsley was in London preparing for a tour of East and Central Africa; as a potential influence over Catholic missionaries in Nyasaland he met with the approval of the Colonial Office.

He is a charming man, and I think will be able to help us in education matters as far as the Catholic Missions are concerned . . . The Pope, he tells me further, is acquainted with our education policy and wishes that all education given in catholic mission schools should help towards the true realisation of the aims and objects set forth in our memorandum on education policy.[139]

His visit to Nyasaland began unspectacularly on 19 June 1928, with a small reception on the corner of Port Herald station, during which his secretary, Father Giesbach, distributed Holy pictures.[140]

The Holy pictures disguised a very astute and forceful personality. In his short tour Hinsley managed to convince the priests in both vicariates of the need for a change in attitude towards education. He made them understand that if improvements were not made quickly and with good grace, the accusation could be levelled against the Church that priests had deliberately kept people in ignorance in order to dominate them. He saw educated Christians, not as threats, but as 'a leaven transforming the rest', and stressed that 'if our schools cannot, or will not, give the lessons and education that meet their (the Africans') demands, others—Government or the sects—will'.[141]

Aside from any missiological considerations, Hinsley also suggested that improvements should be made in the material side of education. He wanted to see solid, well-lit constructions, and one Central School at each station to provide facilities for reaching higher standards. Priests were to learn English as quickly as possible. While he was only giving voice to the education policy of the Colonial Government, coming as the advice did from a prestigious cleric the Catholic missionaries were more inclined to listen than they were to the blandishments of the Education Department.[142] The first four Catholics went for training to the Jeanes School at Domasi in 1928. Both the Montfort candidates, Peter Cinseu and Benito Ntwana,[143] passed, though only Mattias Kalibotona finished the course from the White Fathers' Vicariate.[144]

The situation at the beginning of the 1930s looked very difficult for the Catholic Missions. At the St. Joseph's Normal School, Nguludi, there were Fathers Bossard and Driessen working with a second-grade certificate teacher, Jonas Chimbalanga, and Vito Ntwana who had a third-grade certificate. They were teaching 104 boarders for a three-month term that ran from June to September.[145] The total number of schools in both vicariates was 960 for which the Catholics provided 6 second-grade teachers, 31 third-grade, and 29 teachers with honorary certificates and over twenty years teaching in the Catholic schools.[146] Teachers with first- and second-grade certificates were later known as English grade teachers and were proficient in English. Five of the Catholic second-grade teachers were seminarians who had been withdrawn from the

White Fathers' Minor Seminary at Likuni.[147] In comparison, the two Scots missions, with 590 schools between them, had 6 first-grade teachers, 74 second-grade, 307 third-grade, and 63 teachers with honorary certificates.[148]

The Catholics made tremendous efforts to catch up in the period before the Second World War. Father Villy wrote a teachers' manual, *Mapunzitso a Ecclesia* and Father Driessen produced a Botany book, *Zomera ndi Zolengedwa*, a students' guide, *Bwenzi la Ophunzira*, and a geography book in 1934.[149] In the same year the Normal School at Nguludi was provided with electric light. By 1939 the total number of Catholic schools financially assisted by the Government gave a revenue of £2,000 per annum, and, as priests came back from training courses in Europe, the number of qualified African teachers rose steadily. This was against a background of a large number of unassisted bush schools, made legal by the 1930 Education Ordinance.

TABLE VII[150]

Examination successes 1931–8

Mission	No. candidates vernacular grade	Passes	%	No. candidates English grade	Passes	%
White Fathers	178	141	79	5	5	100
Montfort Fathers	342	257	75	37	27	73
Livingstonia	254	82	32	107	47	44
Church of Scotland	268	114	43	150	52	35

The production of vernacular grade teachers, at the rate of fifty per annum, on an education budget of less than £2,000 throughout the depression years of 1932–5, was an achievement that could not have been predicted from the previous educational efforts of the Catholic missions. It meant that when it came to bush schools the Catholics were able to field an impressive force of teachers in the vernacular. Although 1927 represented a turning point for Catholic education in Nyasaland the policy of widespread bush schools staffed by teachers with no knowledge of English continued unchanged. For the majority of Africans, Catholic education provided just enough learning for mine work or domestic service with Europeans. For many the bush school was the first step towards emigration and the colonial economy beyond the borders of Nyasaland.

The anxiety of the Colonial Government that Africans should have the right sort of education would have been more credible to the Catholic missionaries had the administration given them sufficient money to maintain a workable system of rural schools. The first Catholic Jeanes inspectors, holding one of the most important jobs for Africans in education, were paid at the rate of 24/- per month.[151] Government clerks were earning 30/- at the time, good cooks in European houses 40/-, and mineworkers in Rhodesia from 50/-.[152] Furthermore £1,000 did not go very far in two very large vicariates. Such low payment was self-defeating; no sooner was a teacher trained at great expense than he would emigrate in search of better pay. In 1939, 800 of the 2,500 Catholics around Nsanje emigrated, including nine qualified vernacular grade teachers.[153] Mission diaries in the 1930s were dotted with complaints about 'defections' of catechists and teachers to the mines.

Finally, the same liberalism cum pragmatism that led successive Governors to decline to intervene in interdenominational rivalry, resulted in the Nyasaland administration taking a head-in-the-sand attitude to the greatest single impediment to widespread education in the country, the nyau societies. The first English Education Secretary of the Montforts, Father, later Bishop, Hardman from Preston, seems to have immediately suspected that there was something equivocal about the Government's championing of education for Africans.

> Those who go to the nyau, do not go to the army, produce nothing, and die of hunger the year round . . . having worked too hard during the night they can do nothing during the day. The few well-thinking Natives in the said districts draw the conclusion that since the Government tolerated this state of affairs, it does not wish schools to be opened. The fact is that where there is Zinyau, schools empty themselves automatically.[154]

As long as the societies felt threatened by village schools, and this fear has been a constant feature of village life from the First World War until the present day, they kept up an active campaign to dissuade children from going to school.

Statistics collected in the Chikwawa district on the educational attainment of local nyau society members provide a useful indication of the influence of the Catholic Mission and of literacy on membership. In a total of twelve villages there were 597 nyau members; 516 (87 per cent) of them were illiterate and 81 (13 per cent) were semi-literate. Most interesting was that 13 per cent of the members were baptized Christians.[155] While there was not an exact correlation, the impression that semi-literacy and Christianity were linked seems correct. The majority of the semi-literate nyau members were lapsed Catholics. The population providing recruits for the societies was illiterate pagan villagers. Small wonder the societies fought the bush schools.

At the beginning of the Second World War, Hinsley's hopes had been partially realized. Despite the continued opposition of the nyau societies and a chronic lack of funds, Catholic educational standards had risen in many areas at the cost of a small decrease in the amount of religious instruction carried out in prayer-houses. The Central and Normal Schools had vernacular and English textbooks and the electric light to read them by. The first African priests were coming back from Kipalapala with sixteen years of intensive education behind them; English-speaking Montforts had begun to arrive and most of the older Fathers were speaking heavily-accented but passable English. As pupils reached standard VI, thoughts began to turn to secondary education. It was the Catholic misfortune that the frantic efforts of a decade could not make up for the neglect of a quarter of a century.

Even before Hinsley's impetus to Catholic education the first small beginnings of an articulate African 'middle-class' were already evident. And its members were without exception Protestants. Only occasionally, as in the

Chiradzulu Native Association, under the leadership of Dr. Daniel Male-kebu,[156] were Catholics to be found. Pio Ntwere and Eugenio Matuta held important positions in the Association, but to 'put the Catholic point of view'[157] rather than for more straightforward political motives. Catholics were prominent in no other association.

On arriving, the Catholics had seen their task as religious instruction with secular education to sugar the pill. Their non-élitist view of education had been given the backing of Government and planters alike. They tried to give every villager a small amount of education in their bush schools. The changes of the 1920s caught the White Fathers and Montforts unprepared. If anything they were expanding rather than concentrating their educational efforts, offering the Three Rs, to increasing numbers of villagers.

Because Hinsley represented the thinking of the Vatican, his ideas, which many of the older priests thought were newfangled and overliberal, had been put into action. *Roma locuta est.* . . . Only, by the time the first well-qualified teachers began coming out of the Catholic Normal Schools in the 1930s, the future social contours of modern Malawi had already been sketched in. Nothing the very diligent Catholic missionaries could do, could possibly reverse the process begun in Blantyre and Livingstonia in the late nineteenth century. Whatever the relationship between capitalism and Protestantism in the sixteenth century, in colonial Nyasaland, the Protestantism of the Scots missionaries had slotted Africans into the market economy more effectively than their Catholic rivals.

REFERENCES TO CHAPTER VII

[1] Guillemé to Nyasa missionaries 12 March 1919 in *Règlements et instructions* ibid.

[2] Rev. E. D. Bowman. Comments on Gaunt's notes on J. H. Oldham's memorandum on Native Education in Nyasaland. 2 April 1928. S1/666/28. National Archives. Zomba.

[3] Letter to Members and Friends from Bishop Cathrew. January 1928. S2/2/28.

[4] *Rapports annuels* Dupont's report 1905-6

[5] Nzama Diary 3 February 1902

[6] *Chroniques trimestrielles* No. 129 July 1906

[7] 'The Word of God'

[8] Guillemé to Nyasa missionaries 15 December 1909. Circular found amongst loose papers, Mua mission.

[9] Kachebere Diary 6 April 1909

[10] Unlike the Protestant Churches where members were usually required to be able to read the Bible

[11] Winnen A. *Za Mpulumutsi* St. Peter Claver Missionary Press. Salzburg 1906. Copy at Montfort Archives, Rome.

[12] Literally 'About the Saviour'

[13] Literally 'God alone' i.e. One God

[14] The Dutch Reformed Church also used Bible stories until a ChiChewa Bible was produced in the 1930s.

[15] *Katekismu wa Akatolika* Apostolic Vicariate of Shire 1922

[16] ibid. 41 'Kodi kupereka nsembe kwa mizimu nkucimwa? Ea, kupereka nsembe kwa mizimu nkucimwa, cikufkwa nkupembedza zolengedwa.' 'Do I commit a sin if I offer

sacrifice to the spirits? Yes, to offer a sacrifice to the spirits is a sin because you are praying to creatures.'

[17] *Règlements et instructions* ibid. Baptism and Catechumenate.

[18] ibid.

[19] 'There is no salvation outside the Church'

[20] *Bulletins trimestriels* September 1928, 5

[21] The personal conversion elicited by the 'kerygma', the 'trumpeting forth' of the Gospel message

[22] 'Économe's' report for 1908. Loose papers, Mua mission. cf Chapter III, note 22.

[23] Nzama Diary 10 February 1903. cf page 138.

[24] *Rapports annuels* Mua 1905-6

[25] Dedza District Book 1907 Vol. I. National Archives, Zomba.

[26] Paradis E. 'Notes on the White Fathers' Mission' MS WF Archives Lilongwe

[27] Colonial Office Report No. 574 for the Nyasaland Protectorate, cited in MacDonald R. J. *A History of African Education in Nyasaland: 1875-1945* Doctoral Dissertation, University of Edinburgh. Appendix B.

[28] Minutes of Catholic Education Meetings, Shire Vicariate, 18 March 1937. Catholic Education Archives. Catholic Secretariat, Limbe. By the 1940s when secondary education was beginning, standard VI was the end and standard I the beginning of primary education.

[29] Auneau to Director of Education 5 November 1934 ibid.

[30] Minutes of Catholic Education Meetings 7 October 1930

[31] MacDonald *A History* 33, 122

[32] Mua Diary 4 March 1909

[33] Personal Communication. Rev. J. Blaney s.m.m.

[34] Annual Education Report of Montfort Fathers 1930, Catholic Education Archives, Catholic Secretariat, Limbe

[35] Paradis ibid.

[36] Claude Boucansaud was ordained in 1908 at the age of 27. He became Father-Superior at Likuni in 1920 but left for training and teaching at Bishop's Waltham in England. He returned to Nyasaland in 1930 to teach in the Minor Seminary.

[37] *Notes nécrologiques* 1959 Joseph Mazé. WF Archives, Rome.

[38] Mua Diary 27 February 1911

[39] *Rapports annuels* 1914-15 Mua

[40] Kachebere Diary 4 February 1909

[41] Louis François Villy was ordained in 1910 at the age of 24 and arrived in Nyasaland in 1913. At the time of writing he is still alive and reasonably well at Kasina mission. In his long missionary career his most important work was a ChiChewa translation of the Bible.

[42] Pirouet L. M. 'The First World War—An opportunity missed by the missions'. Paper presented at the University of East Africa, Social Sciences Conference, Kampala, January 1969-70.

[43] Salaun N. 'History of the Catechist' *Catechist Research* Gaba 1969, 10

[44] Guillemé to Nyasa missionaries 12 March 1919 ibid.

[45] ibid.

[46] *Compt. Rend. Synod of Bembeke* 22-24 August 1921. WF Archives, Lilongwe.

[47] Blantyre Diary 22 June 1921

[48] Nsanje Diary 19 July 1921

[49] ibid. 26 September 1921

[50] Nguludi Diary 12 September 1921

[51] Centeno to Bourget 10 June 1920. Montfort Archives, Blantyre.

[52] Gebhard to Auneau 8 July 1921 ibid.

[53] Auneau to Centeno 6 May 1922 ibid.

[54] Oral Testimony, Auguste Baslé s.m.m. Pirimiti mission, Zomba October 1970

[55] Auneau to Gebhard 29 September 1922, and Raphael to Basle 20 October 1922 ibid.
[56] Gebhard to Bourget 7 April 1921 ibid.
[57] Baslé ibid.
[58] Querel ibid. Cahier III.
[59] Nankhunda Mission Diary 2 February 1925 Nankhunda Minor Seminary, Zomba
[60] Between 1918 and 1939 the White Fathers opened six new stations. In the same period the Montforts opened fourteen: Chikwawa (1918), Limbe (1921), Port-Herald (1921), Namuno and Porto Amelia (1922), Zomba (1924), Mulanje (1925), Mwanza (1927), Nsipe (1928) were opened before the 1930s.
[61] Interviews conducted by Kachebere seminarian, Valens Khoriyo, December 1969 with Antonio Katole, Bondo village, Mulanje, Mang'anja, and Pio Samikwa, Mtendereni village P.E.A. Alomwe. We are very grateful to Rev. Khoriyo for conducting these interviews for us.
[62] Oral Testimony, Marko Reid, Catholic catechist, Mang'anja, Mulanje. Interviewed at Likulesi Catechetical School, November 1969.
[63] Mulanje Baptismal Registers, Cisitu mission, Mulanje
[64] Pretorius An Introduction 372
[65] Governor Smith to Colonial Office 27 November 1916. Memorandum attached to Draft Legislation for the regulation of the operation of the missions. S1/1494/19. National Archives, Zomba.
[66] W. H. Murray to Superintendent of White Fathers 19 December 1910. White Fathers' Archives Lilongwe.
[67] Travers to W. H. Murray 2 January 1911 ibid.
[68] Kachebere Diary December 1905
[69] Travers to W. H. Murray 27 February 1911. White Fathers' Archives, Lilongwe
[70] Bernard Onstenk was from Arnhem near Utrecht. He was ordained in 1903 at the age of 25. By the end of 1911 he had returned to Carthage as Professor of Moral Theology.
[71] The Provincial Commissioner
[72] Kachebere Diary 29 April 1911
[73] The popular name for the Dutch Reformed
[74] 'Witches'
[75] Travers to W. H. Murray 24 January 1912. White Fathers' Archives, Lilongwe.
[76] Mua Diary September 1936
[77] Personal Communication, Rev. R. Saffroy w.f. Bishop's House, Lilongwe
[78] Kachebere Diary June 1909
[79] Memorandum to District Commissioners from Acting Deputy Governor, H. L. Duff 25 March 1919. S1/1494/19. National Archives, Zomba.
[80] Our italics
[81] Attorney-General, R. W. Lyall-Grant to Acting Deputy Governor, H. L. Duff. Memorandum 9 September 1910. S1/1494/19.
[82] Rev. Frylinck to Msgr. Guillemé 23 July 1912. White Fathers' Archives. Lilongwe.
[83] Resident at Chiromo to Zomba Secretariat, March 1919. S2/18/27. National Archives, Zomba.
[84] Both referred to in a letter of Governor Smith to Secretary of State for Colonies, March 1916. S1/1494/19. He died in 1923 at the age of 65.
[85] Andrew Bonar Law was Secretary of State for the Colonies in 1915-16, and subsequently Prime Minister.
[86] Bonar Law to Governor Smith 3 August 1916. S/1/1494/19.
[87] Régent to Mulanje Resident 1 November 1925. Catholic Secretariat, Limbe.
[88] Mulanje Resident to R. H. Murray, acting-Provincial Commissioner 7 December 1925. S2/18/27.
[89] Mulanje Diary 26 December 1925

[90] Baslé ibid.
[91] Annual School Report 1926 Mulanje Catholic mission S2/18/27.
[92] Gaunt to Zomba Secretariat 2 November 1927. S2/18/27.
[93] Manser–Barlett Papers, Chancellor College Library, University of Malawi. Papers of a planter in the Mua area 1920–69.
[94] Leopold S. Amery, born in India, pursued a classic career in British Imperialism to become Secretary of State for India in 1940. He was Colonial Secretary 1924–9.
[95] Governor to L. S. Amery Confidential Dispatch, May 1926. S2/18/27.
[96] *Nyasaland Times* 1 February 1924
[97] Quoted in MacDonald *A History* 241
[98] *Rapports annuels* Paradis Report 1926–7
[99] *Nyasaland Times* 25 April 1924
[100] *Rapports annuels* Paradis Report 1926–7
[101] Zambesi Industrial Mission
[102] S1/381/19 National Archives, Zomba
[103] Mumba, another graduate of the Overtoun Institute, was the guiding force behind the North and West Nyasa Native Associations. He became head storekeeper in the Public Works Department at Zomba and, in 1933, the first African member of the Advisory Committee on Education. In 1944 he became the first President of the Nyasaland African Congress.
[104] *Nyasaland Times* 14 March 1924 'Native Education: Scientific management of difficult problems.'
[105] Governor's speech to Executive Committee of the Board of Education 24 June 1930. Quoted in memorandum of 22 July 1930 to Paradis. Catholic Education Archives, Catholic Secretariat, Limbe.
[106] *Nyasaland Times* 16 May 1924
[107] R. H. Murray to Zomba Secretariat 10 December 1925. Marginal comment made at Secretariat. S2/18/27.
[108] ibid.
[109] A translation of 'touche', also in inverted commas in the original
[110] Mua Diary 26 March 1911
[111] ibid.
[112] Guillemé to Governor 5 February 1926. Comments on proposals by the Advisory Committee for Education in the Colonies for vernacular teaching: 'The recommendations are quite right, practical, and the only ones well adapted to the general mentality of the Natives. They show that the members of the committee are perfectly acquainted with the matter of native education in Africa.' White Fathers' Archives, Lilongwe.
[113] For example Sister Alice de la Sagesse who arrived in 1921 and Sister Adelaide-Marie who arrived in 1922
[114] Interview, Edward Michongwe Yao, Zomba, December 1968. Amongst his other children are a nun, an American Ph.D., and another with an important position in the Civil Service.
[115] Interview, Vito Ntwana, Yao, Nguludi, September 1969
[116] Report on Native Education Conference, May 1927, S1/342/27 and Confidential Memorandum, Gaunt to Zomba Secretariat 8 March 1927. S2/18/27.
[117] Rotberg *Strike a Blow* 64
[118] Mua Diary 25–26 July 1926
[119] Draft Education Proposals, S2/18/27. Gaunt to Zomba Secretariat 8 April 1927 wrote that the Bishop's unwillingness to wait until after the Conference would appear to disclose a desire firmly to establish a number of inefficient "schools" before the promulgation of an ordinance than might exert an irksome control S2/18/27.
[120] Final Draft Education Proposals Paragraph 4. 3 February 1927. Catholic Secretariat, Limbe.

[121] Auneau to Gaunt 1 March 1927 and 31 March 1927. White Fathers' Archives, Lilongwe. This was very much in line with the thinking of Attorney-General A. Hogg who suggested to Governor Smith in 1916 that it would be better to spend more money on an improved police force than on the suggested Education Ordinance. A surprisingly contemporary thought. S1/1494/19.

[122] Governor to Auneau 20 April 1927. S2/18/27. The importance of the victory to the situation at Mulanje can be seen from the fact that the news was appearing in the Mulanje diary only six days later on 26 April 1927.

[123] In a memorandum from Gaunt to Zomba Secretariat of 8 April 1927. S2/18/27.

[124] ibid. 'The chief need is for a name for village mission houses which will distinguish them from schools proper.' The name coined in the end was 'church classes'. It was typical that the 172 Catholic institutions around Mulanje in 1927 were referred to by Gaunt as 'prayer-houses' and in the Mulanje Diary by Father Régent as 'schools'.

[125] Report of Native Education Conference 17–22 May 1927. White Fathers' Archives, Lilongwe.

[126] The Federated Missions comprised all the Protestant denominations run by Europeans in Nyasaland. The Universities' Mission to Central Africa with its Anglo-Catholic background in the Oxford Movement had always declined to join.

[127] MacDonald A History 273–300

[128] Port-Herald Diary, January 1927

[129] Interview. Father J. Eyssen S.M.M. Likulesi catechetical school, October 1970.

[130] Port-Herald Diary January 1927

[131] Oral Testimony Mattias Kalibotona, ex-Jeaner Kachebere, August 1969

[132] Interview, Francois-Xavier Lapointe W.F. Mtendere, August 1969

[133] This was Father Jean Swelsen, the brother of the William Swelsen almost killed at Nguludi in 1915. Both Swelsen and Eyssen were Dutch.

[134] Executive Committee of the Board of Education. Minutes of the meeting on 2 December 1927. Each recognized European teacher was worth £200 per annum, or £150 per annum if a woman, to the mission. S1/1547/27.

[135] These were Fathers Braire, Morissette, Paradis, Chateauvert, Roy, and Audet, all Canadians with degrees from Laval University, Montreal; Honoré and Louis with French degrees; and Darot with a degree in canon law from Rome. The nuns recognized were: Sister François-Régis (French certificate) and Sisters Louis-Marie and Louisa (Canadian certificates).

[136] The Advisory Board of Education took on this title.

[137] Executive Committee of Board of Education Minutes of the meeting 30 August–1 September 1927. The voting was 8–2 with only Paradis and Thériault for a re-opening of the question. 'Fr. Paradis protested that but for religious competition this question would never have arisen. His mission could not institute numbers of schools at once; they had not the necessary qualified teachers.' White Fathers' Archives, Lilongwe.

[138] Recommendations of the Apostolic-Visitor 10 August 1928. Catholic Secretariat, Limbe.

[139] Colonial Office to Bowring 26 January 1928. S1/1054/26.

[140] Port-Herald Diary 19 June 1928 and Nyasaland Times 22 June 1928.

[141] Hinsley to Guillemé 5 July 1928 in Le Petit Écho No. 188 1 May 1929. Le Petit Écho is the popular mission magazine of the Society of Our Lady of Africa. However Hinsley also pleaded for unassisted schools in a meeting with the Governor and was rewarded in the 1930 Education Ordinance.

[142] R. J. Gaunt, who died, tragically, of an appendicitis operation while on leave in England in 1928, was remarkably patient with the Catholics, but firm. Another Scot, he had formerly been a school inspector in Kenya.

[143] The brother of Vito Ntwana. The amount of work undertaken by Jeaners was tremendous. Each one supervised twelve to fourteen schools and had to spend a lot of time travel-

ling around visiting them by bicycle. They were worth only £15 per annum to each mission in a Government grant.

[144] Kalibotona ibid.

[145] Annual Education Report of Montfort Fathers 1930 Catholic Secretariat, Limbe

[146] Report of Education Department, Zomba, for 1930, 17, ibid.

[147] François-Xavier Lapointe ibid.

[148] As Reference 146

[149] From a list of Montfort publications compiled by Bishop Auneau for a report to the Propaganda Fidei in 1943. Montfort Archives, Blantyre.

[150] Quoted in MacDonald *A History*, 383. Made from statistics in annual education reports 1931–8.

[151] Kalibotona ibid.

[152] We have not been able to check these figures.

[153] Annual Education Report of Montfort Fathers 1939 Catholic Secretariat, Limbe

[154] ibid. 1940

[155] For details see Schoffeleers J. M. and Linden I. 'The Resistance of the Nyau Societies to the Roman Catholic Missions in Colonial Malawi' in *The Historical Study of African Religion* 263

[156] Dr. Malekebu was fortunately out of the country during the Chilembwe rising and was allowed to begin the Providence Industrial Mission again when he returned in the 1920s. Many of the Catholic missionaries looked on the rebirth of the P.I.M. with the gravest suspicion. The P.I.M. is now a thriving mission with branches in Rhodesia and South Africa, and still under the very able leadership of Dr. Malekebu.

[157] Pio Ntwere ibid.

CHAPTER VIII

Nuns and Priests

> There took place today, March 25th, 1924, the feast of the Annunciation of Our Lady, a very touching ceremony in our oratory. Our first five African girls took the habit. After having done their level best to respond to the wishes of their mistresses during the last two years, to work zealously to combat the practices and habits of paganism, they gave sufficient satisfaction to be allowed to begin wearing religious dress.
>
> *Bulletins Trimestriels* September 1924[1]

One of the most significant features of Catholicism, both in the young Churches of the missions, and in the longer established Churches of the West, has been the division of the *civitas dei* into what might be called first- and second-class citizens. Priests, Brothers, and nuns, by virtue of their vocation to the celibate state, were commonly and authoritatively thought to be practising a higher calling than other Church members, the laity. The Church was therefore able to accommodate varying degrees of commitment to the Christian life. Around the clerical sect was an ill-defined penumbra of more-or-less dedicated laity. This gave to the Roman Catholic Church a structural resilience not shared by smaller Protestant denominations that demanded a sect level of commitment from all its members.

The secular clergy were overtaken by celibacy in the fourth century when the monastic spirit became a norm for Christendom. The ascetic practices and celibacy of the monks of the first three centuries implied a high degree of commitment to otherworldliness. The monastic ideal made inroads on the Church. This was a natural result of the prevailing theological climate, whose moderate Monophysitism[2] emphasized the Divinity of Christ to the detriment of His Humanity. Augustine's belief in the intrinsic sinfulness of all human sexuality provided a moral backing for the Christology propounded by the Alexandrian theologians,[3] which finally triumphed in the fifth-century Council of Chalcedon.[4] If sexual acts were sinful, it followed that those in the most intimate contact with the Deity, at the altar, should remain celibate. Its syllogistic simplicity was enshrined in the law of the Roman Catholic Church; all marriages contracted by priests were considered to be invalid.

The rulings of the Councils of Nicea, Elvira, and the Lateran, together with intermittent Papal directives, testify to the antiquity, and therefore the strength, of a tradition which linked celibacy with service at the altar. Only, in the

Western Church, celibacy was never thought of as merely a strong tradition. Despite the Vatican's recognition of the validity of orders held by married Uniate and Orthodox clergy, celibacy was assumed to be necessarily linked to the priesthood.

The nineteenth-century aftermath of Jansenism,[5] far from undermining the Roman Catholic position on celibacy, resulted in a further extension of the monastic ideal into even Christian marriage. An exemplary French Catholic like the father of St. Thérèse de Lisieux intended, on marrying, to practise a Josephite marriage, 'unsullied' by sexuality. He was only deterred by his wife's insistence that it was the duty of a Catholic couple to provide celibates for the Church.[6] This was an extreme example of nineteenth-century attitudes to sexuality and womanhood. None the less, it was generally held by pious Catholics that the role of women in society was either child-bearing or service to the Church as a nun, with the former very much second-best. The female stereotypes that loomed over French society are personified in the plaster Virgins of church art, and in Toulouse-Lautrec's prostitutes, the pasty symbols of purity and motherhood, or the tragic victims of unbridled lust. There can be no doubt that these stereotypes survived the journey from Europe and Canada to Africa undertaken by the early Catholic missionaries.

The Montfort Fathers, members of a Religious Order that had grown up in reaction to Jansenism,[7] were certainly imbued, both with a belief in a first-class citizenship in the Church, and with a firm conviction that celibacy was a superior way of life. They had begun as an Order for women and the Montfort Fathers had formerly been chaplains to their convents. They were therefore in no doubt as to the value of women in the mission field. Within four years of their arrival the Montfort Fathers were being assisted by ten Sisters belonging to the 'La Sagesse' Order, the Daughters of Wisdom.[8] All came from France except Sister Marie-Reine de Jésus, born Philomène Cecile Sako in Mosul, Iraq. After reading Grignon de Montfort's treatise, 'True Devotion to Mary' quite by chance, and after much discussion with her parish priest, she was still sufficiently enthusiastic about de Montfort's ideas to undertake an arduous camel journey across the desert to Beirut, whence she continued to Marseilles and a *La Sagesse* convent in France. She was a woman of considerable dynamism and strength, working consecutively as nurse, cook, and teacher; villagers around Nzama paid tribute to her energy in their nickname, 'Mai Moto' (Mother Fire).[9] Until her death at Mulanje in 1945, she never became fully accustomed to sitting on chairs, preferring to sit cross-legged on the floor in Arab style. Amongst the early Sisters, Sister Thérèsine returned to France, after beginning a school at Nzama; Sister Charité de Montfort died of malaria at Nguludi within months of arriving in a second caravan in 1905, and Sister Maximus was to die in 1911.[10]

The importance of these women in the Catholic attempt to penetrate and influence village society should not be underestimated. The amount of contact between priests and women in the villages was naturally limited. Not only did the Fathers respect the normal segregation of the sexes in traditional society, but the regulations drawn up by the two bishops bristled with prohibitions concerning contact 'avec le sexe'.[11] Their prudence was well-advised as most European men approaching women were assumed to be looking for mistresses.

The nuns used to go into the villages freely, and would sit on the mat with important women such as Manga, the chief wife of Njobvualema, and Anaphiri, his mother. They distributed presents and were widely accepted. They were able as nurses to go into Protestant and Muslim huts, never hesitating actively to seek out the sick and to proselytize. Although the wives of the Dutch Reformed ministers did accompany their husbands on visits to the villages, they usually had family responsibilities. Without any family ties, the nuns were able to give the Catholic Missions an important advantage in evangelization by working through the female population and its leading women.

Women past the age of childbearing, visited frequently by the Sisters, were the principal educators of younger girls in the village. They taught girls traditional patterns of behaviour, about menstruation and childbirth, how to treat their husbands, and how to make themselves sexually attractive. Education for the next stage in the life-cycle was an important element in the female initiation ceremonies. And neither Chewa nor Ngoni women showed any readiness to abdicate their responsibility for education, whether to priests, to nuns, or to women designated for the purpose by the local Church. Girls were not encouraged to go to the mission school. The interest of boys in elementary education was usually accorded greater toleration. Attitudes to women's education were very resistant to change, as may be inferred from the following diary at Mua in 1946.

> We had special difficulty in getting two girls into the boarding school at Bembeke. The Mother-Superior insisted on their going as they were intelligent and promised to make good future teachers. But the mother and grandmother wanted none of it. There were many different reasons given; the real one was that they did not want them to grow up at Bembeke. There was a risk of their not getting a husband if they had not been initiated in the village; they might even die. Was it not said that Gilberta, a graded teacher who grew up at the boarding school, died before giving birth because she had been reared away from the village at the house of strangers? The old women took it upon themselves to stuff her head with the usual rubbish when she got married. Eight days confinement to her hut without Sunday mass even, and drums and nyau all night. She was given a rude introduction to the Amaravi customs.[12]

A few years earlier women had to be threatened with excommunication to get them to attend the maternity clinic.[13]

Districts in which African societies remained intact, and European penetration very slight, such as the region around Nsanje, gave a pronounced difference in the ratio of the male to female baptisms. In the first ten years of the Nsanje Mission, women never formed more than 20 per cent of the total number of neophytes each year. The ratio of boys to girls at school at Likuni, a Chipeta area, between 1919 and 1928 was 2:1. In areas where Ngoni influence was strong, for example Kachebere, the number of boys and girls attending school was nearly equal.[14]

This reluctance of women to enter the orbit of the mission stations in the principal Chewa/Mang'anja districts seems to have been correlated with the prevalence of *chinamwali*, the Chewa transition rites for women at puberty and first pregnancy. Catholic missionaries in both vicariates, finding it impossible to eradicate the rites, attempted to modify them. Guillemé wrote:

> Chinamwali will have to be tolerated as it is impossible to suppress it. However missionaries should recommend to their christians that they suppress anything immodest in this ceremony.[15]

Auneau had got round to thinking about a substitute Christian ceremony for the Yao *unyago* and the Chewa *chinamwali* by the beginning of the Second World War. The result of his suggestion was to direct Christian matrons to instruct girls and forbid them to undergo any manipulation of the genitalia, as was the normal practice.[16] The priests did not like the initiation rites but they were aware of their importance in village life. Unlike their reaction to the nyau societies, their opposition to *chinamwali* was usually characterized by moderation.

Much of the priests' outrage at the nyau societies, and to a lesser degree the initiation rites, came from their feeling that women were being abused. One of the few occasions on which the Fathers would intervene in Government matters, on behalf of African interests,[17] was when women were involved. While they confided to other priests their disapproval of the chaining and beating of men that went on during the tax forays, and did nothing, they took positive action when they encountered similar treatment of women. There was a spate of cases during 1935–6 in which young women were taken off to Bomas for allegedly failing to pay their taxes. Many instances of wives being punished instead of their defaulting husbands also came to the missionaries' attention. Auneau, inundated with complaints from his clergy, whose sense of chivalry was aroused, was obliged to reassure his vicariate that:

> Neither the DC, Headmen nor Native Authorities have any right to detain a tax defaulter's wife, or send her to work for anyone, to raise money for her husband's tax.[18]

Father Champmartin had been successfully lodging complaints with the District Commissioner at Dedza on behalf of girls around Mua, a year earlier. He was told:

> It is perfectly clear that respectable unmarried girls under 18 years of age do not pay tax even if they have their own hut. I am very glad that you have brought the matter to my notice.[19]

In most cases the Boma police were acting without the knowledge of the District Commissioner. In other instances the young women were anything but respectable and were using their hut for professional purposes.

Catholic missionaries saw tax collection, not in holistic political terms of colonial domination, but from a narrower viewpoint as individual cases of mistreatment of Africans. Their moral values were centred on the family, more than on society as a whole, which they saw as a huge Family, and they saw the suffering of Africans as the result of the bad behaviour of a few individuals. They never concluded that colonial society necessarily entailed exploitation. But when individual instances of bad behaviour affected their most cherished symbols of womanhood, the unmarried virgin and the mother of a family, they reacted strongly.

The nuns took their work amongst African women to be their most important contribution to mission work, apart from being of more general assistance to the Fathers. Their contacts with women paid immediate dividends; the persistent visiting by Sister Marie-Reine to NaPhiri, the third wife of Njobvualema, resulted in the Ngoni's baptism, a day before she died in 1907.[20] The nuns made a very unfavourable assessment of the role of women in traditional society.

> Our principal task is the raising up of women, who in this country are regarded and treated as slaves.[21]

A militant but not entirely balanced assessment. It was true that in the nineteenth century a combination of slavery and Ngoni raiding had reduced women to the level of barter goods of little more value than good cattle. In the colonial period African women were often reduced to being sexual objects for planters and the occasional colonial official, being offered in some instances by their husbands, in order to gain compensation. But many of the older Ngoni and Chewa women were far from being slaves in their villages. The Chewa grandmother was often the priests' most formidable opponent. They bore little resemblance to any of the Victorian stereotypes of womanhood. Knowing only patrilineal France and Holland, the priests treated them as they would a powerful French 'grand' mère'. The *mulier fortis* of matrilineal Chewa society was something of an enigma to priests and nuns alike.

There was one similarity. A life-time of child-bearing was the lot of every woman in the village, if for no other reason than to make up for the depredations of disease. Despite the provision of maternity clinics at some of the stations in the 1930s, child mortality remained high. Discounting stillbirths, in the fifteen years after the First World War at Mua, there were 2,237 registered births; 808 children out of these died before the age of 2 years, 132 between two and five years, and 53 between five and fifteen years; 44 per cent mortality. The comparable statistics over the same period in the more Ngonized community around Ntaka-taka, were 3,160 live births; 695 out of these children died before the age of two years, 166 between two and five years, and 142 between five and fifteen years; 32 per cent mortality.[22] With such mortality amongst Christians who had access to some medical facilities, and in most cases enough education to use them, child mortality amongst the general population along the lakeshore can be imagined.

The demands of a large family, young children on the back that cried and needed feeding, reduced the concentration of the average woman even on a simple catechism lesson. Priests had usually to bellow above the sound of crying babies, and dreaded classes that included married women. Despite high mortality, the population of villages was largely composed of children. In the 84 villages around Bembeke Mission in 1920, there were 4,169 huts with 12,901 inhabitants; 5,908 of these, almost 50 per cent, were children between the ages of one and fifteen. To look after them there were 3,490 married women and 598 widows, at least one child for every woman over fifteen years of age.[23]

In Chewa society a man gained acceptance in his wife's matrilineage with the birth of his first child. He became part of the village through his children. The only brake on the number of conceptions was a taboo on sexual intercourse during lactation, and on a number of other ritual occasions. From baptismal registers, this seems to have produced a two to three year spacing between children. The only hope for a girl wishing to avoid a life-time of pregnancies was to marry an older polygamous man. This solution was not permitted to Christians. In the value system of village life, a large family, together with a good herd of goats or cattle and productive gardens, were the *summum bonum*. These Old Testament values were readily embraced by the first missionaries, many of whom could themselves count over ten brothers and sisters, and for whom the terms womanhood and motherhood were equally synonymous.

Marriage was regulated by traditional law, which ensured that matrimony was primarily a contract between two lineages rather than between two individuals. This contrasted strongly with the more individualist notions of marriage held by the missionaries. The Fathers felt strongly that even young girls were free to choose, and that consent was an important element in the contract.[24] Superimposed on traditional law was Protectorate legislation, which in the 1902 and 1912 Marriage Ordinances had tried to introduce English law to govern marriages between Christians. The 1902 Ordinance was framed with the European population in mind,[25] while that of 1912 was designed, on the instigation of the Protestant missionaries, to cover Christian marriage between Africans. Christian marriage was given a special status, with divorce proceedings in the High Court at Blantyre, a five-year penalty for bigamy, and English laws of inheritance. Christian ministers were supposed to have their churches licensed and themselves registered as civil registrars of marriage.

There was, though, a gulf between a piece of paper signed in Zomba and the reality of the marriage contract in the village. Neither Roman Catholics nor priests of the Universities' Mission to Central Africa were willing to point out to couples the legal procedures for divorce. Africans marrying under the 1912 Ordinance found themselves legally subject to procedures and penalties that might have been reasonable in Edwardian England, but were ludicrous in Nyasaland. The Livingstonia missionary, Fraser, felt that the Government was gratuitously enforcing 'the Law of Christ with fines and penalties'.[26] Moggridge, then District Commissioner at Mzimba, went so far as to say: 'The 1912 Ordinance pleases not more than 25% of the worst class of missionaries.'[27] The Roman Catholics ignored the Ordinance altogether.

When it became apparent to the Government, in the wake of the findings of the Commission of Enquiry into the Chilembwe Rising, that none of the

Catholic priests had bothered to register, and were therefore liable to prosecution, some rationalization of the procedures was felt to be imperative. If the Catholics were unwilling to act as registrars, it meant that the work would have to be done by District Officers. However, if couples were married by the District Commissioner, with a ceremony that lasted thirty minutes, he would have had time for little else.[28] A missionary conference was held in Zomba on 7 April 1920 to formulate a new Marriage Ordinance, and was attended by three Catholics and seven Protestants.[29] Government, Roman Catholics, and Universities' Mission to Central Africa were united in wanting the traditional marriages performed in the village to be civilly recognized, and the religious ceremony to be optional. This fitted the Catholic conception of the separation of Church and State, and suited the Government as it meant no extra work for the District Commissioners. The Protestants wanted traditional law to be modified for Christians so that divorce was only possible in cases of desertion and adultery. The less complicated Catholic position carried the day; priests merely had to explain that traditional village marriage was legally binding in the eyes of the Government.[30] There is no evidence that they ever did.

Marriage issues between Catholics, or in which one of the partners was a Catholic, became the responsibility of the mission. The District Commissioner was a final court of appeal for the civil aspects of divorce only. Having been delivered from the marriage laws of Edwardian England Catholic villagers now found themselves subjected to the laws of mediaeval Rome. The extraordinary complexities of canon law were brought to bear on the marriages of uncomprehending peasants. On occasions, marriage cases would work their way from the mission, through the Bishop, to Rome. There, it might be decided after lengthy deliberation by the leading canon lawyers that a couple living in technical concubinage could be legally married in church. When the good news finally got back to the mission, some two years later, it was more than likely that the unhappy couple had separated.[31]

However great the respect for family life that led priests strongly to oppose the emigration of men from villages to the mines, the Catholic stand on the indissolubility of marriage proved a two-edged sword. At Kasina mission in 1930, it was calculated that forty-six out of 170 heads of Catholic families were absent from their villages, working; five had been away for several years and showed no further signs of life. In the eighteen villages around Likuni mission forty-eight heads of families were away, and thirty-six of these had dissolved their former marriages and remarried. From a total of sixty-six men away from these eighteen villages, only £46 was sent back each year for the support of their families.[32]

The pressure for divorce by deserted women had become so great by 1928 that the Provincial Commissioner for the Central Region called a conference of headmen to discuss the issue. It was decided that if the husband failed to send money home, or if he had been away longer than two years, the woman was entitled to divorce.[33] The refusal of the Catholic Missions to recognize divorce between Catholics validly married in church resulted in intolerable hardships for deserted families. While the missionaries did everything they could to alleviate the attendant problems, acting as a post-office for letters to and from the mines and using lay Catholics to help deserted mothers, the ban on divorce increased hardship. The natural and sensible thing for a deserted woman to do was remarry. Furthermore, the ban clashed with traditional law. Old women readily counselled divorce in the case of marital discord,[34] and Principal Headmen had promptly agreed with the Provincial Commissioner in 1928 that changes in traditional law were required for the new circumstances of widespread family breakdown. They even concurred in the ruling that if the brothers of the departed husband made no effort to help his wife, divorce was in order, a logical conclusion from the premise that marriage was a contract between two families. This was, of course, quite unacceptable to the Fathers.

The result of the Catholic stand was that a third class of citizens of the *civitas dei* came into being, men and women who had some marriage 'impediment', and were therefore excluded from the sacraments of the Church. Many such people were lost to the missions. The obdurate attempt to play King Canute, and by outright prohibitions turn back the waves of social disruption caused by emigration, proved very costly to the Church in time and members. Not only did it result in a loss of baptized Catholics from full Church membership, but it took hours of the priests' and catechists' time, as they tried together to find some loophole that might release a woman from the intolerable choice between penury and loneliness, or exclusion from full participation in Church life.

It is not without significance that the first Religious Order for African women in Nyasaland began at the height of this disintegration in village life in the 1920s. Its two founder members were women separated from their husbands. In April 1922, two women who were living next to Nankhunda mission, and employed to look after orphans at the station, were sent to Nguludi in the hope that they would become the nucleus of an Order of African Sisters. One of them, Elizabeth Nyambala, had been married at the age of 14–15, but had refused to accompany her husband to his village. She had later moved close to the mission dispensary to get regular treatment for severe sores on her legs. The second woman, Martha Phiri, also nearly 30, had been abandoned by her husband as a result of suffering from disfiguring sores. Both of them continued to work with orphans at Nguludi under the supervision of the Daughters of Wisdom. Within months they were followed by a young girl from Nzama, Amartha Sibwi, who had enquired from the Father-Superior how she might avoid marriage. A fourth candidate, Eulalia Phiri, an orphan who had been cared for in the boarding school at Utale, was sent to Nguludi, to be followed soon after by a coloured girl, Maria Maya, who had been brought up by the Daughters of Wisdom at Nguludi.[35]

A rule modelled on that of the Daughters of Wisdom was drawn up by Bishop Auneau, and after three weeks' retreat in complete silence with a series of lessons twice daily from the Bishop, the women were allowed to take the habit and formally begin the religious life. Approval for the proposed Order was received from Rome and the noviciate at Nguludi was ceremonially inaugurated in August 1926. The novices were taught to read, write, and sew. On 15 August 1928, the Feast of the Blessed Assumption, they took the next step, the profession of their first solemn Religious vows.[36] By then, the thirteen novices of 1925 had dwindled to seven, one of whom left within five years of profession.

The seven 'Little Servants of the Blessed Virgin Mary' were obliged to take their title quite literally; four stayed at Nguludi, cooking and caring for orphans, while the remaining three were sent to the new European girls' boarding school at Limbe to perform menial tasks.[37] At least in theory, they were destined for the same kind of mission work as the Daughters of Wisdom.

> The aim of this work is to make them capable of doing everything the Daughters of Wisdom do in the Shire, and then to put them into the hotter stations where we are unable to go ourselves, especially those with orphans and without Sisters.[38]

But the African Sisters continued in domestic work for some time. In the spirituality of the Daughters of Wisdom the girls were learning in the school of humility, followed without flinching by their foundress, Marie-Louise Trichet;[39] in the minds of the African Sisters, it was an unnecessary brake on their advancement as women and nuns.

After the opening of a new convent and boarding school at Mulanje in 1933, and an increased Government interest in women's education, the first African novices began to pass vernacular grade examinations, and later English grade, to become teachers. There was a growing need for women teachers and the African Sisters were eager for intellectual work. The first African community with its own Mother-Superior was opened at Mulanje in 1949. Although the 'relèvement' of women announced by the European Sisters was a slow process, something tangible had been achieved in this small Order of nuns whose numbers increased yearly.

'Relèvement' was a relative term though. The training of the African Sisters was marked by a concern lest material, rather than spiritual, progress should characterize the Order. The attempt was made to keep the Sisters as close to African village life as possible. Novices worked in the gardens, but, on the other hand, African Sisters did not carry out mission work in the villages. The order was begun at the time when the Daughters of Wisdom were becoming increasingly institutionalized and fully occupied in educational and medical work. The closeness to village life was carried to extremes in a ban on shoes and knives and forks that only ended in 1957. In the 1950s and 60s, the number of nuns doubled from 75 to 165.[40]

The religious training given novices included many of the special features of Montfort spirituality. The role of the Virgin Mary as the Mother of God was emphasized. Even communion was said to be received 'through' the Mother of God, and the communicant was supposed to return Christ in spiritual form to his Mother. These strange Mariological doctrines resulted from seeing Mary as a personification of the Church. Christ always, and only, came to the communicant through the Church. Whatever the theological niceties, it was a theology that teetered on the brink of implicit heresy when not handled by sophisticated theologians, and gave even Pius XII some qualms after his canonization of de Montfort. It must have been a strange introduction to the

Religious Life for the African Sisters. None the less, the Virgin Mary, a woman, was held up as an object of veneration and admiration. However alien the plaster statue that adorned churches in Nyasaland, with its cream complexion, blue eyes, and roses, grown men would fall to their knees before it and consider it a representation of a woman second only to Christ. While certainly an archetype of Western Catholicism, it represented an elevation of womanhood which profoundly impressed African Catholics. They soon saw that African women could aspire to, and live successfully, a conscious imitation of the life of the Virgin Mary.[41]

The idea of a bride of God was not unknown to Chewa religion. Women used to be chosen to serve Chiuta at the important rain-shrine of Msinja, at the foot of the Dzalanyama mountains,[42] and M'bona, the guardian spirit of the Mang'anja, had to be supplied with a wife by Chief Lundu.[43] Although at Msinja, Makewana might have ritual intercourse with the Mbewe clan official, Kamundi, it was generally held that she slept with an incarnation of Chiuta in the form of a python.[44] Chewa women could, and did, achieve considerable fame as 'Mangadzi', rain-shrine prophets, or as *mfumumkazi*,[45] female chiefs such as the Mwali at Mankhamba.[46] However, it seems unlikely that any of the first Sisters would have accepted these ancient practices. Certainly the later nuns treated such beliefs with suspicion and rejected them as superstitions. They came from upwardly mobile families which valued education and had largely repudiated traditional ways of life.

An analysis of the occupations of fathers of today's Malawian nuns belonging to the order the 'Servants of the Blessed Virgin Mary',[47] shows that less than 25 per cent were simple subsistence farmers. Three-quarters of them held positions that ranged from Village Headman and tobacco farmer, at one end of the scale, to civil service posts at the other. The majority had been teachers at some stage in their career. Nearly all the Sisters had had some contact with European nuns before they joined the Order, and most were eager for education and personal advancement. A survey of convents at Nguludi, Nankhunda, Limbe, Mulanje, and Nzama showed that 35 per cent of the Sisters came from 'Ngoni' families, 30 per cent were Alomwe, 25 per cent Achewa, either Nyanja, Chipeta, or Mang'anja, and only 10 per cent were Yao.[48] The figures accurately reflected the overall ethnic responses to the Catholic missions, except for the high percentage, 35 per cent, of nuns from 'Ngoni' families.

Ngoni women seem to have held privileged positions in their society in the past. Women sorcerers, NaMagagula and NaNdumbu, were consulted when war was considered, and undertook the rain-sacrifices.[49] NaMlangeni was a powerful figure at Chikusi's court, and his wives dressed well and were treated with respect. The power of the *wachinusi* sorcerers amongst the Maseko naturally declined when the paramounts became Christian during the colonial period. Similarly the past widespread intermarriage with large numbers of Chewa wives became a threat to the authority of Ngoni women from the Swazi clans. By the Second World War, Ngoni women were in a very ambiguous position, caught between Chewa and Ngoni patterns of life. Unlike Sena women who were able to express their grievances by way of spirit possession cults,

Ngoni women, in the same type of patrilocal, patrilineal society lacked such quasi-religious means of asserting themselves and despised them as of Chewa origin. At the same time it was very difficult to escape into any European style career as a teacher when married. They got the worst of all worlds.

Although Bishop Auneau told the first African novices that they had 're-nounced riches',[50] he was talking of a religious idea of poverty, the lack of personal possessions. The Sisters were renouncing not European but African riches, a family, perhaps a far greater sacrifice. The spotless convents offered a way of life equal, and probably superior, to that of most secondary school teachers. An element in the success of the Religious Order for Ngoni women in the Shire Vicariate was that it provided a much superior life-style to the daily drudgery of village life, to women who aspired to something more than a life-time of pounding maize and bearing children. Another was that the Religious Life offered a way of expressing genuine religious sentiments that found no outlet in colonial Ngoni society.

It is plain that the Little Servants of the Blessed Virgin Mary gave Catholic girls one of the few channels for female independence in colonial Malawi. Convent life was humanly, materially, and spiritually, an improvement on village life; it gave women a dignified and personally fulfilling existence. That achievement of status, liberation from the constraints of a male-dominated society, and religious sensitivity, should be linked is not surprising when Sena spirit mediums, Chewa rain-shrine priestesses, and Ngoni sorcerers and diviners, are recalled. African religious consciousness seems never to have suffered from the peculiarly Western habit of dividing life irreducibly into the Religious and the Secular.

This is not to say that the response of Malawian women to the Christian celibate vocation can be explained exclusively in terms of a sociology of religion. Human behaviour can be understood against a number of different horizons, without contradiction. It is no less true to say that the intention of today's Malawian Sisters, when they became novices, was to serve God with total dedication. Yet the successful recruitment of Alomwe and Ngoni women into the Order may be placed meaningfully in the context of the pre-colonial past and the religious spirit of the tribes around Lake Malawi. The Roman Catholic call to the celibate vocation did not fall on some *tabula rasa*, but on complex societies with living cultural and religious systems. That it came at a time when these societies were under considerable stress, and showed signs of disintegration under the impact not of a colonialism that operated far beyond the borders of Nyasaland, should be ignored. The recruits for the Religious Life were not dis-embodied souls, but African women, at a very critical stage in the history of their societies.

In Guillemé's Vicariate the impact of European nuns was less. The first White Sisters arrived in Nyasaland only in 1911, and remained four lone women, two French and two Canadian, until reinforced in 1921. One of the first Sisters remembered the impression they made:

The people were very surprised to observe that several women could live together in peace and harmony without the presence amongst them of a man to stop them quarrelling.[51]

A boarding school for girls was founded in 1924 at Kachebere, but at this time only the Northern Rhodesian administration had any interest in women's education and no Nyasaland girls attended. An order of African nuns, the Theresian Sisters,[52] was begun in 1929, and the first Sisters professed in 1932. Because there were very few White Sisters until the 1930s, and the Order started late in a Chewa area, recruitment into the Theresian sisters was slower than in the south. Educational standards for admission to the noviciate were slightly higher than in the Shire and there were only seventy-five professed Sisters by 1970.[53]

In both vicariates, the presence of nuns turned the station into a centre for outcasts from the villages. After the Spanish Influenza outbreak of 1919, when over 300 people died around Nzama mission, an orphanage was started there by the Sisters. Nuns at Nguludi, Utale, and Nankhunda also took in uncared-for children. In the inter-war period each vicariate began a leprosarium, one at Mua, the other at Utale, at great financial cost.[54] Government subsidies never covered more than 15 per cent of the running costs, and each leprosarium, staffed by nuns, was a constant drain on the resources of the vicariate.[55] The lepers made their own bricks and sold maize to survive. Neither was there anything romantic about caring for lepers; the different tribal groups quarrelled and during the Second World War the Sisters could never get enough food to cope with the numbers. The medical work that had originally been undertaken by the Fathers was progressively taken over by the nuns. The Daughters of Wisdom regularly visited Zomba gaol. These were the 'Corporal works of mercy'.[56] The Sisters did them with little training and not usually with much recognition.

The Catholic missionaries had little difficulty in recruiting women to become the first-class citizens of the Malawian Church. The noviciate of the Servants of the Blessed Virgin Mary is still full today. This success was not repeated in recruitment for the priesthood. If the life-style of the European priests was as attractive to men as that of the nuns to women, Catholic boys showed little evidence of it. The development of an African clergy began later than that of Sisters, progress was painfully slow and the Major Seminary at Kachebere, which was built in the country during the Second World War, was not an unqualified success. There were a number of attractive jobs in colonial Malawi that did not demand the great sacrifice of a family and the many years of training of the priesthood. The celibate vocation for men held little attraction and comparatively few African priests were trained.

It was not for want of trying. Both Guillemé and Auneau took the Papal directives on the building up of an indigenous clergy with the utmost seriousness.

The mission has as its goal the development of the local Church, and the local Church in its normal functioning recruits its clergy, all its clergy, from amongst its own members.[57]

177

Every available resource was put into the seminaries, even to the extent of withdrawing priests from normal mission work, sometimes against their will. The belief that the Western style of priesthood, in the particular form in which it was exercised in the post-Reformation period, was an immutable and universally valid expression of the sacerdotal ministry, meant that the future African priests were required to reach the same standards as their European counterparts. This included being competent in Latin. Father Villy in the north and Father Arnaud in the south both produced a 'Latino-Chinyanja Grammatica' for use in Minor Seminaries, where pupils were spectators of the remarkable linguistic feat of teaching Latin through the medium of a Bantu language.

The first attempt to produce an African clergy was made by the White Fathers at Mua before the First World War. In 1912, two devout young men, Fidelis Muyeye and Mikael Msiyapanje, joined the seminary and were baptized a year later. When Mazé, Boucansaud, and Paradis returned from the front in 1918, Muyeye and Msiyapanje were selected as the most outstanding pupils, and the Bishop was asked if they could begin formal training for the priesthood. Guillemé agreed that the two students could be tonsured on Holy Saturday that year.[58]

The reaction of Muyeye's family after the ceremony of tonsuring was typical of the type of opposition encountered by young men who wanted to take steps towards ordination.

They began wailing as is the custom when someone is on the way to the graveyard. 'We are crying for you today, as when you die in a foreign land, we will be unable to mourn you,' they said. Fidelis was unable to stem the emotional outburst; Father Mazé managed to dry some of the tears by getting Abbé Fidelis to solemnly swear in front of his relatives that he would always live amongst them at the mission.[59]

The relatives thought that being a priest at least entailed going away to Europe, if not being transformed into a European. When priests, trying to stimulate vocations, approached boys and asked them if they had ever thought of becoming a priest, they often were given the reply: 'But how could I become a European? I am an African.' The degree to which Christianity was still seen as the Europeans', rather than a universal, religion can be gauged from these remarks. Seminarians' families often made every effort to keep their sons at home. It was assumed that they were being bought, body and soul, by the European missionaries. Boys would be punished for too close a contact with the mission and, on occasions, seminarians were deliberately introduced to attractive girls when they went home.

Owing to the shortage of staff at the seminary, nothing came of these first attempts. The Minor Seminary was closed later in 1918 and all the pupils dispersed. Muyeye married and became one of the most dedicated catechists in the history of Mua mission. Minor Seminary training was resumed in 1920, and in 1927 Cornelio Chitsulo from Njoro's village, near Mua mission, left a completely pagan family for Kipalapala Major Seminary and ten years of further study. He returned to be ordained Nyasaland's first African priest at Bembeke in 1937. A year later two Montfort-trained seminarians, Alfred Finye and Andrea Makoyo, both Alomwe, were ordained amidst much splendour at Limbe Cathedral.

After November 1939, pupils leaving the Minor Seminaries in each vicariate went to Kachebere Major Seminary, founded by a White Father with a degree from the University of Laval in Montreal, François-Xavier Lapointe.[60] He was joined in 1941 by Father Bernier, an experienced teacher with a degree in theology from Rome. The first fifteen seminarians were housed in an empty girls' school vacated by the nuns, on an enormous 2,200 acre plot of land on the border between Nyasaland and Northern Rhodesia. Serving vicariates in both countries, the missionaries' numbers were brought up to five, for a handful of seminarians. A grant of £2,000 from the White Fathers' Generalate allowed new blocks to be added to the original building by a team of Brothers[61] working with students. When finished it was one of the largest buildings in Nyasaland.[62] The Kachebere Mission beside it continued its normal work.

The privations of seminary training in Nyasaland were no greater than in Europe. The seminary régime ensured that, like their contemporaries in the Religious Orders for women, students developed in a spiritually rather than materially rich environment. Where Kachebere differed from a small seminary in rural Italy was that shoes were forbidden and food was African, poor quality, and mass-produced.[63] If the aim of this austere régime was not to separate students more than was necessary from village life, it was a hopeless under-taking. They spent up to sixteen years in all away from their villages, and nothing in the seminary programme could make up for this absence. Latin lessons occupied eight or nine hours a week, since nearly all the seminary manuals in the early days were in Latin.[64] Discipline was strict. Training for the priesthood was an arcane apprenticeship, as related to village life as a spell in an English Public School.

Conditions in the Minor Seminaries were mostly worse than in Europe. At Nankhunda, in an almost Dickensian atmosphere, classrooms and sleeping quarters were in the same room, and sleeping mats were suspended from the ceiling. As at Kachebere in the beginning, there was a permanent shortage of books.[65] Until the 1930s there were no teachers trained in educational techniques. It was hardly surprising that many students dropped out to look for paid work, once they had absorbed a rudimentary education. A percentage of pupils regularly failed to return from their holidays and the Minor Seminaries were quick to cut down on the amount of time a pupil was allowed in his village away from clerical control. As at the Major Seminary, holidays came to be taken in the company of a priest at one of the mission stations. As a result seminarians spent long periods away from their families, another source of grievance against re-cruitment for the priesthood.

The intellectual formation required for the priesthood was not modified in any way in Nyasaland. The time taken to complete it was longer, though, than in Europe. At the beginning the course consisted of three years' philosophy and six years' theology, interrupted by a break of one year's probation when the seminarian was allowed to return home for the first time since he entered the Major Seminary. While there was some leniency towards students who had to struggle with philosophical concepts, and a few abortive attempts were made to teach philosophy through ChiChewa at Kachebere, every student was expected to reach a certain minimum standard no different from that of small seminaries in France and Italy of the period.[66]

After prolonged training in seminaries, with their thoroughly European atmosphere and training, African priests had a psychologically difficult time when they were ordained and began work in the villages. They were placed with European priests and carefully supervised to ease their re-entry into what was by then the outside world. Some of the older priests in the Shire Vicariate initially experienced some difficulty in accepting the new African clergy as equals. Their relationship had begun as teacher/pupil and old habits died hard. Auneau's instructions for African clergy might easily have been interpreted as racist, were it not for the fact that regulations for his European clergy were almost equally restrictive. All European priests had, for example, to wear 'missionary attire; bare arms, legs, or chest, are to be avoided'.[67] They had also to avoid 'all meetings of a worldly kind which necessitate an absence from the mission'.[68] On no account were women allowed into a priest's bedroom, even to make the bed after he had left for an outstation.

But African clergy suffered additional restrictions. For some reason, doubtless the practice of humility, nobody at all was allowed to make their beds, and they were not permitted to invite friends to eat at table in the mission. They were obliged to ask for money for articles as trivial as a comb, and their finances came entirely from the Superior of the mission where they were working.[69] The African clergy were considered to be on a period of extended probation during which time they were to be closely supervised by the European missionaries. This put African priests in a very embarrassing and awkward position. They were ill at ease at the mission, yet after the Europeanization of seminary training, they were little more at home in the village. They were, in fact, caught between two cultures. It says a lot for their determination and self-discipline that most persevered, often feeling not fully accepted in either world. The greatest irony was that the partial Europeanization that they had undergone was the product of a seminary training which demonstrated more than any manifesto that the Catholic Church believed in the most rigorous racial equality. When the European Bishops introduced the new priests to their people, they invariably emphasized that the African priest held the same position in the Church as their European counterparts. The first African priests were very much pioneers of the Indigenous Church and suffered greatly because of it.

Under such conditions of tension, it might be expected that a small number of African priests, taking their lead from Protestant ministers in a similar predicament, would have broken away from the Roman Catholic Church to form their own Independent Churches. Some priests did leave, marry, and reject the celibate vocation, but they made no attempt to muster any personal following; several made good use of their long education in a profitable secular career. This lack of Independency amongst Nyasaland Catholics can be correlated with the late arrival of the missionaries, the inaccessibility of the Bible to Catholics,[70] and the uniquely Roman Catholic view of authority in the Church.

The Catholic teaching on authority given in religious instruction lessons was readily understood by African parishioners because of its similarity to their institution of chieftaincy. In patristic writings,[71] the bishop was thought of as the 'pleroma'—fullness—of the Church, in a way analogous to that in which a Maravi chief personified his land and people. While authority was not handed down through a lineage, the non-genetic idea of the Apostolic Succession was not difficult to understand. Individual Bishops still talk of their 'ecclesiastical genealogy' which traces their authority back to a particular Pope.[72] Priests held their authority immediately from their bishop. Apostolic Succession was to chieftaincy as the Protestant concept of inspiration was to spirit-mediumship and prophecy.

For a Catholic to break with the Church and use his authority *qua* priest to assemble a following, was easily seen to be impossible. His authority derived from the Church, not from any personal qualities. The central event of Catholic worship, the mass, with its stylized rubrics, had the effect of removing almost all personal elements from a priest's actions at the altar. Apart from speed and personal tics, one priest's mass was literally, as well as theologically, as good as another's. Since mass was said facing the wall at the end of the church, there was little possibility of the priest's using the liturgy to become anything more than an anonymous celebrant. People were obliged by church law to attend, and the size of the congregation was not related to the ability of the priest as an orator. Preaching was an important but not prominent part of the Sunday service at the mission.

Most committed African laymen were, furthermore, outraged at the thought of a 'fallen priest'. While they were willing to forgive an occasional sexual peccadillo, any attempt to publicize an open separation from the Church would have been unthinkable. Great shame fell on the family of a laicized priest, and many families were unwilling to allow a son to go off to the seminary for fear that he would bring disgrace to the family at a later date.[73] Lay Catholics did not read the Bible avidly as their Protestant neighbours did, but would see collections of Bible stories. There was little chance, therefore, of lay people following a priest off into the wilderness, under the inspiration of a Biblical passage which they took to be the word of God addressed directly to them.

If there was a danger of Independency it came from men such as Muyeye, the lay catechists, who led prayers and preached at outstations the priest was unable to visit. The sermon was often given on the *bwalo* by men with very little theological training. The catechists had a more intimate knowledge of village life than even the African priests. They knew the parishioners and, often, were able to see intuitively whether a marriage was likely to last in difficult cases. They could find out who went to the nyau, who had the abortion, and who stole the chickens. While on occasions catechists did refuse to work for a particular priest, and struck for higher pay, they never formed break-away Churches in Nyasaland. They relied on the support of the mission for their authority in the villages and most of them had a genuine commitment to the work of the Church.

Only in Zambia did an ex-seminarian, a catechist named Emilyo Mulolani, form the Church of the Sacred Heart and defy the Church authorities between 1955 and 1962.[74]

The tremendous efforts made by the Catholic missions between the wars to bring an indigenous clergy into being had to be coupled with their attempts to upgrade schools. Missionaries were trying to do three things at once after Hinsley's visit, train teachers, recruit and teach seminarians, and maintain an extensive network of prayer-houses in the bush. Something had to suffer. From 1927 to 1937, when catechists were being withdrawn from the villages for further training, money was scarce because of the Depression, the missions overextended in the Shire Vicariate, and the first African priests yet to return from Kipalapala, there was a temporary but marked weakening in the Catholic hold over their villages. The scramble for Government-assisted schools was undermining the solid foundation of a peasant Church that had been so assiduously developed before Hinsley came. The Montfort response to the problem, shortening the period of catechumenate to make up for the lack of evangelists, was disastrous. There was a revealing comment in the Chikwawa Diary in 1929:

> On every side young Christians are entering illicit marriages. They have been baptized too quickly.[75]

The tightening up of the system of lay leaders in the villages by the introduction of supervisors proved effective in both vicariates.

The system that grew up in the 1920s varied from mission to mission, but involved fundamentally a division of labour into catechists, with a more roving ministry, and Church Elders who looked after a particular village. Each village had its selected 'Akulu a Mpingo',[76] who were in charge of Catholics in their neighbourhood. They kept a register of births, first communions, and other details about Catholics in their immediate vicinity, as well as preaching the Sunday sermon in the absence of the priest, and leading the prayers. The 'Agurupa', or 'Akapitao' as they were called in the south, supervised a number of different villages, linking them with the mission station. This system was later paralleled by the *praesidia*[77] of the Legion of Mary. These committed Christians were reinforcements for the old-style catechists, many of whom were training as teachers in the Normal School, or teaching with Honorary Certificates in Government-assisted schools. They were the effective leaders of the Catholic community, mediating between both Europeans and the first African priests, and the villagers. They formed another rung in the hierarchy which extended from women banned from the sacraments to nuns.

There were two other attempts at forming celibate or Religious communities during this period. The Oblates of the Holy Family, African Brothers whose function it was to assist the clergy, began at Nankhunda Seminary in 1928. The Brothers were chosen from boys who did not seem to be academically suited for training for the priesthood. Very few persevered. They had the demands of the celibate vocation without the consolations of the priesthood. Another confraternity of men who took vows of celibacy proved a total failure. Most of its members left to start small businesses, and its most pious member, a hunchback, went off in great style on a pilgrimage to the tomb of the Uganda Martyrs, and never returned.[78]

Despite teams of devoted lay people in the villages, who were keeping the Church alive, the two bishops persistently went in search of the golden fleece of *sacra virginitas*. In the first twenty-five years of Kachebere Seminary's existence only sixty-four priests, who had to serve both Nyasaland and Northern Rhodesia, were ordained. Yet the priesthood had immense status in the eyes of the laity. It was obvious from the varying degree of failure experienced by the Fathers in recruiting for the priesthood, the Brothers, and celibate lay confraternities, that the celibate state for men was simply an alien institution to the African societies in Nyasaland. The question asked by boys who were interested in the priesthood, 'How can I become a European?', was perfectly reasonable. The priesthood, as it had been imported, with Latin rubrics and Gregorian chants, philosophy, theology, and celibacy, was European. The fact that Catholic missionaries came to Nyasaland with the accumulated preconceptions of centuries, that they were representatives of a Church with a cultural and theological heritage that had moulded the history of Western Europe, meant that any adaptation in this most central of all institutions, the priesthood, was out of the question. African priests were priests of God first, and Africans second.

The drop-out rate from Kachebere between 1939 and 1964 was at least 25 per cent of students getting through the first few years of training at the Major Seminary. In the early years, 1920–30, Nankhunda seminary sent on almost 20 per cent of its best pupils, who completed the course in the Minor Seminary, to Kipalapala. Between 1930 and 1940 this dropped to 10 per cent and then to 2 per cent in the next decade.[79] The intensification of selection was designed to stop unsuitable candidates getting through to further training, as happened in the enthusiasm of the 1920s. But the reverse side of this high failure rate was the large numbers of Catholic boys who went through seminary training and who were not to become priests later.

The seminaries were far more important than mere training grounds for priests; they were a major formative influence on large numbers of ambitious lay Catholics. Until the beginning of secondary schools in 1941–2 they provided the most advanced education available to Catholic boys. The Major Seminary at Kipalapala provided the only real post-primary education for Nyasaland Catholics. And if the pupils were able to adapt to the severe discipline and compulsory Latin they were, on the whole, taught by better and more sympathetic teachers than they would find in the Catholic Central and Normal Schools. A high percentage of seminarians undoubtedly saw the seminaries as a way into 'white-collar' jobs.[80] The names of several prominent Catholics today can be found on the seminary registers of the 1930s and 1940s. The most ambitious Catholics were therefore being trained in an authoritarian atmosphere designed to prepare boys for the discipline of the clerical life. Until the 1930s they were taught by priests without any training in educational methods and, if they persevered to the Major Seminary, they were given three years of philosophy presented as apologetics. They grew up at a time when the influence of Pius XII, and a profound fear of communism, was beginning to dominate the Church in every country. After the Second World War it was above all atheistic communism that the Church opposed, just as before 1917 it had been liberalism and modernism.[81] This was to have an important influence on the reactions of lay Catholics to the events of the 1950s and 1960s, Federation and Independence.

The insistence of the Catholic Bishops of Nyasaland that the Westernized celibate clergy had to be imported whatever the cost had the ironical long-term result that the Malawian Church was effectively run at the village level by married men, 'Akulu a Mpingo'. It still is today. By 1966 a total Catholic population of 705,000 had only managed to produce seventy-five priests. There were 227 European priests and 228 European nuns in the country to help them. On the other hand there were 1,194 married catechists working in the villages. The lack of success in recruitment to the priesthood is highlighted when the number of African Brothers is compared with the number of African Sisters: six compared with 256.[82] It was not that Nyasaland Catholics rejected the idea of a first-class citizenship in the Church. This was just what the catechists and *Akulu a Mpingo* used to be, and to a certain degree still are. It was simply that celibacy was an undesirable vocation for most men while there were so many other careers open for the educated.

The constant emphasis, stimulated by Papal Encyclicals, on the development of first-class citizens for the *civitas dei* rebounded on the Church. Malawian lay people were, and still tend to be, neglected. Except for a few years after Hinsley's visit, if there was a choice between training priests and training lay people, the former won. Father Lapointe, the founder of Kachebere, was withdrawn from his position as head of the Teachers' Training College to start the seminary.[83] Many of Malawi's Catholics came to feel themselves not only second-class citizens of their Church, but also of their country. Catholics staffed the lower echelons of the Civil Service, the police force, and the army, and the village headmanship level of local government. Today, still, a disproportionately small number of Catholics get through to secondary education and the University.

On the other hand the experience of the Anglican Church has not been that a married and less well-trained clergy, and greater lay participation, has been entirely satisfactory. Married priests have great difficulties in combining support for their families with full-time ministries, and the wife of an Anglican priest is not necessarily an asset in his Christian ministry. The Anglican Church has suffered from a greater number of break-away Churches, and lay participation in situations of ethnic and local conflict is a disadvantage. So it would be rash to dismiss the Roman Catholic efforts as totally misguided. Today, with Civil Service jobs filled, the Major Seminary is full and the crisis may only be temporary. Only, in the long term, the cost of a well-trained celibate African clergy has proved very high indeed.

REFERENCES TO CHAPTER VIII

1 *Bulletins trimestriels* September 1924, 12

2 A doctrine that Christ had but one nature, the Divine. It was first associated with Apollinarius of Laodicea c. 390, and in the fifth century with Eutyches c. 450. The Monophysites formed a separate Church after the Council of Chalcedon.

[3] The Alexandrian theologians, of whom the most famous was Origen, were greatly influenced by Platonism and its later advocates such as Plotinus. The Platonic emphasis on the reality of the spiritual world and the transience of the material naturally resulted in accentuation of the Divine element in the person of Christ. St. Cyril of Alexandria, for example, was quite ready to say that 'God suffered on the Cross'. Christ tended to be seen as God covered with the accidental trappings of the material world.

[4] The Council of Chalcedon was held in Asia Minor in 451 to counter the Monophysite heresy. St. Augustine of Hippo lived from 354 to 430 and was influenced in his views of sexuality, not only by Platonism, but by his personal experiences before conversion.

[5] See Chapter II, Reference 86

[6] Görres *Hidden Face* 33

[7] See Chapter II

[8] See also page 70 and note 29 to Chapter III. The first five sisters arrived at Nzama on 8 December 1904, the second at Nguludi, 15 August 1905. The second caravan consisted of Sisters Marie Thérèse de St. Yves, Charité de Montfort, Maximus du Sacré Cœur, Sainte Caroline, and Sylverie. Montfort material on the nuns was kindly collected for us by Sister Marie-Thérèse of Providence Teachers' Training College, Mulanje, to whom we are most grateful.

[9] Bishop Dupont was also known as 'Bwana moto-moto'

[10] Notes made by Sister Marie-Thérèse and kindly lent to us

[11] In ecclesiastical documents put out by Bishop Auneau, women are usually referred to as 'le sexe'. For the White Fathers it was 'les personnes du sexe'.

[12] Mua Diary November 1946

[13] Interview, Sister Victorine, Lilongwe September 1971. Sister Victorine was the first-born of seven children and from a farming village in Quebec. She arrived with the first contingent of White Sisters in 1911 aged 25 with no practical training except dressmaking.

[14] Nsanje Baptismal Registers, Nsanje Mission, and *Rapports annuels* 1919–28

[15] Minutes of the Synod of Bembeke 28–30/8/13 in *Règlements et Instruction*

[16] Auneau was very cautious about this. For example, in a letter to the Montfort missionaries 6 October 1937 he said: 'On the matter of customs and inveterate practices, it would be true to say that one destroys only what one can replace successfully. In certain districts it does seem that we shall be unable to get rid of Cinamwali and Unyago until we replace them with a Christian Unyago and Cinamwali. I invite Superiors of missions who have the opportunity to try this.' However, nothing equivalent to the Anglican modification of the *Jando* rites attempted at Fort Johnston and Masasi was carried out, see text. For missionary adaptations of this kind see T. O. Ranger 'Missionary adaptation of African Religious Institutions: the Masasi case' in *The Historical Study* 221–51.

[17] It was simply that the Fathers saw the extension of the Catholic missions to be more in the interests of the Africans than anything else, because it had an effect on their eternal destiny and salvation. It was unusual for priests to intervene on politically sensitive matters, see Chap IV. If it was within the context of acts of charity e.g. the work of the leprosarium, they might attack Government decisions. During the Second World War it became apparent that the restrictions on buying maize were going to cause a shortage at the leprosarium, and the Fathers put up a spirited resistance.

[18] Auneau to Montfort missionaries 23 January 1936. Education Archives, Catholic Secretariat, Limbe.

[19] Philips, District Commissioner at Dedza, to Champmartin 23 October 1935. Loose letter in Mua Diary.

[20] Nzama Convent Diary 18 December 1907, Providence Training College, Mulanj

[21] *Bulletins trimestriels* June 1909, 1: c.f. the Portuguese in the seventeenth century

[22] *Rapports annuels* 1934–5 Mua and Ntaka-taka

[23] *Rapports annuels* 1920–1 Bembeke

[24] Port-Herald Diary 28 January 1930. A case of a Christian girl, Magdalena, who was being forced by her family to marry someone she did not want to. 'In front of the Akulu the Father declared that even a young girl is her own master.'

[25] Rev. Fraser of Livingstonia's notes on Native Marriage Ordinances. S1/1622/19, National Archives, Zomba.

[26] ibid.

[27] Moggridge to Registrar-General 10 June 1916. S1/1622/19.

[28] ibid.

[29] Bishop J. Fady Notes. Fathers Mazé, Régent, and Martin, attended for the Catholics.

[30] Report of missionary conference held at the High Court, Blantyre 7 April 1920. S1/1622/19.

[31] Personal Communication, Rev. Kalenburg W.F.

[32] Reports on emigration sent to Bishop Guillemé from White Fathers missions, 1930 Kasina Report, White Fathers Archives, Lilongwe

[33] Dedza District Book. Vol. III Minutes of District Council Meeting 31 March 1928, National Archives, Zomba

[34] Wellens C. 'The influence of village environment on the stability of Roman Catholic marriages in a rural parish of Malawi' Africa Theological Journal No. 2. 1969, 84–93. The matrilocal Chewa had a higher divorce rate than the Ngoni, who regretted the increase in the incidence of divorce, see Barnes, J. A. Marriage in a changing society Rhodes Livingstone Papers No. 20. Oxford 1951. 122–3.

[35] Handwritten undated notebook 'Débuts des Vierges', Providence Teachers' Training College, Mulanje

[36] The final profession of perpetual vows was made several years later Bulletins trimestriels September 1928, 4

[37] As Reference 35

[38] Bulletins trimestriels September 1924, 13

[39] Sister Marie-Louise Trichet subjected herself to the most degrading mortifications—for example she was known to lick the spittle off the floor of the hospital where she worked, as a penitential exercise

[40] Lavoie J. 'Recruiting of New Members for the Religious Congregations in Malawi' Pastoral Survey Zomba, March 1970

[41] Bulletins trimestriels December 1926, 9, and see also Douglas M. Purity and Danger London 1966, 158

[42] Rangeley W. H. J. 'Two Nyasaland Rain-Shrines. Makewana the mother of all People' Nyasaland Journal Vol. 5 July 1952, 31–50

[43] After the installation of a new Chief Lundu in 1969, a bride for M'bona, Salima, was sent by lorry from Mbewe to Khulubvi thicket, and promptly returned by the rain-shrine officials; she was expected to walk from Lundu's capital in traditional fashion. Personal Communication, Rev. Dr. J. M. Schoffeleers.

[44] Rangeley Makewana 32–3

[45] Oral Testimony, Epiphanio Kankhumba, Headman Kafulama's, July 1970

[46] During this interview the Mwali was known either as a female chief or as the high priestess, the terms were used interchangeably

[47] A survey undertaken by questionnaire, followed by interview in convents within an eighty-mile radius of Blantyre. The Sisters were randomly placed geographically and not sorted into convents according to district of origin. The sample included convents in bush and peri-urban areas.

[48] The word 'Ngoni' is put in inverted commas as it does not imply that the Sisters were drawn from aristocratic Swazi-clans. The implication of this designation is that they came from Ngonized villages where 'bride-price', lobola, was paid, and society was patrilocal.

[49] Personal Communication, Inkosi Willard Gomani III

[50] As Reference 35.

[51] Personal Communication, Sister Victorine, Mlale Mission, Lilongwe

[52] Named after Countess Teresa Ledochowski, sister of the Cardinal Prefect of the Propaganda in 1901, founder of the St. Peter Claver Missionary Society and benefactor of the missions.

[53] Lavoie ibid.

[54] In 1927 there were nine small leprosy treatment centres run by the Protestant Missions together with the Mua leprosarium. The Utale leprosarium opened in 1931 after Auneau had been impressed by a slide show on leprosy at the 1927 Education Conference.

[55] The Government grant for Utale leprosarium in 1935 was £118. 10s. The actual running costs that year were £838. 19s. 8d.

[56] These comprised the care of the sick, the dying, and those in prison. Although there was an emphasis on Otherworldliness in Catholic mission practice this was set against a background of material help for Africans in the parishes on an individual basis.

[57] Pope Benedict XV 'Maximum Illud', published in 1919

[58] Mua Diary July 1942. A biography of Fidelis Muyeye written by Father J. B. Champmartin on his death.

[59] ibid.

[60] Father F. X. Lapointe was born in 1898, the last of nine children, in a small village outside Montreal. He was ordained and came to Nyasaland in 1925 to leave immediately for Northern Rhodesia where he visited the Teacher Training Centre at Mpangwe mission. He returned to Nyasaland in 1928 and was put in charge of the Teacher Training School at Kachebere, which was later transferred to Likuni. He founded the Major Seminary at Kachebere in 1939.

[61] Brothers Paul Camire, Peter-Claver Van der Hoorn, and Henri Renevey, see a booklet published in 1964, '25 years. Kachebere Major Seminary', Kachebere. Fort Manning (now Mchinji).

[62] ibid. for pictures

[63] Personal Communication, Bishop Patrick Kalilombe w.f. ex-Rector, Kachebere Seminary

[64] Rev. François-Xavier Lapointe ibid.

[65] ibid.

[66] ibid.

[67] Minutes of the First Diocesan Synod. 23 October 1928. Education Archives, Catholic Secretariat, Limbe.

[68] ibid.

[69] Auneau L. 'Clergé Indigène du Vicariat du Shire' Undated. Circular to Superior of Missions. Nsanje Mission. Regulation 15. 'C'est d'ailleurs à l'Économe-Général, ou Supérieur-local, qu'ils s'adressent pour quelque achat de *quelque nature qu'il soit*'. Perhaps no more than inveterate caution but very galling for those who had to live under such a régime.

[70] See Barrett D. B. *Schism and Renewal in Africa* Oxford 1968, for a useful measure of the likelihood of independency. Also for a local study, Wishlade R. L. *Sectarianism in Nyasaland* Oxford 1965, very out-of-date now, though, for Churches in southern Malawi.

[71] A useful summary in *De Ecclesia* Catholic Truth Society, London 1965 27–41. Especially the writings of St. Gregory Nazianzen.

[72] Personal Communication, Bishop J. Fady

[73] Personal Communication, Father Kalenburg

[74] Oger L. *Mutima Church of Emilyo Mulolani: 1955–1962* MS White Fathers' library. Totteridge, London

[75] Chikwawa Diary 31 January 1929

[76] For details of their work see 'Mkulu wa Mpingo ndi Nchito Zace'. Undated booklet for

Church Elders written by Father Mohr S.M.M. Nsanje Mission, and Chapter IX.

[77] Local groups of a pious association for lay people devoted to good works and prayers, see Chapter IX.

[78] Querel *L'histoire* Cahier IV

[79] Nankhunda Minor Seminary records, Nankhunda, Zomba

[80] Personal Communication, Father Andrea Makoyo, Nzama Mission. Father Makoyo first went to the seminary in order to get training as a clerk and only later felt a call to become a priest.

[81] Few of the priests had much idea of what communism meant. Many had left Europe before the Bolshevik revolution. For example in the reports on emigration sent to Guillemé from Kasina in 1930, a priest writes. 'Some hotheads come back with communist ideas, the country belongs to the blacks, the whites ought to be chased out.' As today in South Africa the label 'communist' was given to anything alien or even mildly inconvenient. Champmartin put down the Maize Board's refusal to give extra rations to the leprosarium as a result of 'idées communistes'.

[82] Education File, Catholic Secretariat, kindly lent to us by Rev. G. Van Asdonk S.M.M. At that date there were 91 European brothers working in the country. The priest to laity ratio was 1:2,350. This compared unfavourably with Tanzania's 1:1,500 but was better than Uganda's 1:3,330, see Hastings A. *Church and Mission in Modern Africa* London 1966. The figures for the whole of Malawi had increased to 1:2,645 by 1970. The comparable figure for another Protestant country like England is 1:700, while very adverse ratios are typical of the Latin American States. Excluding priests not involved in parish work the figures for 1971 are 1:4,400. Report on 'Financial Self-Support'. Pastoral Survey January 1971.

[83] François Xavier Lapointe ibid.

CHAPTER IX

Mua: A Profile of a Mission Station

It is the fiftieth anniversary of the founding of the mission. We now have 6,140 baptized Christians, 1,579 families; 639 of these are broken marriages. Only 2,100 of our 3,324 adults are allowed to receive the sacraments; 2/5ths of our parishioners never receive communion. Out of a total of 2,516 children and youngsters, 750 are illegitimate, from adulterous liaisons. And this is only the children we know about. For the Christians who remain faithful, what indifference to the things of God. Let us hope that 1952 will see an increase in their fervour.

Mua Mission Diary 1 January 1952[1]

Since this book opened with the claim that mission activity would be studied mainly at a village level, it would not be fitting to end before focusing down to the interaction of one station with its local community to see if any patterns emerge. It was quite by accident that the White Fathers' stations at Mua, and later at Ntaka-taka, were sited a few miles from Mankhamba, the capital of the Maravi under Karonga. None the less the choice of Mua for a micro-study can be justified by the fact that this station was situated in the Chewa heartland, a region still called 'Malawi'.[2] Quite apart from its historical significance the area was a hotbed of local politics into which the missionaries were unwittingly drawn. The response to Catholic Christianity around Mua may be instructively analysed in terms of the intrusion of the mission into the complicated struggle for power between Chewa and Ngoni, a struggle influenced by the past structure of Chewa society with its Phiri chiefs and Banda religious officials and commoners.

The local history of the Mua region is rather like the profile of an excavation. In the surface layers there is the Catholic Mission and a loose topsoil of Christianity. Apart from visits from District Commissioners and Boma police, one or two modest European plantations, a railway, and a forest reserve, the European presence in the area was largely felt through the activity of the Catholic Mission. Underneath the European topsoil runs a thin stratum representing the period of Ngoni colonization, and extending below this to a bedrock of bushman-type Akafula culture, is Chewa society. Features of the bottom-most layers, the Chewa rain-cult and nyau societies, still emerge on the surface in modified but recognizable forms. The profile is dominated by the vast and poorly differentiated pre-colonial past of the Chewa.

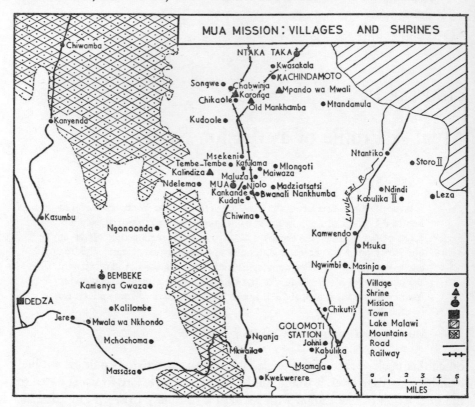

Because of a high mountain range to the west and the lake to the east Mua was geographically somewhat isolated from the rest of the country. There was a path over the escarpment leading to Bembeke mission near Dedza, and numerous rivers draining the mountains divided the lakeshore plain into segments. Dry season gardens could be planted along the river beds in *madimba* where there were layers of fertile silt, and it is easy to understand why the region supported the first major settlement of the Chewa. There was even the added bonus of acacia trees that automatically provided fertilizer for the soils by fixing nitrogen. The missionaries were attracted there precisely because of the dense population the plain was able to sustain and was, in fact, supporting when they arrived.

The traditional religious system of the district was part of a complex of territorial rain-shrines that extended into Zambia and south of the Zambesi amongst the Shona. The shrines were controlled by Phiri chiefs whose power was balanced by Banda prophetesses or wives of the High God. Each village had its own shrine where lineage spirits were worshipped but it was only the main territorial shrines which had a hierarchy of priests and were particularly associated with the spirits of deceased Phiri chiefs and heroes, as well as with the High God.[3] At Mankhamba the spirit-wife was known as Mwali, said to be married to Karonga, or in other traditions, to a mythical snake. Associated with the shrine was a sacred pool near Ntaka-taka mission where Mwali probably interceded for rain. The shrine ceremonies negotiated the unity of the different Chewa clans by means of simple symbols; each matrilineage had to make a token offering of food and grass for the building of a spirit-house. The sacrifices at the spirit-house were believed to bring about rainfall, so control of the shrine by a designated official of the Karonga was an important aspect of Phiri rule.

For the Catholic missionaries, the rain-cult, since it was believed to influence rainfall, was superstition. None the less they accepted that the shrine liturgy reflected genuine religious aspirations—unlike their outright rejection of the nyau societies' ceremonies. Their informants, seeking some analogy to convey the religious significance of the spirit-houses described them as 'little churches'. Although the priests knew that prayers were directed to spirits of deceased chiefs or commoners, according to the shrine, they were also aware that the repeated supplications addressed to Chiuta or Mphambe for rain at the territorial shrines indicated that the Chewa had a definite concept of the role of a High God. Since supplicants approached the shrines in a reverent fashion asking for forgiveness and pleading with a Supreme Deity, the priests were willing to see the cult as an expression of Natural Religion and a preparation for the Christian Revelation. For this reason, and for the more mundane one that ceremonies at the royal shrines were rare and the spirit-houses were hidden in sacred thickets, the missionaries were rarely actively hostile to the rain-cult.

This peaceful state of affairs was largely the result of depredations by both Yao and Ngoni in the nineteenth century. The missionaries were entering a situation in which the Phiri royal house had already been destroyed as a political force. When Anglican missionaries attempted to settle on Thyolo mountain in the 1860s they were hounded off by enraged officials of the M'bona cult.[4] But when the White Fathers pitched their tents at Mua the Karongaship was in abeyance and there were no Phiri chiefs in the area to shore up the territorial cult, as there were in the Lower Shire Valley. Furthermore the decisive battle fought in 1894 between the two most important war divisions of the Maseko Ngoni had driven the loser, Kachindamoto, on to the lakeshore plain. He was saved from death only by British intervention.[5] A descendant of the last Karonga gave him land; so an Ngoni chieftancy had superseded that of the Phiri at Mankhamba.

British rule which had saved Kachindamoto was also to be his downfall. A number of murders by the chief were reported to the Boma and he was finally arrested. His brother, Ndindi, was passed over in favour of a sister, Nyathei, who became regentess from 1899 while Ndindi moved south into the region of the Dutch Reformed missionaries. The son of Kachindamoto's murdered leading nduna moved down from the mountains to settle.[6] Although he was from a family that was culturally Ngoni he decided to take the Chewa title Njoro to please his subjects. He offered sacrifices at the shrine in his village 'to make peace with the land' and made a number of concessions to the Chewa.[7]

Njoro's deference to Chewa public opinion and his tactful rule was a product of Ngoni weakness in the region. Instead of a uniform imposition of the Ngoni's cultural pattern there was a spectrum of tribal interaction. In the immediate vicinity of Ntaka-taka a handful of Swazi-clan Ngoni ruled over assimilated captives who had largely adopted the Ngoni way of life. At the opposite extreme were 'pure' Chewa villages around Mua.[8] Other villages lay between the two.

Kamwendo's village was made up of Chewa captives taken by the Ngoni in the period 1870 to 1890 who had largely held on to the Chewa marriage and child-rearing practices. Other villages with captives taken from Tanganyika while the Ngoni were at Songea[9] were naturally more 'ngonized'. Njoro's was a typical example of a village in which the Ngoni and Chewa had come to some compromise.

The importance of this rough category of 'intermediate' villages is that the first catechumens, Christians, and catechists, at Mua were drawn almost entirely from them. Until the First World War the villages under Njoro and Kamwendo produced more than one quarter of the station's Christians.[10] There was little response from the more ethnically homogeneous villages. Even when the Ngoni regentess finally agreed to the Fathers' opening a school at Ntaka-taka one of her leading *nduna*, who came from a clan with important religious and ritual functions, still persisted in opposing it.[11] Similarly it was only in 1924 that the village headman who lived on the site of the old Mankhamba and had an entirely Chewa village allowed a school to be built there.[12] The other Chewa headmen were no less hostile but often granted a school and then forbade their children to attend.

On the whole those who entered the orbit of Mua mission most readily were people of Chewa origin who did not fit into the Ngoni aristocracy. The old Maravi–Phiri political and religious structures were fragmented as a result of two major invasions and people sought a new alternative in the highly-structured *corpus christianum*. From Njoro's village with its Ngoni headman who lived in many respects like a Chewa, came the first Mua catechists, the first African priest in Nyasaland who later became its first African Bishop, and several other priests as well.[13] The first African Rector of Kachebere Major Seminary grew up at Ntaka-taka and later moved to settle next door to Mua mission in a Chewa area.[14] Far from creating a group of 'marginal men' by Europeanization and Christian teaching, the Catholic Mission in this district attracted the marginal men produced by a process of purely African colonization.

The Church's first recruits were Africans who found in the Church salvation, not so much from the alien concept of Original Sin as from the very real problems of life in a society where two types of African culture clashed. The missionaries found the partially assimilated Chewa hopeful that the Europeans would side with them in the restoration of their lost chieftancies and free them from the restrictive aspects of Ngoni domination. The great success of both Dutch Reformed at Magwero and Catholics at Kachebere in recruiting Chewa under the rule of Mpezeni's Ngoni perhaps provides some measure of the relative strength of the two Ngoni polities.[15] The Chewa at Mua simply did not need the mission as badly as those around Kachebere. The disproportionate number of 'Ngoni' nuns further highlights a situation in which the worst deprivation of Ngoni rule was felt by women living in Ngonized villages.

This role of the Church in assimilating those unable successfully to manipulate a village-level power structure that effectively excluded them has wider application than Ngoni colonization. At Nsanje during the first ten years of mission work, from 1921 to 1931, the politically powerful Mang'anja made up only 10–20 per cent of those baptized, while according to a census taken in 1922 the Mang'anja formed 67 per cent of the population of the Lower Shire.[16] The Church's neophytes were more than three-quarters new arrivals in the area, Sena immigrants who had fled from the Zambesi sugar estates in large numbers after the 1917 Makombe rising.[17] The Mang'anja chiefs and leading shrine officials at M'bona's shrine refused baptism although they lived amicably alongside the mission. The first woman in normal health to be baptized at Nsanje typified the pressures at work on the immigrants. She belonged to a Sena clan, and had been obliged to live in the village of her Mang'anja husband. Against strong protests from her husband's family, who believed the priests wanted to take her as a wife, she went off to work at the mission. She was suffering both the disadvantage of patrilocal residence and the difficulties of being a Sena woman in a Mang'anja village where the other marriages would be uxorilocal. The mission provided her with a way to attain status within society and she is today a respected Catholic matron.[18]

The period of the 1920s at Mulanje when the Catholic mission recorded an unprecedented number of baptisms in the space of five years provides another striking example. Although in 1905 Catholic missionaries were rejecting the Mulanje district as underpopulated,[19] by 1925 immigration from Mozambique by Alomwe labourers had made it a desirable mission prize. By 1927, it was estimated that 32 per cent of labour in the Shire Highlands was Alomwe.[20] These immigrants had the dual problem of finding a place under Mang'anja headmen and working under European planters on the new tea estates. In both *milieux* they were the underdogs and subject to abuse.[21] The second and third priests to be ordained in Nyasaland came from immigrant Alomwe families, as did the first Archbishop, Rt. Rev. James Ciona.[22] Today the Church in the southern region of Malawi might without exaggeration be called the 'Alomwe Church'.

In each station, Mua, Mulanje, and Nsanje, the *corpus christianum* provided an alternative society in which Africans could attain positions of authority and prestige denied to them elsewhere. At a deeper level, the explanatory framework of Catholic Christianity allowed people to make some sense of, and adapt to, an environment in which values and social structures were changing. While they might still remain as outsiders in the long-established Protestant churches they were welcomed with open arms by the Catholic missionaries who were themselves new arrivals. The tremendous influx of Alomwe into the Mulanje area which continued into the 1930s finally gave rise to a large number of Independent Churches which answered needs that the Institutional Churches were unable, or unwilling, to satisfy.[23]

It might be argued that the variations in response to Catholic missionary effort were related at Mua, not to tribal and social factors, but simply to a village's distance from the mission station. This would be to underrate both the tenacity of African cultural institutions and the missionaries' extraordinary capacity for walking. The Fathers tramped thousands of miles on foot each year so that the most distant of the outstations received as much attention as the villages next to the mission. The priests kept to a schedule in which each missionary spent periods of up to three weeks in the bush visiting outstations and living in the villages.

A Mang'anja chief living within half a mile of Nsanje mission has remained a pagan until this day while Sena headmen on the periphery of the parish were baptized in the 1930s. In 1920, the Mua parish boundaries enclosed 3,945 people; 2,121 of these villagers lived within a five-mile radius of the mission, 1,824 between five and twenty miles distant. 609 of those living within a five-mile radius of the mission were baptized; 387 of them were adults. Between five and twenty miles distant, there were 699 Christians, 392 of them adult baptisms.[24] Despite the higher population close to the mission there were fewer Christians; the critical factor was not proximity to Mua but the relative strength of Chewa cultural institutions, in particular the nyau societies.

Just as at Kachebere the young Ngoni paramount Mpezeni quickly accepted baptism, so Abraham Kachindamoto entered the catechumenate in 1907 in the teeth of considerable opposition from his *nduna*.[25] The principal role of the Ngoni paramount was to provide a focus for life in his territory. A constant supply of food was expected to be on hand at the *inkosini* for visitors. Quite apart from the socio-religious aspects of royal polygamy simple functions such as this modest but unfailing hospitality depended on the chief's polygamous wives who cooked for, and served, the visitors. The older *nduna* rightly feared that the missionaries' insistence on monogamy as a condition for baptism risked undermining the Ngoni way of life. They warned the young chief that disrespect for the customs of his ancestors would result in disrespect for the chief himself.[26]

The social structure of an Ngoni village was so intimately bound up with the institution of polygamy, even down to the arrangement of huts, that the missionaries' insistence that all but one wife should be renounced was unlikely to be heeded. The priests were not just asking, as they thought, for a personal conversion but for the transformation of a society that had survived for almost a century. Some Ngoni did choose one of their wives, supported the rest, and submitted to a Church marriage, but usually they relapsed. The majority remained polygamous and perpetual catechumens. For Abraham Kachindamoto the catechumenate lasted from 1907 until his death on 2 December 1931. He had fifteen wives, attended mass regularly, and always summoned a Catholic catechist to accompany him whenever he went shooting in case he was wounded mortally in a hunting accident and died without baptism.[27] In 1910, the regentess was caught by her husband drinking with men in the local store. She was promptly divorced but remarried quickly, and it was only in 1934 on her deathbed that she was finally baptized.[28]

Polygamy may have been some buffer against the worst effects of labour migration. In the severe famine year 1912–13 one-third of the men were away from their villages in the Mua district.[29] Government attempts at sponsoring cash crops were a failure. The mission had distributed free seed as requested by the Boma but villagers were unwilling to grade the cotton they produced and felt cheated when Government-appointed buyers refused to give them top prices for inferior produce.[30] Unhampered by a high density of European planters, Government attempts to stimulate cash crops might have achieved more success had they been willing to subsidize keen farmers. The mission set a good example in its gardens but the Brothers' agricultural techniques required capital and rarely travelled beyond the confines of the mission grounds. An exception was at Kachebere where Brother Willibrord's use of ox-drawn carts became popular amongst a few of the richer farmers in the area.[31] But for most, a period of two to three years labour migration became something akin to a test of manhood. For the Ngoni it was a pattern of behaviour that had proved successful before the Europeans came; the young Ngoni mineworkers 'raided' the cash economy and returned with their booty to marry. But for the Chewa, who had responded to Ngoni overrule by paying tribute in agricultural produce, labour migration was a new experience that tended to disrupt family life. Chewa husbands refused to leave their wives unless they agreed to move to the man's village where they would be under his sisters' surveillance,[32] and even the Ngoni lamented an increase in divorce.[33]

In the midst of the 1912–13 famine, Governor Manning arrived at Ntaka-taka in full cock's feathers to enthrone Abraham Kachindamoto. In his speech the Governor pointedly referred to the 'suppression' of Kachindamoto's father by the British authorities.[34] The ceremony of enthronement was designed to emphasize the Ngoni's dependence on the Europeans. Manning made a courtesy call at the mission after the official function and it must have been plain to all Chewa spectators that the Europeans were masters of the much-feared Ngoni. In 1913, leading Chewa accepted the Cross and entered the catechumenate.[35] To what extent these conversions represented an astute reading of the signs of the times is hard to assess. The Chewa could have been in no doubt as to the power of the Europeans and some may have felt that a polite gesture towards their religion was required. None the less some Chewa headmen still kept up fierce resistance to the mission, one virtually on the priests' doorstep.[36]

The heavy settlement of Chewa villages around Mua did not allow the few 'pure' Ngoni at Ntaka-taka to maintain complete control of the territory nominally under their jurisdiction. The first Njoro resigned because of old age and was replaced after Manning's visit by a headman far less adroit in village politics. Njoro II became widely despised as being 'nothing but a messenger boy for Kachindamoto' and was barely able to exert his authority over his villages.[37] By 1938 the power of the headmanship had declined further and the contemporary Njoro was resorting to repeated *mwabvi* ordeals to impose his will. Complaints to the District Commissioner resulted in his deposition and imprisonment. His successor, Modeste, began to champion Chewa customs to ingratiate himself with his villagers.[38]

The mission had always passively opposed the Chewa female initiation rites of *chinamwali*. Not only did they involve the nyau dances but practices the missionaries found immoral such as manipulation of the *labia minora* and ritual intercourse with a man known as *fisi*, the hyena. Before the First World War there had been instances of Christian girls being snatched from their huts to be initiated forcibly, but as the mission gained in strength the rites were increasingly limited to pagan girls. The Ngoni genuinely shared the mission's repugnance of the rites. Their own initiation rites were acceptable to the missionaries since they lacked the overt physical acts of Chewa customs. The mission attempted to counteract the pagan ceremonies by developing a Christian 'initiation' for girls. This was little more than private instruction in sexual matters and marital conduct by older Catholic matrons known as *alangisi*, and lacked the communal public dimension of acceptance into the reproductive community of traditional initiation.

The Christian *alangisi* bypassed the traditional *namkhungwi*, who resented handing over responsibility to the mission. More important, the village headman, who was traditionally responsible for all *rites de passage*, and received payment for each girl who reached puberty, bitterly opposed the encroachment of the mission on his former preserve. Within a short while, Modeste had become embroiled with a Catholic mother who had insisted that her daughter refuse *chinamwali*. His behaviour towards her was sufficiently insulting for a court case to ensue. Behind his anger lay the problem of the *corpus christianum* as a separate and challenging institution which eroded the already limited power of traditional authorities.

On the other hand, for the Ngoni, the political power of the mission was a useful weapon against their Chewa headmen. Over a wide range of issues priests and Ngoni *nduna* were natural allies. After the 1924 District Administration Ordinance village courts were recognized officially and were able to judge petty criminal cases and *milandu* involving points of traditional law. Resort to the District Commissioner provided a final court of appeal. Chewa villagers therefore found themselves at the mercy of an Ngoni Principal Headman and a parish priest, often working hand in hand. Kachindamoto made skilful use of the Njoro case to emphasize that the Njoro chieftancy was originally Ngoni.

Kachinda then turned to Njoro with a smile on his lips and asked him to what tribe he belonged. 'The Abanda.' 'Banda is the name of a place not a tribe,' replied the chief. 'Amaravi,' Njoro hazarded. 'You come from the mountains yet you call yourself Maravi, a native of the lakeshore! I don't understand. This Maravi *chinamwali* with all its filth, does it belong to your people? No. You borrowed it from others. Why couldn't you have left it to them? Your people are right and you reprove them for wanting to do the right thing.' [39]

Whatever Kachindamoto's precise feelings about the cultural and moral issues involved, the case provided him with an ideal stick with which to beat a headman who was siding too much with the Chewa faction.

The enthronement of Kachindamoto III, on 26 May 1932, presented the Chewa with an impressive display of Ngoni/mission solidarity. Priests attended from Mua, Ntaka-taka, and Bembeke missions. The new chief, wrapped in a black cloth, was borne through the bush on a *machila* carried by eight young men and taken to a hut built specially for the occasion. After the usual war dances had been performed, the *nduna* called for the chief to come out of his hut. He was formally admonished by all his councillors and obliged to stand throughout their speeches, according to custom, on one leg. [40] The homily given by the last *nduna* contained the sage advice that the chief should always refer to the Catholic priests before he took a major decision now that the missions had come to stay in the land. The Father-Superior at Ntaka-taka was called forward to speak last.

> He told the chief to go back to standing on both legs, and said that everyone was to respect the chieftancy for this was a commandment of God. He asked the Christians to pray for him. Then the chief returned home carried triumphally by the young men while the women sang war songs. After eating alone in his hut, he was then supposed to visit the hut of the ancestral spirits. But he refused to, saying that all those things were now finished. The old people were unhappy about it but that part of the ceremony did have to be suppressed.[41]

The Maravi headmen present could scarcely have asked for a more pointed demonstration that the Ngoni-mission alliance was permanent. The two colonizing powers were seen to share common interests.

The alliance was in many ways counter-productive for the mission. As *mzinda* proliferated around the station the local Chewa increasingly found a new tribal identity in the nyau societies. Although eighty to two hundred pupils were registered for schools serving three major Chewa villages around Mua, attendances in 1930 never exceeded eight pupils.[42] To be Chewa began to mean nyau membership, opposition to mission schools and to Ngoni political control.

The Ngoni, who had no illusions about the power of the nyau, treated cases involving dances with some circumspection. In October 1924 a Catholic was almost throttled to death for singing the secret nyau songs in public. He had been warned repeatedly by the society but foolishly failed to heed the threats of nyau members. The mission brought the case before Kachindamoto who cannily deposed the headman whom he disliked and replaced him with a man of his own choosing.[43] A year later, while the mission was making an all-out attempt to get the dances finally banned, charges of immorality and indecency were brought before the District Commissioner.[44] Catholic catechists had hidden in the bush by the *mzinda* and were willing to testify to the obscenity of the songs and that naked dancers had appeared in front of women. A case of public indecency was made against a *kapitao* and the District Commissioner decided to depose him. On this occasion Kachindamoto pleaded for the man and he was later reinstated.[45] He came from Kafulama's, the most powerful of the neighbouring Chewa villages, and a little magnanimity on the Ngoni's part towards this important Banda clan village may have seemed expedient.

Kafulama's power came from the fact that his lineage was the provider of the Mwali at the rain-shrine at Mankhamba. The Chewa attempted to revive the Karongaship as part of their opposition to the Ngoni but were thwarted in the 1920s both by the missionaries and by the opposition of the Banda clan. A mission *kapitao* at Ntaka-taka claimed to be the legitimate Karonga. But Kafulama did not want to see his power lost to a Phiri pretender and demanded that the *kapitao* marry a designated Mwali from Kafulama's village in accordance with the tradition that the Karonga had to marry the Mwali. The *kapitao* was already married and the priests vetoed the proposal that he marry again. As a result no Karonga was reinstated and all Chewa resistance continued to remain under the leadership of Kafulama as the prerogative of the Banda. Once again the Banda had reacted by opposing centralized authority and this opposition was shown to the Phiri, to the Ngoni, and to the missionaries.[46]

After the 1930s the balance of power shifted further in favour of the Chewa. Statistics drawn from census returns for the Central Region can be interpreted as showing a marked decline in the status of Ngoni in Nyasaland. There were 64,023 'Ngoni' in 1926, 46,309 in 1931, but only 14,243 by 1945. The sharp drop in the 1930s was not registered in the north where the number of villagers claiming to be M'belwa's Ngoni actually rose in the same period by 20,321. Even allowing for the inaccuracy of such census returns and heavy labour migration from the Central Region Ngoni, the difference is striking. While the Tumbuka in the north were increasingly willing to be identified with the Ngoni there was something akin to a resurgence of Chewa identity over and against the Ngoni in the Central Region. This dissociation of many Chewa from their former colonial rulers was largely the product of the growth of the nyau as a powerful force in intertribal politics.

The Maseko paramount, Gomani II, did manage to ban nyau successfully in his territory with the help of Protestant missionaries, but, although Kachindamoto was boasting in 1946 that he would emulate this, it was four years before he summoned up the courage to press for a total ban. Supported by a decision of the combined chiefs of the Dedza district that made the permission of the local Native Authority mandatory for the holding of dances at night, Kachindamoto banned the societies in 1950. He had not done so before through fear of his Chewa subjects.

He does not want to displease his subordinates and always wants to be 'the good chief' come what may. His other deep-rooted preoccupation is poisoning.[47] He is frightened they might just be capable of it. It is not impossible either. There have been enough examples in the past.[48]

The result of the ban was predictable. The Chewa headmen were incensed and defied Kachindamoto's instructions while making a number of approaches to the Boma in the hope that the order would be countermanded. By 1952 the antipathy between Chewa and Ngoni was reaching breaking point. A court case involving dancers triggered a confrontation between the protagonists that almost led to violence.

Angoni and Achewa arrived at the chief's court with sticks and clubs ready for a fight. The Angoni were shouting, 'We don't want these dances', and the Achewa replying that they belonged to their customs. The Angoni warned them that they were prepared to fight if necessary. The chief, hearing of the trouble, arrived just in time as sticks were being raised. But the nyau remain forbidden at Kachindamoto's and the people are a little cold towards us because of it.[49]

The Chewa were in the ascendancy in the Mua area and ready to challenge the Ngoni openly. Kachindamoto himself was suspected by the Boma of supporting the Nationalist movement.

The highly successful opposition of the Mua Chewa to the combined central authority of Ngoni and mission, led by the Banda clan chief, Kafulama, grew out of the dynamics of pre-colonial Chewa society. The powerful centralized Phiri chieftancies of the Maravi Empire were checked by the 'centrifugal' Banda headmen who led clusters of villages and asserted their authority through such institutions as nyau societies and Banda rain-shrine prophets.[50] Ngoni and European colonization changed the character of the central authority by replacing Phiri chiefs with Ngoni Native Authorities and European priests. With its central political superstructure destroyed, the Mankhamba shrine was superseded by the mission, while Kachindamoto continued to occupy the position of Karonga.

If the role of the shrine was easily replaced by the authoritarian mission, this was no less true of its religious functions. During the drought of 1912–13 the priests held a Novena, nine days of prayer, for rain. On the third day there was an enormous downpour. The older people in the church were most impressed and requested the priest that they be allowed to continue the Novena to make sure the rain did not stop. At the end of the nine days the priests asked the large congregation to make a Confession of Faith in God and a public repudiation of the cult of ancestral spirits.[51] Again in 1922, a day of prayer for rain was conducted at Mua by Father Mazé and ended in a cloudburst. Mazé had openly challenged villagers to bring rain by means of a local shrine and when they failed proclaimed his own day of prayer. The shrine became defunct shortly afterwards.[52] Thus the demand made of African traditional religious systems that they should offer some apparent control of the world could, on occasion, be answered by the Institutional Churches. If the High God, Chiuta, repeatedly failed to provide satisfaction but prayers to the Catholic God appeared to be efficacious, villagers were prepared to give up the traditional cult. Unlike the nyau cult the shrine ceremonies occurred rarely and were largely the preserve of religious officials. An entrenched hierarchy of priests such as that at Mankhamba could maintain a spirit-house from year to year, but had little control over popular support for the rain-cult and were unable to organize resistance to the mission.

The Catholic Mission at Mua and the Ngoni Chief were not just nominally and metaphorically a replacement of central Phiri authority. In such an isolated district the Father-Superior was effectively a Catholic chief in his own right and of far greater importance in the daily life of villagers than the District Commissioner. Priests were normally moved from mission to mission, rarely spending more than five years at a particular station, so that it was the office rather than the man which commanded respect. Mua was an exception in that one man, a French priest, Jean-Baptiste Champmartin, worked there from 1906 to 1949 with an occasional break because of illness, accidents, and the required one-year Retreat for White Fathers back at Maison-Carrée in Algeria. He was a thin, sallow man with a stentorian voice which he used to announce his presence on getting back from *ulendo*.[53] There was something very typical of the spirit of the White Fathers in his return from the year's Retreat, the most prolonged and intense spiritual exercise undertaken by any missionary, loaded down with a water-turbine engine for use in the Mua carpentry shop. He spoke fluent Chi-Chewa and could hold congregations spellbound, stopping his sermons only to take snuff and growl at the little boys fidgeting under his pulpit. He was also a skilled carpenter. Intellectually he was below the level of most of his colleagues, but made up for a simple-minded dogmatism by an intense love of his parish and the people in it; his only academic enterprise was the production of a colloquial translation of the Gospels. 'Chamare' behaved and was treated like a chief.[54]

What success the mission had in Chewa villages can be ascribed to Champmartin's chiefly attributes, in particular his ability to win the respect and confidence of villagers. He never underestimated the power of older women and was careful to court the favour of village elders whenever possible.[55] The day Njoro I retired Champmartin 'took the opportunity to give a little catechism on the love and respect which are due to chiefs and old people'.[56] When he discovered that his elderly catechumens were finding the catechism lessons too difficult and coming in for ridicule from youths in the class, Father Mazé was commandeered to write a simpler catechism and classes were separated.[57]

A training in canon law admirably fitted the priests for the task of unravelling the complexities of traditional law and men like Champmartin became experts in litigation. He was also the cause of successes amongst the Ngoni. For more than ten years Mua mission tried to gain the allegiance of the Ngoni chief, Ndindi, on the Livulezi. Attempts by Kachindamoto to win him over only stiffened resistance; Ndindi clung to the Dutch Reformed to assert his independence from Ntaka-taka. When Ndindi brought a case involving a Christian to the mission for judgement, Champmartin brought all his diplomatic skills to bear.

There must be some punishment; an imprudent act has taken place and an example must be set. But the punishment ought not to be too severe as no offence took place. There can be no question of an offence having taken place as Emilida was pregnant and her friend had a child a few weeks old. Under these circumstances, according to custom, an offence would have resulted in the death of either the child or the husband. This is just a case of childishness and misplaced familiarity. 'Quite so,' said the *kapitao*, 'but Bambo Ndindi wants to know how much they should pay.' 'For such things,' said the Father, 'Bambo Ndindi is master of the land and not I. His decision will be absolutely proper.'[58]

Within a year Mua mission was allowed to build its first school at Ndindi's. The only condition made by the chief was that he wanted a teacher from Likuni Normal School who would be 'quick witted' and not like the old catechists.[59]

Such honeyed treatment of traditional authorities was entirely dictated by expedience and the evangelical goals of the mission. In private the Catholic missionaries were unhappy about the power wielded by chiefs and headmen who opposed Christianity. A Montfort priest had this to say about the anti-Christian Mang'anja chiefs of the Lower Shire Valley.

It has never been properly understood in this country that there is a temporal power which belongs to the chiefs and spiritual power towards which the chief is merely to be well-disposed. People go on allowing it to be thought that the chief is all-powerful. I do not think that London herself would want to give these headmen more authority over their subjects than the British Government has over hers in England.[60]

When a chief favoured the mission as did all the Kachindamotos the missionaries had no quarrel. When the chief was pagan, forbade church marriages and stopped children going to school, as did most of the Mang'anja, the Fathers fell back on direct appeals to District Commissioners and complained about the ill-effects of Indirect Rule.

The authority of a Father-Superior as Catholic chief came to lie not primarily in a share in the power of the European colonial superstructure but in his control of the extensive infrastructure of the *corpus christianum* of African Lay Catholics. Pius XI's plea for more lay involvement in the life of the Church was received sympathetically by missionaries in Nyasaland. To oppose the twin evils of atheism and communism the Pope had reiterated in the 1930s his predecessors' appeals for 'Catholic Action' in a secular world. The joint meeting of Catholic Bishops at Chilubula in Zambia in September 1938 saw Catholic Action in Central Africa in terms of laymen helping their priests to evangelize districts in depth.[61] This provided a mandate for African Catholics to intervene in village life in an attempt to Christianize their environment.

The response of the mission at Mua to these directives was to diversify the already existing organization of lay Catholics. The Agurupa were divided into two groups, one under an ex-seminarian, Fidelis Muyeye, who was named *Akulu Akatholica* for the region around the mission, the other under Mikael Mbunama, who supervised Agurupa working beyond a five-mile radius of the mission. As a concession to lay involvement in the affairs of the Church both men were elected by ballot amongst the Agurupa. Edel Quinn, the promoter of the Legion of Mary in Africa, came to Mua in 1940 and Champmartin readily agreed to found the society in the parish.[62] The legionaries met weekly for prayer and decided on secret 'action'; this ranged from collecting wood for an infirm woman to guarding funerals of Christians from attack by the nyau. Each week the legionaries reported back to the meeting whether the action has been successfully accomplished. Although the Legion was a pious and innocuous association for prayer and good works, it provided yet another channel for the mission to influence the daily life of villages.

By the end of the Second World War, Mua had an infrastructure of overlapping groups and individuals at the village level. They were answerable only to the priests and enjoyed a degree of independence from both nyau and village headmen. Their leaders, Agurupa like Muyeye, were highly respected members of the community able to challenge the authority of headmen. A record was kept of every Christian family in the district in a *status animarum*. At the mission office were a large assortment of registers in which the Christian life of the parish was translated into statistics. Registers of births, baptisms, confirmations, marriages, deaths, banns, catechumens, and marriage cases, were maintained with scrupulous care. The Agurupa visited villages armed with a copy of the *status animarum* and new entries were written into the main record at the mission office. Every soul was accounted for. Even if the shifting population of the lakeshore never had the makings of the stable organic society of priestly dreams, it could at least be reduced to canonical order in the station records. There was something very touching about the missionaries' careful returns of annual totals of communions and confessions sent to their bishop when they were at a loss to explain what made their parishioners turn up for, or absent themselves from, weekly mass.

It was this regulated *corpus christianum* with its records and officials, reaching into the villages with its indigenous leaders and societies, that expressed and sustained the political power of the European missionaries. The points of inter-action between the mission as a centralized authority and the villagers came at a 'periphery' where Agurupa clashed with village headmen. Although the priests' representatives could only claim spiritual authority, this authority was exercised over important areas of life such as marriage, where the distinction between 'secular' and 'spiritual' was neither meaningful nor readily understood by most villagers.

An example of a case tried at Njoro's illustrates the influence skilful well-trained catechists could exert over headmen. A Christian from a Chewa village had fled to the mines after almost killing his wife. When he returned some two years later the case was brought before Njoro who fined the man 7/- with 5/- compensation to be paid to the woman.[63] The headman declared the couple divorced and told the husband never to go back to the village again. Since they had originally been married as Catholics the divorce was contested by the mission and the Akulu Akatholica sent to Njoro to impose the priests' ruling. Muyeye's forceful presentation of the case is given below.

Bambo, you are the chief. Nobody questions that. But today we have two *milandu*. One stems from the fight between these two young people in which blood flowed. You judged that case, Njoro, and we have nothing to say against your punishment. But there is also a second *mlandu*, the divorce of these two people. And here it is a question of their souls, their very salvation, the very commandments of God. Over these matters you have no jurisdiction. You have nothing to say, chief. When it is a question of souls their chief and *nkhoswe*[64] is Bambo Chamare, and today myself who represents the Father. I order you to allow this man to eat and sleep with his wife.[65]

Njoro, of course, obeyed. In a situation in which the authority of headmen was being undermined by well-paid mineworkers returning to their village and the rising power of the nyau leaders, this type of conflict with mission employees further eroded traditional leadership.

On the other hand the mission was willing to shore up weak chieftancies such as that at Ntaka-taka when the Native Authority was favourable to Christian practice. This siding with one faction inevitably polarized society around the mission. When the Kafulama headmanship became vacant the legitimate heir was a leading Catholic catechist, Zacharia. He was forced to step down in favour of his younger brother. It would have been impossible to reconcile an important position in mission employment with headmanship over the leading nyau *mzinda* in the district. It was widely rumoured that he would have been poisoned had he tried to eradicate dancing from the village. The catechist was obliged either to choose the Ngoni–Christian camp or to seek power within the nyau. Only Chewa of great personal prestige such as the contemporary Mwali, Rita Kafulama, were able to maintain both traditional office as the descendant of the shrine prophetess and a position as head of the women's section of the Legion of Mary.[66]

The fact that the *corpus christianum* represented an alternative to traditional village life for active laymen and women meant a failure of the Church's avowed intention to become incarnate in African society and culture. Ambitious men were forced to make a choice between mission and village or the escape to the towns and mines. But for the majority of Christians it was not a question of either/or, rather of and/and. Christian practice did not displace Chewa culture but grew up alongside it. The growth of the Church at village level was more a process of juxtaposition. Older explanatory frameworks tenaciously remained. Villagers would attend mass but they also might participate in nyau dances; a girl might receive her first communion in white dress after detailed instruction and later secretly undergo *chinamwali* to ensure that she got a husband. Inasmuch as the mission was a centralized chieftancy the Church found a niche in Chewa society and became part of it. But at the level of the village cluster and matrilineage the Church was resisted throughout the colonial period.

The Catholicism that reached Nyasaland villages in the twentieth century had been filtered through centuries of contact with pagan and peasant societies in Europe. In the Catholic Church's authoritarianism, her sanctions, her priests and ritual, there was an appeal to religious consciousness that cut across cultural barriers. While the Catholicism of a mission like Mua was superficially Westernized and unadapted to village life, at a deeper level it retained many features of rural European village religion, features that the Protestant Reformation had studiously tried to eliminate from Christianity. Most readily acceptable to African villagers was the importance accorded in the Catholic Church to the Communion of Saints. The Church was presented as containing both living and dead; in much the same way a villager saw himself related with equal significance to deceased as well as to living relatives. Some of Champmartin's notes for a retreat sermon show how the ever-present reality of the dead and their existence in a continuum with the living was in no way denied by simple Catholic teaching.

The example of Our Lord, Mary, the Apostles and Saints, in particular St. John the Baptist and the missionaries each of whom keep one hour a day free for prayer not to mention an examination of conscience one day a month.[67]

One of the most popular celebrations of the liturgical year was a procession held on the feast of the Holy Souls in Purgatory on 1 November; its unfailing attraction for villagers was a source of pleasure to the Fathers.

The graves have been well-kept and the cult of the dead has begun to reduce the number of superstitions on the subject especially offerings to the spirits.[68]

The Catholic concept of Purgatory was paralleled by a Chewa belief that a period equivalent to three generations elapsed before a person became a pure spirit who would not bother the village.[69] Villagers were able to participate in these ceremonies without any strain on their own conceptual framework in which the reality of a spirit world was fundamental.

African villagers were presented by the mission with a rival set of symbols in which to express religious consciousness; it was easy in the Catholic Church for them to avoid any change in *Weltanschauung*. For the high proportion of Catholic villagers who continued to feel during the colonial period that older patterns of thought still had validity little synthesis with Christian ideas was achieved. Very little conscious adaptation of Christianity took place and a village life, already shattered by the effects of labour migration and nineteenth-century invasions, seemed not to offer a great deal that the Western Church could in good conscience baptize. The teaching of the Church from mission pulpits and the structure of the Church did in some ways challenge the society and world-view of Africans in colonial Malawi but the challenge was easily overlooked or avoided.

Over against the Church's revolutionary proclamation of love and brotherhood stood a strict moral law that sanctioned by hell-fire, and a hierarchical institution that ran from Pope, Bishop, Father-Superior, to village-catechist, an ecclesiastical image of the line from Boma police to the Governor of Nyasaland and King of England. The fear which missionaries decried as the scaffolding of traditional village life was not foreign to the Church's teaching. Champmartin's notes provide an exaggerated example of a type of sermon that was at this time as common in Central Africa as in Western Europe.

> Then the impediments to the eternal destiny of man, salvation, peace in heaven—in great detail. Sin and its consequences. The first payment of sin, death. In the afternoon after instruction: death leads to eternity, payment for sin expanding a little on the Judgement, what it is to be alone with God, the terrible silence of the vengeful Deity . . . the poor Agurupa paled a little when they heard that the blood boiled in the brains and veins of the damned, even in the marrow of their bones and that for all eternity.[70]

While the missionaries often opposed restrictive taboos, they did not ultimately question their sanction, the fear of transgression, but applied this sanction to their own moral code.

This is not to say that the change from traditional to Christian symbols and codes of conduct represented no progress, a move from one prison to another. One of the most damaging taboos observed by pagans until well after the Second World War was a ban on sexual intercourse while a member of the family was sleeping away from the village. A daughter was not allowed, for example, to cohabit with her husband while her father was absent from home. If the father was polygamous and visited wives in another village, or left for the mines, for long periods, this could put an intolerable strain on the daughter's marriage. The taboo was sometimes circumvented by the introduction of a formal substitute father but often abstinence was the only alternative. A priest like Champmartin rarely bothered to argue the case but if she was Christian simply ordered the girl to cohabit. The issues resolved into the authority of the mission over against that of traditionalists.

> Today you will sleep in your husband's hut. If there is to be a death let it be on my own head. I am not a bit afraid. All this is Satan's work and nothing to do with Christianity. Off to your husband. A Christian marriage, an indissoluble marriage.[71]

Yet the breaking of such taboos was essential if children were to be permitted to attend boarding schools. The priests' opposition liberated Catholics for life in colonial Nyasaland; but it also pre-empted the natural evolution of village life towards adaptation and solutions to the difficulties of labour migration.

The mission was able to eliminate some restrictive customs and reduce the frequency of female initiation rites but it could never be a completely satisfactory substitute for the old social and religious system. While Institutional Christianity offered substitute *rites de passage* and could vie with Chewa ceremonies liturgically, it generally failed to answer the ever-present needs of villagers to control their world, predict misfortune, and explain why misfortune had fallen here rather than there. Priests were expected to be rain-callers and witch-finders and generally they refused. Occasionally an eccentric like the Canadian Father Roy achieved fame as an exorcist, he had reputedly cured an ailing herd of goats by sprinkling them with Holy Water, but deliberate attempts to rival religious institutions like the rain-shrines, such as occurred at Mua, were exceptional.[72]

Yet while the older world-view remained so did the demands made on the prevailing religious system. Christians simply chose in the Christianity presented to them the elements that were meaningful and helpful to them, and ignored the rest. Sena women at the two Lower Shire Catholic Missions took the casting out of the Devil at baptism quite literally to the exclusion of the rest of the symbolism in the rite. In a remarkable parallel to the Sena spirit-possession cults, women often fell into a trance during baptism and went into spasms on the floor as the evil spirit left them.[73]

The most attractive feature of Christianity was its most central tenet, that Jesus Christ formed a bridge between man and the High God with whom some sort of communion was possible.

Although the spirit-world, interposed between man and the otiose High God in Chewa traditional religion, was thought to intercede for rain and stop epidemics, the idea of man as such being in contact with God was limited to religious officials and to a particular spirit-possession cult. The shrine prophetesses were considered to be married to the *kapitao* of Chiuta, the snake *thunga*, who could also sometimes possess villagers. Since the High God was totally distant from man it would have been inconceivable for them to have been married or possessed directly by Chiuta himself.[74] It was precisely the idea of Christ the mediator that was taken over by shrine officials at M'bona's from the body of Christian teaching. Under Christian influence the Phiri hero became a 'Black Christ'.[75] The effect of Catholic teaching on the Trinity was also to produce a personalization of the Chewa concept of God. Chiuta was no longer described as living in total aseity above the clouds; a description of the meaning of the various names for God given by Epiphanio Kankhumba, a baptized Catholic and headman at Kafulama's, is very different from the classic impression of a *deus otiosus* reported by the early Scots missionaries to Nyasaland.

> Leza is merciful and sends the rainbow; the rain ends the drought. Prayers are made to Mphambe so that he should not be angry and send a drought ... Chauta looks after the world; his name comes from 'kuuta' to look after property.[76]

It was the Christian idea of a personal and active Deity who became incarnate that answered a need which a royal cult, in which a hidden and revered priestess alone had access to a representative of Chiuta, left unsatisfied amongst villagers. At First Communion Catholic children were told that they would 'meet Jesus' and that Jesus was God, whereas in the rain-cult only a special priesthood was allowed contact, and that remote, with the High God. Chewa religion may well have been moving towards this 'democratization' of religion in the spirit-possession cults like *UChiuta* and the *Avirombo-a-Chisumphi* in which ordinary villagers were possessed by God's messenger.[77]

But if Catholicism gave the radical promise of communion with God it failed miserably in the other important religious task of rooting out evil in the form of witches. Anxiety and guilt continued to be articulated in terms of witchcraft accusations until after the Second World War, and indeed until today. In the war period droves of villagers went off to *mapondera* in Portuguese East Africa to take the poison ordeal and demonstrate to their neighbours their innocence from witchcraft. The missionaries had always fought against the ordeal but it was rare for the colonial authorities to share their extreme concern.

> Mr. Kenyon-Slaney honoured us with a short visit on his way to the monthly meeting at Mankhamba and Ntaka-taka. He dwelt at length this time on the evils of *mwabvi*. 'The habits and customs of your ancestors are now dead and buried. You must follow the new order now and listen to the missionaries. There is nothing to fear from their teaching.' It was a long time since we catholic missionaries had heard as much from a government officer.[78]

The new order never became a reality at the level of Chewa villages; epidemics and crop-failures continued and hundreds of men annually left their villages for the mines. The number of deaths from *mwabvi* in the Mua area is difficult to assess from mission records alone but it must have run into several hundreds since the first arrival of the priests. The first sign of modernization was that villagers from Mua would go by train rather than walk the eighty miles to *mapondera* in Portuguese East Africa at Mtengo-Mbalame. It was only after the War that the poison ordeal began to be displaced by a more harmless method of witchcraft detection.

In many of our outstations there has been some kind of superstition growing up. Many Christians, *Akulu a Mpingo* and even Legion of Mary members, have been going to get rid of their 'ufiti'.[79] They take the train to Lirangwe and then walk across the border into P.E.A. The witch-doctor charges 7/6d. He makes them vomit up their 'ufiti' and will even send them a sort of vaccination if they cannot attend in person. We have not been refusing any of them the sacraments. If we had the church would have been empty.[80]

There was an equally impressive response to wandering *Apulumutsi*, itinerant preachers who put villagers through a symbolic death and resurrection by making them lie prostrate on the ground.[81] Purifying movements of this type, *mchape*[82] and witchfinders, never failed to capture the interest of the mission congregation. The missionaries had preached the reality of Satan and Evil in the world but, in the eyes of their parishioners, had never provided adequate protection against it.

In the short period of evangelization changes in the daily life of villagers were slight.[83] The changes that did occur were largely the product of labour migration rather than mission interference. If the quality of village life did change then, ironically, it was in an overall direction of increasing secularization. Like the first Christians in Rome, the Catholic missionaries could have been accused of atheism by the pagans around them. The mission contributed to the decline of the rain-cult and to the transformation of the nyau societies from a leading Chewa religious institution to a secret society harbouring the least progressive members of society. The priests' insistence in legal issues on the distinction between the secular and spiritual realms provided intellectual backing to a process of desacralization already begun. It was the profoundest irony that the missionaries came from a Western world in which the sense of the numinous had virtually disappeared to preach God to societies in which it was very much alive.

Yet, over several generations and in families rather than districts, the mission could claim that through their efforts transformation and Christian conversion was a reality. The first of the Kafulamas was baptized in old age. Her successor, Rita Kafulama, died a Christian death in 1971 having provided the mission with a long-serving clerk and catechist whose own son was in turn ordained priest in the 1960s. The grandfather of the present Bishop of Lilongwe refused a Catholic school. His father was a prominent member of the Legion of Mary. To talk about tangible changes in the quality of life produced by the mission is to discuss a handful of distinguished African Catholics. For the majority of Chewa, though, the mission remained a Western enclave set alongside normal village life. The worlds of the Church and of the village remained separate with different horizons. Christians who lived in both required an existential pluriformity that fitted them for the dissonances of life in mine-compound and towns. They remained second-class citizens in both the *civitas dei* and the secular city.

The missionaries' insistence on strict adherence to Church laws on marriage resulted in hundreds of Catholics being driven into an even looser relationship to the Church. They formed a large group of third-class citizens debarred from the sacraments and on the edge of the Institutional Church. Mission policy therefore achieved the strange feat of replicating the structure of the Catholic Church in Europe, huge numbers of nominal members forming a penumbra around priesthood and dedicated laity. By the Second World War the missionaries had successfully transplanted the European model of the Church on to African soil.

Like the Irish and Italians in the United States, the Catholics in Nyasaland were late arrivals. They clung to the past for security, taught a Gospel of other-worldliness, and staffed their stations with the most down-to-earth of men. They earnestly desired a Church of the *status quo* both at the village and national level, but found themselves fanatically sectarian when Protestants or nyau societies threatened what they saw as the salvation of souls. Because the Church looked backwards to the Middle Ages and heavenwards, and so shared a world-view as ahistorical as pagan traditionalists, Catholic Christianity never fundamentally transformed village life. The campaigns against nyau, *chinamwali* and taboos were directed against epiphenomena while the Protestant demands for self-help, thrift, historical change, and education, attacked—albeit with little success—the underlying world-view.

For the early Catholic missionaries there was One True, Catholic and Apostolic Church. It was *semper idem* and they belonged to it. The missionary task was physically arduous but spiritually simple, the baptism of men and the salvation of souls. They had come to Nyasaland to save the country from Protestantism and to turn the base metal of African villages into the gold of the *corpus christianum*. In the timeless African village was to be built the timeless Catholic Church. To this end they offered a dedication of a lifetime. Some, refugees when they left Europe, died at their mission stations some forty years later happy men but complete strangers to the continent they had left. Many were escaping a Europe they found repugnant and constraining. For the nuns the missions were a way out of the triviality of European convent life; for the priests the freedom to pioneer as Catholic chiefs of large areas.

The Church they produced in Nyasaland was a remarkable replica of the one they left behind in Limburg, Quebec, or Brittany; it was profoundly conservative and made up largely of peasants. Throughout the colonial period it was a small but powerful brake on the development of political consciousness amongst its membership, for its apolitical stance was always a tacit acceptance of the *status quo*. The growth of the young Indigenous Church in the post-war period was slow and shared the character of the Mission Church that had brought it to life. With a continued emphasis on authority and hierarchy in tribal, national, and Church, life it is unlikely that the historical role of Catholicism in modern Malawi will differ in any important respects. The character of the Malawian Church was defined for a long time to come in the formative period 1889–1939.

REFERENCES TO CHAPTER IX

[1] Mua Mission Diary 1 January 1952
[2] Travellers coming south from Tongaland or crossing the escarpment eastwards from

Dedza still refer to this as 'going to Malawi'. Around Mua people still use the term 'Maravi' when wishing to distinguish Chewa from Ngoni.

[3] The shrines were connected with the three main Phiri chieftancies of the past. At Mankhamba was the Karongas' shrine, at Msinja that of Undi, and near Nsanje that of Lundu.

[4] See Schoffeleers J. M. 'The interaction of the M'bona cult with Christianity' *Chilema conference on the interaction of Christianity and African Societies* August 1971

[5] Linden *The Maseko Ngoni* 244

[6] Oral testimony, Jakobi Mbalule, Chief Gwaza's Bembeke, interviewed in Mua hospital, May 1969

[7] Details of the villages are contained in a summary written in the Mua Mission Diary, November 1913

[8] For example, Maiwaza, Tembe-tembe, Kafulama, Kalindiza, Bwanali, and Maluza

[9] For example, Mganja's was made up of Matengo people from Songea, see Linden I. 'Some oral traditions from the Maseko Ngoni' *Society of Malawi Journal* Vol. XXIV No. 2 July 1971, 71 for details of Maseko migrations.

[10] Many others came from Kanjobvu's whose headman was the son of one of Chifisi's brothers' captives and a thorough-going Ngoni, and from Mganja's

[11] Oral Testimony, Gwiranimaondo, Catholic catechist interviewed in July 1970 in a village under Headman Nkwaila. Also Mua Diary, 25 October 1905. Nduna Chabwinja was from the Ngozo clan which had a ritual role in relationship to the Ngoni Paramount.

[12] *Rapports annuels* 1924–5 Ntaka-taka

[13] Bishop Cornelio Chitsulo of Dedza Diocese was ordained in 1937 and became Bishop twenty years later

[14] Bishop Patrick Kalilombe who was consecrated in Lilongwe in 1972 still remembers his feelings of being out of place when he moved as a child from Ntaka-taka to Mua a change from a Ngoni area to a Chewa area.

[15] Oral Testimony of Dutch Reformed catechist Jakobi, Village Headman at Magwero. All the first Dutch Reformed catechists were Chewa, and Mpezeni's Ngoni seem to have been far more successful in dominating the Chewa under them than the Maseko under Kachindamoto. The same type of mission/Ngoni alliance grew up, however, around Kachebere and Ludzi Missions.

[16] Murray S. S. *A Handbook of Nyasaland* London 1922, 72–3. The Mang'anja population of the valley was spread along the Shire River. Almost all the baptized Mang'anja belonged to the Phiri clan (19 per cent of total, the majority being Sena).

[17] Schoffeleers J. M. *The Lower Shire Valley* Limbe 1965, 6, and Oral testimony of Yohannes Simbi, Sena catechist of Mankuso village, Nsanje May 1970. The Makombe rising is well remembered in the region by Sena immigrants—see Ranger T. O. 'Revolt in Portuguese East Africa. The Makombe Rising of 1917' *St. Antony's Papers* No. 15. London 1963, 54–81.

[18] Oral testimony, Teresa Chingesi, Sena of Achizulu clan, Chief Chataika's, Nsanje, May 1970

[19] Nzama Mission Diary February 1905

[20] R. H. Murray Labour Report for 1927, S1/428/27. One of the pressures driving Alomwe people into Nyasaland was the high Portuguese Hut Tax.

[21] As is so often the case with immigrant populations the Alomwe were believed by Nyasaland Africans to eat rats and cats and to live in a subhuman fashion

[22] Oral testimony, Father Alfred Finye and Father Andrea Makoyo ordained in 1939, interviewed on a number of occasions in 1970

[23] Wishlade R. L. *Sectarianism in Southern Nyasaland* Oxford 1965

[24] *Rapports annuels* 1920–1 Mua mission

[25] 'Inkosi' is the title for the Ngoni paramount and *inkosini* his dwelling place

[26] *Rapports annuels* 1912–13 Ntaka-taka

[27] Personal Communication from Father F. X. Villy of Kasina Mission who knew Abraham Kachindamoto.

[28] Personal Diary of Ernest Paradis w.f. 10 January 1910. White Fathers' Archives, Lilongwe.

[29] *Rapports annuels* 1912–13 Mua

[30] The African Lakes Corporation bought unsorted cotton from the Mua area in 1906 at the price of three farthings per pound. Personal Diary Alfred Honoré w.f., August 1906. White Fathers' Archives, Rome.

[31] Personal Communication, Brother Peter, Kachebere Major Seminary, Mchinji

[32] Read R. 'Migrant Labour in Africa and its Effects on Tribal Life' *International Labour Review* Vol. XIV No. 6 June 1942, 628

[33] For differences in marriage stability between patrilocal and matrilocal tribes see Mitchell J. C. 'Social Change and the Stability of African Marriage in Northern Rhodesia' in *Social Change in Modern Africa* ed. Southall A. Oxford 1961, 316–29 and for the Ngoni . . . Barnes J. A. *Marriage in a Changing Society*. Rhodes–Livingstone Paper No. 20 Oxford 1951.

[34] *Rapports annuels* 1911–12 Ntaka-taka

[35] Mua Diary November 1912

[36] Priests visiting Maiwaza's village, a Chewa cluster, in January 1971 were still received in a hostile fashion. Personal Communication, Father J. Coppens, Mua.

[37] Mua Diary November 1913 notes on villages

[38] Mua Diary November 1937

[39] ibid. For the reaction of Inkosi Gomani II to Chewa customs see Read M. 'Tradition and Prestige among the Ngoni' *Africa* Vol. 9 1936, 472. Contempt for the Chewa is tempered by the fear of losing them by labour migration or movement out of the area.

[40] The symbolism of the ceremony conveyed the idea of the re-birth of the chieftancy. One-leggedness was a sign of the supernatural re-birth of the chief.

[41] 'L'intronisation d'un chef Angoni' MS Anon. White Fathers' Archives, Lilongwe. For comparison see details of the enthronement of Inkosi Willard Gomani III, in Nurse G. T. *African Music Society Journal* IV 1966–7, 56–63.

[42] Reports on Schools 1930. White Fathers' Archives, Lilongwe.

[43] Mua Diary November 1924

[44] Dedza District Book 5 September 1925. National Archives, Zomba.

[45] Mua Diary 6 September 1925

[46] Papers of Fathers Braire and Paradis now in the possession of Rev. Dr. J. M. Schoffeleers

[47] The Mua area has a long tradition of poisoning. Some of this pharmacological expertise may have come from association with Mankhamba. Another possibility is that the absence of *mwabvi* trees in the area stimulated the search for other poisons. Even today when offering a calabash a villager may drink first, *kuchotsa mfiti*, to drive away the 'evil spirit' and so safeguard his guest from poisoning.

[48] Mua Diary July 1945

[49] ibid. 10 October 1952

[50] I am indebted to Dr. J. M. Schoffeleers for this analysis of the position of the nyau in Chewa society. The political tension between Banda and Phiri is discussed in Langworthy H. *A History of Undi's Kingdom to 1890 : aspects of Chewa History in East-Central Africa* (Doctoral dissertation, Boston, 1969, 154) but is nowhere analysed in terms of religious institutions.

[51] *Rapports annuels* 1912–13 Ntaka-taka

[52] Oral testimony, Zacharia Kankhumba, Catholic catechist, Mua mission, August 1970.

[53] Personal Communication, Bishop Patrick Kalilombe w.f. and Father Roger Saffroy w.f. 'Ulendo' was the name used for the periods spent travelling by priests or District Commissioners.

[54] *Notes nécrologiques* 1950. Father Champmartin was born on 7 September 1879 and died

at Kasina mission on 3 August 1950. The water-turbine is still in use but was not, as *Notes* state, the first in Nyasaland. A water-turbine generator was in use at Livingstonia in the 1880s according to Mr. Leroy Vail.

[55] Mua Diary 30 May 1912. His adage was 'Bees come to honey not vinegar' on such occasions.

[56] ibid.

[57] Mua Diary 12 August 1913

[58] ibid. July 1937

[59] It is instructive how aware chiefs were of educational standards and differences between the missions. Ndindi 'did not want to have one of the old catechists who were still stuck on the ABC after ten years teaching. He said that sort of school was shameful.' July 1937.

[60] Heraud to Auneau 15 August 1939. Education Archives, Catholic secretariat, Limbe.

[61] Details in Mua Diary March 1939

[62] The Legion of Mary proved popular and proliferated, with sometimes up to thirty *praesidia* per parish. The legionaries recruited many Catholics into the *praesidia* until the Legion of Mary, with its Diocesan Curia and Comitia, began to suffer from all the weaknesses of the Church as a whole, nominal membership and emphasis on hierarchy. In 1968 there were still over 700 *praesidia* in Malawi with a membership of over 10,000. Both Bishop Julien and Bishop Auneau gave the Legion their active support and saw it as an ideal lay organization. Edel Quinn was in Africa from 1936 to 1944 see article by O'Brien S. *Southern Cross* 1 January 1964.

[63] Mua Diary March 1939

[64] The legal guardian and sponsor for marriage and other affairs, usually the maternal uncle

[65] Mua Diary March 1939

[66] Personal Communication, Father Messer of Mua mission. Rita Kafulama died in 1971, see text.

[67] Mua Diary February 1942. The inclusion of St. John the Baptist, Father Champmartin's patron saint, cannot have been without a touch of humour, however.

[68] Mua Diary November 1939

[69] Personal Communication, Rev. Dr. J. M. Schoffeleers

[70] Mua Diary February 1942. When it is remembered that the diaries were regularly read by a Visitor appointed by the Bishop, it is clear that many such passages are included to demonstrate the writer's theological prowess. That they are left untouched by the Visitor shows that official disapproval, if it existed, was not serious enough to warrant comment.

[71] Mua Diary May 1938

[72] Personal Communication, Bishop Joseph Fady W.F.

[73] Oral testimony, Carlos Chipondeni and Simon Tole, Catholic catechists at Nsanje, October 1970.

[74] These conclusions are derived from interviews with Chewa villagers in the Mchinji region. Even amongst Christian informants the idea that *thunga* was an incarnation of Chiuta in the Greek sense was firmly denied. If a Judaeo-Christian parallel is sought then *thunga* would fall into the category of an 'angel'. Father Hovington spends much of his first volume on the Chewa idea of God, and his manuscript, at Ludzi mission, provides a variety of support for the idea of the total aseity of the Chewa High God. This distinguishes the Chewa cults from the Mwari cult of the Shona where the Deity does appear to speak and act directly through officials.

[75] According to Catholic catechists at Nsanje this designation for M'bona antedated the arrival of the South Africa General Mission at Lulwe in 1900. For a full discussion of the Christian influence in the Nsanje area see Schoffeleers *M'bona* 367–73. M'bona is also known as *mwana wa mulungu*, the Son of God.

[76] Oral testimony, Epiphanio Kankhumba, Mua, July 1970

[77] Linden *The Karongas' Shrine* deals with these cults in detail. It seems likely that they

are the product of the break-up of the territorial rain-cult. However they may be seen in the Horton sense of being a pre-Christian evolution of the traditional religious system to respond to the changes that had taken place in the nineteenth century.

[78] Mua Diary February 1941

[79] The prefix 'u' would suggest the writer is talking about witchcraft, an abstract term, rather than *mfiti* the possessing force itself

[80] Mua Diary November 1947

[81] *Rapports annuels* 1930–31 Bembeke. *Apulumutsi* means saviours.

[82] These movements swept across Northern Rhodesia and Nyasaland in the 1930s although similar movements occurred during Independence in Malawi 1960–4. Coloured water was given to the 'patient' to wash away the evil. To understand their impact see Mulaisho D. *The Tongue of the Dumb* Heinemann African Writers Series 1972

[83] See Wilson M. *Religion and the Transformation of Society* Cambridge 1971, for a general discussion of the influence of Christianity on African Societies

Index

O.P.   *Dominicans*
S.J.   *Jesuit*
S.M.M. *Montfort Father*
W.F.   *White Father*

Abushiri Rising, 15, 36n

Adaptation, missionary, 203–4; initiation rites, 185n, 195–6, 205; Lavigerie and, 51–2; Mariology, 53; Mass, 54; morality, 119–20; possession, 205; priesthood, 178–9, 183; religious belief, 191, 199; Religious Orders, 174; Society of Jesus, 3; tact, 58, 71, 140, 200, 208; women, 167–8

Affliction, cults of, 58

African Lakes Company, 13–19 *passim*, 35n, 210n; land ownership, 42; Moirs, 37n, 83n; and Mponda, 22, 24, 28, 30–1

Agriculture, 141, 150; Brothers', 68, 195; cattle, 47, 68; cotton, 194, 210n; DC's and, 123; diploma in, 156; Malawian, 2; oranges, 71; poor harvests, 79, 110; resistance to innovation, 79

Akulu aMpingo, 182, 207; hierarchy of, 201; run Church, 184

Ancestral Spirits, attitudes to, 139–40, 160n, 197, 199, 204; important cult of, 90; intercede for rain, 205; Mang'anja sacrifices to, 46; village shrines, 190–1; Yao, 24; *see also* Nyau, Spirit possession

Anthropology, viii; DC's knowledge of, 123, 127; White Fathers' writings, 71, 127

Apocalypse, 77, 93

Arabs, 1, 2; and Yao, 21, 22, 30; contact with Mang'anja, 121; North Africa, 51; nun, 167; rumours about, 94

Armageddon, 75; First World War as, 80, 93, 101

Auneau, Louis, Bishop, 71; biography of, 72–3; character, 74, 144–5, 152; informs of Rising, 94; evacuates Nguludi, 96; gains prestige, 100; resists war service, 107–8; on education 141–2; warns Nicolas, 150; on schools, 154–6; instructions on women, 167–9; instructions on African Sisters,

173–4, 176; and Indigenous Church, 177, 180

Authority, in Catholic doctrine, 87–8, 181, 197, 203; in colonial society, 90; in seminary training, 183; in Ngoni society, 47, 59; of chiefs undermined, 200–2; of priests, 53, 59; of shrine prophets, 66n, 199; *see also* Father Superior

Banda, clans, 1, 196; authority of chiefs, 114; and nyau, 127; opposition to Phiri, 197–9; religious officials, 189

Baptism, of Bemba in war, 109; death-bed, 60, 61, 107, 129; eligibility for, 52, 64n, 121, 139, 140; as initiation rites, 65n, 140; magical beliefs about, 78; male versus female, 168; mass, 4; at Mulanje, 146; of Ngoni aristocrats, 56, 58; parents' permission for, 70, 77; pre-war slump in rate, 77–8; spirit-possession in, 205; statistics, 74, 75, 113–14, 192–4; by total immersion, 76

Baptist Industrial Mission, 1, 43, 81, 99

Baslé, Auguste, S.M.M., 103n, 145

Beer, Catholic versus Protestant attitude to, 60, 147–8; food converted into, 110

Bemba, 5, 44, 89, 109

Bembeke Mission, 70–1, 114, 168, 171, 179

Bible, imagery, 7, 77, 80, 81, 94; Catholic attitude to, 101, 105n, 147, 181; Chilembwe's use of, 95, 96; and historical consciousness, 87–8; magical attitude to, 77; politics and the, 81, 95, 101; values, 171; *see also* Revelation, Apocalypse, Armageddon

Black Americans, 80, 93, 95

Blantyre Catholic Mission, 68, 73

Blantyre Scots Mission, attitude to RC's, 46, 73, 92, 145, 150; catechists, 94; church,

213